"*Saving Bravo* is the best account I have read of this mission. As a former SEAL I am very familiar with this legendary operation. Talty's research and writing lets you get to know the men and what they are feeling in this tribute to human perseverance. This book proves that real world SEAL ops are better than fiction."

— **Howard Wasdin,** *New York Times* best-selling coauthor of *SEAL Team Six*

"Talty skillfully and engagingly tells the dramatic story of twelve fateful days in the life of then-fifty-two-year-old Air Force navigator Gene Hambleton . . . [He] brings in geopolitical and military strategy issues in this fully realized rescue story that will appeal to those in search of a (mostly) positive event that took place during the Vietnam War."

— *Publishers Weekly*

SAVING BRAVO

SAVING BRAVO

THE GREATEST RESCUE MISSION
IN NAVY SEAL HISTORY

STEPHAN TALTY

MARINER

An Imprint of HarperCollins*Publishers*
Boston   New York

First Mariner Books edition 2019
Copyright © 2018 by Stephan Talty

Mariner
An Imprint of HarperCollins Publishers, registered
in the United States of America and/or other jurisdictions.

www.marinerbooks.com

Library of Congress Cataloging-in-Publication Data
Names: Talty, Stephan, author.
Title: Saving Bravo : the greatest rescue mission in Navy SEAL history / Stephan Talty.
Description: Boston : HarperCollins Publishers, 2018. | Includes bibliographical
references and index.
Identifiers: LCCN 2018006365 (print) | LCCN 2018007171 (ebook) |
ISBN 9781328866271 (ebook) | ISBN 9781328866721 (hardback) |
ISBN 9780358118206 (pbk.)
Subjects: LCSH: Vietnam War, 1961–1975 — Search and rescue operations. |
Hambleton, Gene (Iceal Eugene), 1918–2004. | Search and rescue operations —
Vietnam | United States. Navy. SEALs — Search and rescue operations — Vietnam. |
BISAC: HISTORY / Military / Vietnam War. | HISTORY / Military / Special Forces. |
HISTORY / United States / 20th Century.
Classification: LCC DS559.8.S4 (ebook) | LCC DS559.8.S4 T35 2018 (print) |
DDC 959.704/342 — dc23
LC record available at https://lccn.loc.gov/2018006365

Book design by Emily Snyder

Maps by Mapping Specialists, Ltd.

Printed in the United States of America
23 24 25 26 27 LBC 8 7 6 5 4

For the sixteen who didn't come back:

Wayne Bolte
Robin Gatwood
Charles Levis
Anthony Giannangeli
Henry Serex
Byron Kulland
Ronald Paschall
John Frink
Peter Hayden Chapman
James Alley
John Henry Call III
William Roy Pearson
Allen Avery
Roy Prater
Larry Potts
Bruce Walker

CONTENTS

AUTHOR'S NOTE ix

PROLOGUE: THE RIVER xiii

PART I: GENE

1. Midwestern 3
2. Rocket Man 12
3. Korat 21
4. The Boys in the Back 29
5. The Time of Useful Consciousness 36
6. Ernie Banks 43
7. Blueghost 39 48
8. Tucson 62
9. Blowtorch Jockeys 68

PART II: DARK KNIGHTS

10. Joker 77
11. Yesterday's Frat Boy 86
12. "Their Glowing Trajectories" 93
13. Tiny Tim 100
14. Futility 106
15. "I Know We're Going to Die" 111

16. Low Bird 117
17. The Division 124

PART III: THE SWANEE

18. The Real John Wayne 129
19. The Hurricane Lover 135
20. When the Moon Goes over the Mountain 140
21. The First at Tucson National 152
22. Dark Encounter 159
23. The Grove 165
24. Clark 173
25. Places Like the Moon 179
26. Zeroed In 183
27. Esther Williams 188
28. "Some Kind of Rescue" 200
29. The Sampan 207
30. Journey's End 214
31. "Lay That Man Down" 222
32. Beyond a Normal Call of Duty 232
33. The Returns 242
34. "As Comrades" 247

ACKNOWLEDGMENTS 258
APPENDIX A: CHRONOLOGY 259
APPENDIX B: WALKER AND POTTS 262
NOTES 273
INDEX 298

AUTHOR'S NOTE

Darrel Whitcomb has been researching, writing, and lecturing on the Bat 21 mission since his service as an Air Force forward air controller in Southeast Asia in 1972. He allowed me to use his extensive collection of mission interviews, research material, maps, and photos for this book. Darrel provided key insights on combat, and specifically, rescue operations and military culture, and offered technical advice throughout. His help with this project has been invaluable.

SOUTHEAST ASIA, APRIL 1972

Legend
★ Capital
■ Base
● Town
✈ Airfields

CHINA

NORTH VIETNAM

● Hanoi

N

SCALE

0   200   400 km
0   100   200 mi

Plain of Jars

LAOS

Gulf of Tonkin

Hainan

Vientiane ★

Udorn ✈

Nakhon Phanom ✈

Nam Phong ■

Tchepone ●

Ho Chi Minh Trail

VIETNAM

(aircraft carriers) ✈ ✈

Dong Ha

● Da Nang

THAILAND

Takhli ✈

Korat ✈

Ubon ✈

● Kontum

Pleiku ●

Bangkok ●

U-Tapao ✈

CAMBODIA

SOUTH VIETNAM

Cam Ranh Bay ✈

SOUTH CHINA SEA

Phnom Penh ★

● An Loc

Tan Son Nhut ✈
★ Saigon

Gulf of Siam

POSITIONS OF HAMBLETON AND OTHERS, APRIL 1972

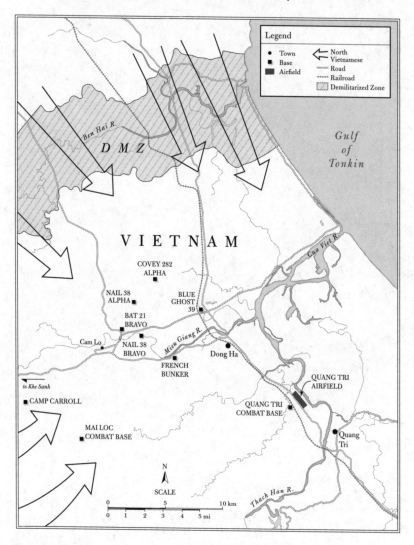

Prologue

THE RIVER

GENE HAMBLETON PUSHED himself away from the tree he'd collapsed against and peered into the jungle. A stray beam of light had passed down between the fronds and thick vines that hung in front of him, illuminating something beyond them, something light among the dark browns and greens. He squinted. It looked like a sandbar.

The navigator managed to lever himself up and stumble over to the edge of the banana grove. He crouched down and placed his fingers on the last of the fronds, and pushed the leaves apart. There it was, a large, long sandbar, glowing in the sun, a slash in the thick foliage.

But a sandbar in the middle of the Vietnamese jungle? It was ridiculous. Hambleton thought, not for the first time, that he might be losing his mind.

He was aware that his condition was deteriorating rapidly. After eight days on the run from the enemy, with no food and fear a constant companion, he couldn't trust his own perceptions. His body was bruised, severely malnourished, and weak. He'd lost about forty pounds on his already thin six-foot-two frame; his once pristine flight suit hung on him, filthy and torn. The hallucinations he'd been experiencing for the past day were growing more frequent and more lifelike. Perhaps this was one of them.

And yet there it was, a sandbar about fifty yards away.

Exhausted, the navigator lay down on the ground and stared in fascination at the line of tan, wishing the daylight were stronger so that he could get a clearer view. It was muggy. Mosquitoes buzzed; gibbons shrieked in the canopy. After four or five minutes, his eyes seemed to adjust and the thing below him swam into focus. Hambleton realized that he'd been mistaken. What he was looking at wasn't a sandbar after all. It was a river.

The navigator was overcome with emotion. He'd found the Mieu Giang at last, which meant he was close to being rescued. He would not be marched to Hanoi, as he'd feared, and tortured to give up his secrets.

Hambleton struggled to his feet, staring at the rolling water. His self-control deserted him and he hurried forward toward the river. He *had* to reach it; his rescuers might be waiting. The stealth he'd practiced so obsessively for the past days disappeared as he thrashed through the foliage, shoving the thick leaves aside and pushing his body through the gaps. As he careened forward, the ground dropped away from under him and he fell heavily. He'd blundered over the lip of an embankment, and now he tumbled down its side, his body turning somersaults. He raised his arms to protect his head as he pounded down the slope. After a few seconds, Hambleton crashed into a tree trunk and stopped dead. He could hardly breathe.

Unable to stand, he began to crawl on his belly. When he finally reached the river's edge, he put his hands into the water and splashed some back and forth, delighting in its texture. It had to be the Mieu Giang. Though he knew Vietnamese rivers were often full of bacteria that caused terrible diseases, his throat was bone dry and so he plunged his face into the water and drank. "Thank you, sweet Jesus," he said. "Thank you."

After he'd been shot down, Hambleton had vowed to himself that he wouldn't be captured. One reason was his desire to see Gwen, his willowy beloved wife, again. The other had to do with the Cold War. In nearly thirty years in the Air Force, he'd worked on highly classified missile systems and specialized in electronic counter-warfare, collecting top-secret information that the Soviets coveted. In his memory lay the inner workings of advanced radar systems and the names of the cities that American nuclear warheads were pointed toward at that very moment. Now he would make it out of the jungle without having to reveal them to the KGB agents stationed in Hanoi. Just by surviving, he would prove to his father and his war-hero brother that he too could display courage under great stress, that he was a man to be reckoned with.

As Hambleton studied the river, however, his mood darkened. He couldn't tell how wide it was but guessed two hundred feet. "What had looked like a godsend only moments before," he later recalled, "now looked like an impassable abyss." He could barely walk. How was he supposed to swim across that?

He rested until the sky turned dark. When he awoke, there were rustling sounds from above. They were coming from the foliage on the edge of the embankment. Something was heaving itself through the underbrush, thwacking its way forward. More than one thing. It could only be the North Vietnamese.

The water was shallow as he hurried into it. The stones cut painfully into his feet, but he couldn't cry out in case the NVA soldiers heard him. The water rose up to his chest as he forged into the current and pushed downstream as fast as he could.

As he rushed downriver, the bottom beneath his feet dropped away and Hambleton plunged into the cold depths, his head sinking under the surface. Underwater, he fought for breath, kicking and flailing, trying to push himself higher. But the heavy survival radios weighed him down, and he only sank deeper into the translucent darkness.

One reason Gene Hambleton believed he was close to being saved was the unprecedented number of soldiers who had been sent out to bring him back alive. For a week, hundreds of American pilots, navigators, door gunners, forward air controllers, and pararescuemen had risked their lives to retrieve him. Never before in the nation's history had so many men or so much materiel—an armada of fighter planes, B-52s, attack helicopters, Navy aircraft carriers—been put into play to save a single person, and they never would be again. But the mission had not gone well. Eleven men were dead and one was missing, while two more were being marched to North Vietnamese prisons. And Hambleton, who was surrounded by thousands of enemy soldiers, remained in imminent danger of being captured.

Because of this stupendous outlay of blood and treasure, certain members of the military had turned sharply against the mission. "You god-damn son of a bitch," one furious commander told a rescue planner. "If anything goes wrong in that operation, you guys are gonna be hung out to dry." Helicopters had been forbidden to make any more attempts to bring Hambleton back. No further B-52 airstrikes had been authorized. In fact, the only force left with a chance of getting Hambleton out alive was a short, slim, soft-spoken twenty-eight-year-old Navy SEAL named Tommy "Flipper" Norris and his small team of South Vietnamese sea commandos.

Norris was an unusual person to be leading such a mission. He didn't come across as very warrior-like; in fact, he looked barely big enough to be in the Navy, let alone in the SEALs. (One soldier who met him years later remarked, "Damn, I didn't know they made 'em that small.") Then there was Norris's friendly expression — he was as polite and affable as a young priest — and his tendency to dissolve into loud, braying laughter when something amused him. But the smile hid a ferocious will. Lieu-tenant Tommy Norris hated, just *hated,* to give up on anything. Once, when bad eyesight threatened to end his dream of becoming a fighter pi-lot, he'd managed to improve his vision through hours of concentrated ef-fort, which no other failed applicant had even thought of trying to do, be-cause most people don't regard *seeing* as a skill you can get better at. And when it came to physical courage, he was a freak, even among his fellow soldiers. "He simply did not seem to notice," one fellow soldier said, "or react to personal danger."

The young SEAL, however, was in trouble. That afternoon, more than a dozen members of his support team had been killed in a rocket attack on their forward base. And as the hours passed, the American realized that he was facing a gathering mutiny among his commandos, who believed with good reason that if they ventured out that night to save Hambleton, they were going to die.

PART I

GENE

1

MIDWESTERN

HIS ORIGINAL AMBITION had been to fly. Ever since he was a teenager living in the heart of the Midwest, Iceal "Gene" Hambleton had ached to get away from its listless plains and into the air. But he was born in farm country, near the Illinois-Indiana border, to a man who discouraged dreaming in his sons.

The family had been in the Midwest for generations. Gene's father, also named Iceal, grew up in the small town of Rossville, Illinois, but had set his heart on becoming a lawyer and getting away from the boredom, the bad crops, and the 5 a.m. milking times of farming life in the early 1900s. After graduating from high school, Iceal Sr. went away to college and was doing well there. Then a letter arrived instructing him to return home immediately; his father had died and he was needed to tend the crops. Iceal packed his law books into his suitcase and returned home to Rossville.

That first dose of bitterness didn't take, not completely. Iceal Sr. was a fiercely stubborn young man — his sons would inherit this quality — and he wasn't about to be easily denied his dreams. He went to work on the farm with his usual zeal and even found enough time to marry a sweet-natured local woman, Stella Wilbur, whom he'd known since he was fourteen. On November 16, 1918, a son arrived and was named Iceal Eugene Hambleton. Iceal Jr. had an older sister, Frances; three years later, a younger brother, Gil, was born.

Iceal Jr. was born near the end of a farm boom. World War I had pushed prices to previously unimagined heights; an Illinois farmer could sell his corn crop for $1.35 a bushel, almost three times the prewar haul. But when the peace treaty was signed at Versailles, profits plummeted, and with a young family to support, Iceal Sr. turned his eyes to agribusiness. By the 1920s, he'd worked his way up through the ranks of a company that bred and sold Percheron horses, a sturdy breed used for farming and pulling carts. Seventy percent of the draft horses in America were Percherons by the end of the decade; they plowed the fields and hauled the corn and wheat harvests for thousands of small-time farmers who couldn't afford the latest tractor from International Harvester. With the country growing and needing to be fed, it seemed like Iceal Sr. had stepped onto the first rung of a ladder leading upward. After working diligently for a number of years, he was even named president of the company.

Then the Great Depression arrived. The price of a bushel of corn fell to eight cents, less than it cost to produce. If you drove through the back roads of certain midwestern states in 1932, you might be startled by the smell of fresh popcorn wafting across the fields. Farmers fed their bushels of cobs into the family stoves to heat their houses rather than selling the crop, lending the air of places like eastern Illinois the scent of a Bijou cinema lobby. Bankers called in their loans and, when farmers were unable to meet them, quickly foreclosed. In Iowa, locals kidnapped a judge and threatened to hang him unless he agreed not to force any more families off their land.

The demand for the Percheron horses melted away and the company folded. Iceal Sr. was left nearly penniless, without even a farm to feed his family. The indignity leached into his character, poisoned his moods, sharpened his already sharp tongue. Nothing Iceal Jr. or his younger brother Gil did was good enough for the old man. "He was opinionated and bullheaded," said his granddaughter Pam. "And he was real hard on the kids. He was just such a dominating kind of a person." Their mother was very different, "soft and fuzzy," but it was Iceal Sr. who set the tone for the household.

From all indications, the elder son had inherited a far sunnier and more personable nature than his father, but the strain of the Depression years and the constant belittling at home wore on him. By the time he reached school age, the family was living in tiny Wenona, Illinois, "a carbon copy of thousands of little communities in the U.S.A." Wenona had a one-room schoolhouse, a town eccentric (his name was Mr. Anderson), and not much else. People depended on their neighbors and knew the intimate details of the lives of dozens of other Wenonians. "By a family's reputation from generations past," Iceal Jr. later wrote, "a newborn baby shall be known." It was hard to outrun your history in a place like Wenona.

As the firstborn son of the brooding Iceal Sr., the young boy grew to resent his given name. "Iceal" didn't fit his gregarious personality. "All my life I've been looking for the guy who tagged it on me," he would later say, knowing full well that the guy who tagged it on him was his old man. At some point during his boyhood, he even began refusing to answer to Iceal. It takes only a little imagination to suppose that he wanted not only to free himself from its un-American weirdness but also to put as much distance as he could manage between himself and his coldhearted father. (How appropriate that the name's first three letters spelled "Ice"!) And so he took his middle name, Eugene, shortened it, and became the far more pleasant-sounding Gene.

Gene was funny, mischievous, and defiant; the word back then would have been "devilish." He was inordinately fond of pranks. Tired of his father's beatings and lectures, Gene acted out, his rebellions mostly taking the form of Huck Finn–type capers. He and his friends attended the one-room school with a potbellied stove in the corner to heat it when the sharp-clawed winter winds swept across the Illinois fields. His teacher was Miss Jones, "big boned and with perfect posture," who carried a leather strap about a foot long to dispel any thought of misbehavior. Gene and his buddies made up their minds one day that the strap was an affront to their dignity as young Christian men and decided not only to carry out a plot to steal it but also to then burn the thing right there in the classroom stove. Gene was chosen to grab the whip while his two friends created a diversion by staging a fight in the schoolyard. When the pair started throwing haymakers and rolling in the dirt, Miss Jones ran out with the rest of the class and tried to untangle them. Once she was fully engaged, Gene slipped back into the schoolroom, grabbed the strap from her desk drawer, opened the stove's soot-black hatch, and threw it into the flames. Miss Jones soon forced confessions out of the boys, and Gene was soundly whipped.

But he was incorrigible. He and his friends put a smoke bomb under the hood of Mr. Anderson's car and cackled gleefully when the fire trucks came speeding down Main Street to put out the "fire." They hid garlic in the high school's heating system and waited for the fumes to circulate. Finding themselves too broke to afford the latest motion picture one night, they occupied themselves by picking up a brand-new Austin car and carrying it onto the owner's porch, where they deposited it, much to the amusement of the more tolerant Wenonians.

When Gene and his friends were lucky enough to be able to afford a movie during the 1930s, they would sit in the cinema and watch the black-and-white March of Time newsreels that preceded the features. Events in Germany were a mainstay of the short films: the famous night rallies, National Socialists goose-stepping through Berlin's streets, dazzling spotlights picking out the blood-red flags imprinted with the swastika. "In the most concentrated propaganda campaign the world has ever known," intoned the narrator of a 1938 reel, "Minister Goebbels has in five years of Nazi rule whipped 65 million people into a nation with one mind, one will and one objective: EXPANSION!" Gene read the newspapers and followed the debate over whether America should get involved in stopping "this man Hitler."

Though he deeply resented his father, Gene shared the man's ambition; he was dying to get out of Wenona. One night when he and some friends were attending a house party in town, the boys were sitting around talking about the news from Europe. "'Hitler' was a name we were hearing more and more often," said Gene. He saw war coming and had decided there "was no way for our country to stay out of the mess." The conversation turned to enlistment, and Hambleton — never shy — jumped in. "'When the time comes, I'm going to get into the action,'" he told the others. "I made up my mind right then and there that I was going to be part of the military." Not only that, but he was going to be fighting the Nazis as that most dashing of warriors, the American aviator. When the final struggle with the Third Reich arrived, Gene Hambleton fully expected to be flying bombers over Germany.

There were, in the middle of the century, two or three generations of young land-bound Americans who angled their eyes upward and away from nearby wheat fields or greasy corner transmission shops and dreamed of flight. The story of one Vietnam pilot who served with Hambleton, Peter "Hayden" Chapman II, could stand in for the men's collective background. Chapman grew up in a plain farmhouse in Centerburg, Ohio, a town given its name because it lay in the exact geographical center of the state. He grew up with six sisters who mothered and coddled and fought with him. "He was so damn cute," said his sister Carol. "We wanted him to look nice. We wanted him to eat nice." It was assumed that Hayden would one day take his place on the farm or, if he was particularly ambitious, in Centerburg itself after four years of college.

But that all changed for Hayden when he was six or seven. That summer, on blazing hot days when the cornstalks on his father's farm appeared as wavering stalks of molten gold, young Hayden would feel a deep thrumming that seemed to rise up from under the floorboards of the farmhouse and vibrate pleasantly in the bones of his chest, like the stirring of some subterranean monster. This would be the signal for the young boy to immediately drop what he was doing and run for the back door that led out onto his father's twenty-five acres; from there he would dash to the farthest corner of the small plot, climb onto the lower rung of the fence, and look up, shading his eyes with his right hand to catch the thrilling and enormous black shape of a B-17 bomber against a cut of blue sky as it roared ten thousand feet above on its way across the country.

Hayden became obsessed with flying. In fact, as a young boy he grew so absorbed in cutting out balsa models from send-away kits that he once carved the shape of a bomber into his mother's best carpet with a pair of scissors, completely unaware that he was slicing a hole through thick wool as well as the paper pattern, for which crime he was exiled to the milk house. When Hayden outgrew the toy planes, he took a job so that he could afford flying lessons.

Chapman's parents took out a loan on their house to finance his pilot training, and he returned the gesture by taking them on trips to Las Vegas and Carlsbad Caverns during his weeks of leave. To have a military pilot in the family was like having a movie star coming home for Thanksgiving. "It was like nothing we from Centerburg could understand," said his nephew Brad Huffman. "A little farm community of a thousand people. He was just the guy everyone looked up to in the family."

Gene Hambleton shared this midwestern obsession with flight. He was, after all, from the same generation that produced the Apollo crews who went to the moon — just three years older than John Glenn. As young boys and teenagers, many of his fellow future airmen were forking over the profits of their newspaper routes or lifeguard jobs to see movies like 1939's *Only Angels Have Wings*. If the Army had John Wayne, the single greatest recruiter of human flesh into the land forces of the United States in the nation's history, the Air Force had the dark-eyed melancholy of Cary Grant playing a pilot in a white silk scarf. Hollywood made flying seem like a rakish dare.

In April 1941, with Pearl Harbor still eight months away, Gene was drafted and shipped off to basic training. The military quickly sent him home for failing the physical; his teeth were bad. Gene's dream of becoming an aviator was dashed for the moment. But the events in Europe did produce one life-altering event for the young man. He found a job at the enormous Joliet Arsenal munitions factory in northeastern Illinois, which was churning out armaments for the war. And it was on the factory floor that he first met Gwen.

Gwendolyn Mae Flessner was brunette, fine-featured, crisply beautiful, and all of eighteen years old. Her smile was radiant and often remarked on, but it hid an inner steel. "*She* was the rock in that family," an acquaintance later said. As Gene and Gwen got to talking after their shifts piecing together land mines and artillery shells, he found this young midwesterner to be very much like his own caring, nurturing mother. She was cheerful and encouraging, and, crucially, she laughed at his jokes. As Hambleton toiled away making the bombs that he'd once thought he'd be dropping on Stuttgart and Düsseldorf, Gwen's gentleness was a balm for his hurt pride. He fell hopelessly in love. It was the first real piece of luck in his life.

Despite the smiling face she turned to the world, Gwen had known sharper tragedies than Gene. She, too, had grown up poor, though the term barely had any meeting in farm country during the Depression, so common was the lack of money. The root pain of Gene's life sprouted from his father's hard, bitter personality; for Gwen, it was the death of her older brother Kenneth, with whom she shared a birthday. When he was nine years old, Kenneth was riding in a tractor when the hired man driving the vehicle tried to negotiate a steep slope. The man misjudged the angle, and the tractor tipped over on itself, trapping Kenneth under its heavy metal frame. Gwen's mother ran from the farmhouse to the road where her eldest child lay pinned, holding Kenneth's hand until enough men could be gathered from the fields and nearby houses to lift the tractor off him. Then she rode with him to the hospital. The boy died on the way.

For years afterward, Gwen's parents found the accident too painful to speak of, except when her father would rail passionately against the hired man, whose negligence he blamed for causing Kenneth's death. From that day, Mr. Flessner never again seemed to enjoy life. He was unable to express emotion — that is, the emotion of love or affection. Sadness and helpless anger he expressed readily. The tragedy hung over the farmhouse like a curse, and all the children were marked by it.

When Gwen met the lanky young man from Wenona, she was taken with his good looks and his irrepressible high spirits. The two became inseparable. To their families and friends, Gene and Gwen seemed like figures out of a Fitzgerald novel, clean-limbed aristocrats of the Midwest. "We always thought of her as a movie star," said Gene's niece. She really was that good-looking: think Donna Reed in *It's a Wonderful Life*. As for Gene, he was a better-looking Hank Williams, lanky and soft-eyed and slow-voiced, a storyteller who kept you riveted until the last word. Relatives and friends jealously waited for their visits and talked about them for months afterward. The Hambletons were fun, kind, attractive human beings.

But as much as they made you feel that you were a special part of their lives, there was one boundary you would never cross. You would never be as important to Gene as Gwen was, not ever, not if you saw a hundred. And vice versa. Her aunts warned their niece more than once that the relationship would never last, but she only laughed. "Gwen loved him deeply," said her sister Mary Ann. The two eloped to St. Louis, where they were married in August 1942.

As friendly and outgoing as he was, Gene was still proud and a bit ornery at times; he remained alive to any hint of an insult. When he argued about his salary with his supervisor at the arsenal and threatened to quit, the man warned him that he would be drafted as soon as he stepped off the assembly floor. Gene scoffed and walked anyway. Within weeks, he received his notice to report.

President Franklin D. Roosevelt had issued a call for American industry to produce fifty thousand aircraft every year, and those fighters and bombers would need pilots. As Germany began its conquest of Europe, the Army Air Corps waived most of its requirements for aviators. No longer would recruits need, for example, two years of college. "We bet there are a lot of taxicab drivers who could be turned into swell combat pilots," noted the *New York Daily News* approvingly. But the Air Corps refused to compromise in other areas. Every applicant had to pass the difficult — some called it "diabolical" — physical, which included not only tests of manual dexterity and problem solving but also a rigorous psychological examination, which included a Rorschach test. Many aviators would later say that passing the exam was the toughest thing they'd ever faced in the Air Corps.

It required bravery simply to sign up for flight school, as the service had acquired the unfortunate habit of killing its own recruits before they even saw combat. Over the course of the war, fifteen thousand airmen — as many men as made up an infantry division — would die in training before they left the continental United States. And once they were in Europe and the South Pacific, Air Corps planners estimated that the force would have to be completely replaced every five months. That is, statistically speaking, everyone in the service would soon be dead. It's no wonder that Hap Arnold, commanding general of Army Air Forces in World War II, stated that every airman needed to be "honest, truthful, reliable . . . [and] possess that *sine qua non,* courage."

Despite the risks, tens of thousands of young men flocked to the Air Corps. Gene Hambleton was one of them. Though he had to have been short on cash, he'd somehow scraped enough money together to pay a dentist to fix his teeth. He now aimed himself at the cockpit of an American aircraft the way a missileer aims a rocket at a distant city.

But it wasn't to be. We don't know whether Gene failed some part of the physical for flight school or whether the competition to become an aviator was simply too fierce, but he gave up the dream of flying bombers over Germany and settled for navigation school. It must have been a searing disappointment.

Meanwhile, Gene's younger brother Gil had completed flight school and was headed to Europe as the pilot of a B-17 heavy bomber. And as the months went by, the family received letter after letter describing Gil's exploits; he flew thirty missions over Germany without a single downed plane or a single lost crew member. In fact, Gil Hambleton was so adept in the cockpit that he was chosen for assignments that pushed ahead the new technology of radar. Secret missions. Quiet, serious Gil didn't talk much about them — in fact he preferred not to talk about himself very much at all — but there was no doubt he'd proved himself to be an exceptionally able and courageous pilot.

While Gene had been working the assembly line, his kid brother had gone out and become a war hero. A sibling rivalry began to smolder. "On top of his resentment over not becoming a pilot, there was my father," said Gene's niece Sharon. Both brothers were anxious to make their mark, but only Gil had excelled among the very best the country had to offer. "It caused an estrangement."

Navigation school did provide one pleasant revelation for Hambleton. He found that he had an almost uncanny sense of cardinal direction, that is, a sense of where north, south, east, and west lay without the use of a compass. He was a natural. "In 1945, I graduated," he recalled, "a smart-assed second lieutenant who knew he was the best goddamned navigator in the whole Army Air Corps."

But the setbacks and the lengthy training at navigation school meant that his journey to the front took longer than he'd anticipated. When he was finally ready, waiting for his first assignment, the *Enola Gay* dropped the atomic bomb on Hiroshima. The war had ended before Gene Hambleton could get into it.

2

ROCKET MAN

After vj day, Gene left the Air Force (keeping a Reserve commission), moved back to Peoria with Gwen, and tried his hand at selling fridges. Like millions of other discharged soldiers, he morphed into Mr. Suburbia.

While Gene was peddling appliances to Illinois housewives, more bad news arrived. After Gwen attempted to get pregnant for months without any luck, they went to see a doctor. He did some tests and told the couple they were unable to have children. It was a shock. "They would have been awesome parents," said Gene's sister-in-law Donna. Gene was good with kids; they were drawn to him. "He was a delightful uncle," said his niece Pam. The fact that his brother Gil had become both a father and a war hero seemed to emphasize that Gene was destined to be the unlucky Hambleton boy.

On June 25, 1950, at four o'clock in the morning, North Korean troops with their Soviet tanks, artillery guns, and even their Russian-stitched uniforms poured across the 38th parallel and invaded the South. The Korean War was under way, and Gene was called back to service. He entered the United States Air Force and was sent away to retrain as a navigator on the B-29 Superfortress, the state-of-the-art four-engine bomber whose development had cost more money than the Manhattan Project itself.

Here was another chance at glory.

He missed Gwen. He sent her frequent, adoring letters. "I love you so damn much," he wrote her in one, "and am waiting for you as patiently as possible." His loneliness was a constant theme; he always wanted his wife next to him, begged her to join him, in fact. During training, he wrote her from the barracks at Ellington Air Force Base in Houston. "No matter what happens, honey, I would like to have you down here . . . That I will love . . . All the other fellows have brought their wives down and moved to town." He would go to Air Force dances and look at the women there and walk back to his bunk and compose a letter to Gwen. "I have been down here so long that some of them are even beginning to look as good as you," he wrote in one. "But not quite . . . I suppose you know I love you dearest and do hope that you get here soon."

Gene was posted to Korea and flew forty-three missions, directing the pilots on their runs to the North, the B-29s loaded with thousands of pounds of high-octane fuel and heavy loads of incendiary, fragmentation, and delayed-fuse bombs, dodging flak and the new MiG-15 fighters supplied by Joseph Stalin. It was Gene's job to get the plane to its drop spot and back, and he was good at it.

When he'd graduated from navigator's school, he'd told friends that he was going to stay in the service "for five years or five stars." That is, if he wasn't on his way to making five-star general by the time he hit his fifth anniversary, he would leave the Air Force. That didn't happen. By his own estimation, he'd reached the top echelons of his craft, but his career hadn't turned out the way he'd imagined. There were no medals, no string of rapid promotions, no headlines back home in Illinois. He was just another airman in a distant war.

After completing his combat tour, Gene was rotated out of Korea and assigned to the Strategic Air Command. The SAC controlled two of the three legs of the nuclear triad: bombers armed with atomic weapons, and land-based intercontinental missiles, or ICBMs. Hambleton would serve in both. After arriving back in the United States, he went to work as an intelligence and targeting officer, and then as a radar-bomb navigator on B-47s at bases in Oklahoma and Texas. In 1961 he received orders to report for navigator duty on the B-52 bomber; at the same time, a friend and fellow navigator was assigned to missiles. Gene didn't want the B-52s, so he and his buddy decided to swap assignments. The Air Force agreed to the switch.

That summer, Hambleton flew to Madison County, Alabama, to begin classes at the famous Redstone Arsenal. During World War II, Redstone had been used as a chemical weapons plant which produced 27 million bombs and other munitions containing lethal poisons such as phosgene and mustard gas. After the surrender of Japan, Redstone switched its focus to missiles. The nature of warfare was evolving, and Hambleton was at the forefront of the change. He'd gone to Redstone to become a Rocket Man.

Beginning at the end of World War II, the secret American program known as Operation Paperclip funneled German scientists who had worked on Hitler's missile programs to the States, including the mastermind of the V2 rocket, Wernher von Braun, and more than 1600 German specialists. They arrived at Redstone and went to work on a series of rockets that would lead to the Saturn V, which would lift American astronauts to the moon. But traveling into space wasn't the first objective of the German scientists and their American colleagues. A potential nuclear exchange with the Soviet Union was. Redstone began producing an array of new weapons: surface-to-air, surface-to-surface, medium-range, and intercontinental missiles.

When Hambleton arrived at Redstone, he began working on the Jupiter family of rockets, designed by von Braun himself, one of which, the liquid-fueled Jupiter-C, was used on the first nuclear-armed medium-range ballistic missile. The airman was then assigned to the two-stage Titan family, which eventually lifted astronauts into the atmosphere during the Gemini program, the forerunner to Apollo. With his security clearance, Hambleton was briefed on the highly classified list of Soviet cities, airfields, and military headquarters inside the USSR that would be struck first in a nuclear exchange. "I'd been in targeting for most of my career," he noted later. "I knew almost every target that was going to get a bomb if we ever went to war."

Once he'd finished his nine-month training at Redstone, Hamble-

ton flew to Turkey and began his duties as a "launch maintenance officer" at the Cigli Air Base, where Jupiter missiles had been deployed in
April. The Jupiters were kept as a deterrent to the Soviet leader, Nikita
Khrushchev, putting him on warning that any invasion of Germany and
the rest of NATO would be met with a fierce nuclear-tipped response.

On October 14, 1962, five months after Hambleton began his tour in
Turkey, Major Richard Heyser, flying above Cuba in a U-2 spy plane, took
a series of 928 photographs of the terrain below. When the photos were
developed, analysts spotted the telltale marks of an SS-4 medium-range
ballistic missile site under construction near the city of San Cristóbal.
Khrushchev had decided to deploy the missiles partly as a response to
the placement of the Jupiters in Turkey and Italy. Two days later, President Kennedy was informed and the Cuban Missile Crisis began.

That week, schoolchildren across America practiced their duck and
cover drills as Cuban families gathered together in crowded Havana
apartments to await "the end of the world." As the standoff intensified,
the missile installation at Cigli became both a flashpoint and a bargaining
chip. Had nuclear war broken out, Hambleton and his men would most
likely have been ordered to launch the Jupiters at their targets deep in the
USSR, if the men and their missiles weren't vaporized by incoming Soviet missiles first. As the negotiations continued, it became clear to both
sides that a quid pro quo arrangement might lower tensions and decrease
the chance of war. On October 28, US attorney general Robert Kennedy
hand-delivered a note to the Russian ambassador agreeing to the terms of
a deal. The Soviet Union withdrew its missiles from Cuba, and President
Kennedy pulled the Jupiters out of Turkey. Hambleton had nearly played
a part in the arrival of Doomsday, but the moment passed.

After spending more than a year at Cigli, Hambleton returned to the
States and began to climb the Air Force ziggurat. He worked his way up
to missile launch officer and then commander at Mountain Home Air
Force Base in Idaho before being appointed squadron commander of the
390th Strategic Missile Wing at Davis-Monthan Air Force Base in Tucson. He was now in charge of several of the enormous, tetchy Titan IIs
that dotted the complex, missiles that carried the largest warhead ever de-

ployed by SAC. As part of his duties, Hambleton strapped a .38 revolver to his thigh; if any of his subordinates disobeyed the order to launch the ICBMs, he was authorized to shoot the man on the spot.

Finally reunited with Gwen, Hambleton bought a comfortable home in Tucson, joined a Lutheran church, and played endless rounds of golf at the local courses.

By 1971, Hambleton was fifty-two years old. He had over two and a half decades of service in the USAF, and he began to think of retiring to enjoy the desert air and his circle of friends. But events in Southeast Asia intervened.

With American ground troops leaving the combat theater in huge numbers as part of Richard Nixon's policy of Vietnamization, the burden fell on the Air Force to support the South Vietnamese army, the ARVN. There was a pressing need for more pilots, more navigators, more helicopter mechanics, more of everything. Hambleton was pulled away from his Titan II facility and arrived at Korat Royal Thai Air Force Base in northeast Thailand on September 4, 1971. He assumed the duties of staff navigator for the Forty-second Tactical Electronic Warfare Squadron.

Hambleton and his fellow officers had been enlisted in the "wizards' war," the secret duel between Soviet and American scientists that was under way in the skies over Vietnam. Southeast Asia had become a proving ground for the technology that would decide the next great battle. In preparation for it, the two adversaries were pitting their advanced fighters, radars, laser-guided bombs, and top-secret electronic-war systems against each other in the field. It was a war within a war, and Hambleton found himself privy to its secrets.

The navigator was hardly the bright-eyed airman who had signed up for flight school three decades before. Most of the men around him were twenty or thirty years younger. He was still rail-thin, but he'd grown overly fond of Manhattans and cigarettes, a three-pack-a-day man. He did keep in shape, with some jogging here and there and the occasional bike ride, but it was exercise more appropriate for a suburban bank examiner than it was for a soldier on the front lines. On his best day, Hambleton probably couldn't run a hundred yards without hacking up a lung.

But Vietnam offered opportunities. Not only could he cap off his career by making full colonel, with all the benefits and prestige that offered, but also he still yearned to prove that he was a significant person, a man who might burnish the ancient name of Hambleton in combat. It was just that all the John Wayne moments had passed him by.

As Hambleton headed to Vietnam, Tommy "Flipper" Norris was already there. Fifteen years younger than the navigator, the Navy SEAL had grown up in the heart of government suburbia, in Silver Spring, Maryland; he'd even had a paper route delivering the *Washington Post*. As a boy, he was surrounded by the pale secretaries and the harried mid-level bureaucrats who made American officialdom hum. But Tommy Norris was, from early on, pointed toward a more extreme vocation.

When he was a young boy, Tommy and his brothers heard on the radio that a rare hurricane was approaching Maryland. While his parents prepared, a thought occurred to the ten-year-old: *What would it feel like to stand in the middle of a really big storm? I would like to know that.* Norris didn't want to experience the hurricane on the ground, watching rain cut horizontally across the beautifully manicured yards; he wanted to feel the storm as if he were part of it. Tommy coaxed his little brother into joining him, then climbed up a large oak tree near the family's house, "high enough so I was above the roof line and could really feel the wind." He waited. The hurricane blew in, its winds shearing across the shingle roofs, snapping branches as they went. Norris felt the storm trying to pluck him from the limb and whip him toward southern Pennsylvania. He thoroughly enjoyed the experience.

It was an ordinary American childhood. Norris's dad taught him to hunt and fish, and he managed to make Eagle Scout, so he had some exposure to the outdoors. But there was one thing that stood out in his childhood, and that was Tommy's willpower. "More than the other boys," his mother said, "he could be just plain stubborn." It showed in his pursuits. Tommy was short and thin, too small to play the popular sports in high school, which were basketball and football, so he took up wrestling. And he was a menace. By being almost demonically resistant to defeat, he managed to win two Atlantic Coast Conference championships while at college. Even at the height of his sports success, however, Tommy Norris was a shrimp, weighing in at only 115 pounds.

Early on in life, Norris had become entranced with the idea of becoming a fighter pilot, and in 1968, he finally applied to flight school. During his physical exam, however, he failed the crucial depth-perception test. Norris was crushed; he'd been so convinced that he would be flying the A-4 Skyhawk that he hadn't even thought of a plan B. But the young man quickly decided on a very Tommy Norris solution: he would refuse to accept the results. He resolved to conquer the test, no matter what it took. Norris went to an ophthalmologist and "worked on" his vision (*how* he did this he never quite revealed), spending hour after hour trying to improve his score. After a great deal of time and effort, he somehow managed to pass the test and went back to Andrews Air Force Base in triumph. He was going to be a pilot no matter what the doctors said.

But the military exam turned out to be tougher than the civilian one and Norris flunked it. So he went to Quantico and attempted to pass the Marine test. No go. He schlepped over to the naval hospital in Bethesda and tried the Navy version. Fail. Norris still wasn't done; he joined the Navy as a navigator, hoping to slip by the eye test down the line and make pilot after all. When he came in for the exam, he stood in line and memorized the answers the guys in front of him were giving. "I rattled off the same thing they were saying . . . and the doctor gave me a thumbs-up." Norris was ecstatic. *He'd beaten the system! He was going to fly jets!* It didn't seem to occur to him that being unable to properly judge depth while operating an aircraft capable of 673 mph might not be a very good idea.

The young recruit entered pilot training. But when he attempted to land his plane on an aircraft carrier that was heaving up and down on ocean waves, Norris's vision problem finally caught up with him. He washed out. "It was devastating," he said. "I'd never failed at something I wanted to do."

At loose ends, Norris remembered an article he'd seen in *Reader's Digest* about a secretive unit known as the SEALs, which was barely known to even most military men at the time. When he found a pamphlet that spelled out a SEAL's duties, he got fired up all over again. "*That's* what

I want to do!" he said. Norris wrangled a transfer to the program and entered the six-month training class.

It was and is a process strongly predicated on failure. Three out of every four recruits never made it through the course, and trainers were initially convinced that Norris would be one of them. Early in the program, they nearly shitcanned him for being "too small, too thin and not strong enough." But it turned out that the Maryland kid was deceptively fit and, as his mother could attest, almost unbelievably stubborn.

During Hell Week, when prospects are denied sleep, forced to swim in ice-cold ocean waters, man boats, and lift heavy logs for excruciatingly long periods, Norris came down with a stomach virus, this during a series of days when trainees are burning seven to eight thousand calories every twenty-four hours just to maintain their weight. Food was the only comfort you were provided, and Norris couldn't keep a thing down. Already thin, he dropped to about a hundred pounds; by the end of the week he was medically malnourished, a "barely coherent" skeleton. But he wouldn't ask to be released.

After doing everything they could to get the recruit to drop out, the trainers realized that his gentle exterior wasn't the whole story of Tommy Norris. He might look like a slightly overgrown paperboy, but it turned out he was "as tough as one man could be," in the words of an airman who knew him. Norris didn't care how big, how fast, how well armed you were; he would not stand down. "Tommy's the nicest guy in the world," said one Air Force officer, Darrel Whitcomb, "but there's something about him that says, '*Don't fuck with me.*'"

There was something else, too. Men who later served with Norris came to believe that he was a psychological oddity, wired differently than they — or most human beings — were. Particularly when it came to what might be called fear management. This was a skill that most SEALs excelled in; these were guys, after all, who *signed up* to be sent into the hairiest, most dangerous scenarios the American military encountered all over the world. But even among this highly select group of young men, Norris was an outlier. You as a SEAL team member might be facing a machine gunner zeroed in on your exposed position and you might think you were doing great by concealing the abject fear you felt; then you looked over at Tommy Norris, who didn't seem to comprehend what fear *was*.

Of the approximately seventy-five men who began the course that year, fifteen graduated, and one was Tommy Norris. He certainly stood apart from the other fourteen. He rarely drank, and if he did, he always stopped at one beer. He didn't curse — this became a source of wild amusement to the other SEALs, who could be almost unconscionably foulmouthed — and he had a donkeyish laugh that could make those unacquainted with him think he was a little simple, which he wasn't. "A real gentleman, very engaging, always smiling and giggling" is how one airman portrayed Norris, a description perhaps never applied to another SEAL, living or dead. Only Norris's thick, muscular neck and a certain stone-breaking look that came into his eyes when he was angry indicated that he might be something other than the quiet young division chaplain. He even ended up setting several records in the training course, though there was one area related to the Hambleton mission that he did not excel in: the dude from Silver Spring always came last in swimming.

Still, Norris had made it. "Probably more than any of the rest of us," said one of his classmates, "he wanted to be a Navy SEAL."

3

KORAT

THE MORNING of April 2, 1972, Gene Hambleton awoke in his hooch. He could hear the hum of air-conditioning as he lay between fresh white sheets and rubbed his eyes. The navigator got up and readied himself for the day. He took a shower, soaking his lean frame under a steady stream of hot water, then had a leisurely shave with his electric razor plugged into the base's grid. As he did so, he might have spotted in the corner of his mirror the Thai maid assigned to his hooch flitting soundlessly here and there in the background. He knew that when he ventured out, the maid would take the time to collect his dirty clothes, launder, fold, and return them, while at the same time refilling his refrigerator with fresh pineapple and other delights. Did Gene prefer the taste of Tiger Beer (imported from Singapore) or perhaps the smoother yet still potent San Miguel (brewed in the Philippines)? Whichever it was, chilled bottles would be waiting for him on his return, along with clean sheets on the bed.

He hit the latrine, careful to avoid the snakes the Thais nicknamed "two-steppers" because by your second step after being bitten by one, you'd be dead. After making his way back to the hooch, he donned his freshly washed flight suit, then strolled out onto the base grounds. At the dining hall, which was perhaps the finest of its kind in Southeast Asia, he greeted his squadron mates and chose from a buffet that featured SOS (creamed hamburger on toast), eggs scrambled, fried, or soft-boiled, pancakes, sausage, toast, fried potatoes, and much more. He selected bacon and eggs with coffee and took the tray to a nearby table. There he ate leisurely while shooting the shit with some aviators.

After his last cup of java, he headed out. Maybe he dropped a letter to Gwen at the post office, or jumped on a bicycle — you could buy one cheap in the nearby town of Korat — and pedaled around the base. Did he want a new bespoke suit? Gene was careful with money, but you could go to the tailor's shop and pick out any material you desired (a light cotton blend was popular with the squadron dudes) and soon be the owner of a sharp-looking jacket and pants that would cost you a fraction of what they did back in Tucson. He could even snap up a bolt of Thai silk for his wife to have a few dresses made.

Had an American war been fought from such an enchanted place, ever, in the history of the republic? It was hard to imagine. Movies? Nightly at the base cinema. Gems? Jewelers from Bangkok arrived regularly to sell the airmen pearls, opals, emeralds, and sapphires for their wives and daughters back home. A spot of exercise, perhaps? The swimming pool sparkled in the bright Thai sun. Bronze statues? Hand-woven tapestries? Siamese dancing dolls? Elephants carved from ivory tusks? They were all at hand, and for a song.

When the warm evenings arrived, you could stroll over to the Officers' Club. What *didn't* the dudes get up to in that place? The club was filled with go-getters and former college quarterbacks and hot-rodding speed freaks turned Air Force pilots and navigators; it was like walking into an exceptionally rambunctious foreign chapter of Chi Psi. At the top of the social pyramid were the fighter jocks, instantly recognizable by the way they used their hands to describe a particular maneuver, flattening their hands out and holding them together and away from their bodies, imitating their aircraft as their fingers ducked and soared in a circle of cool-eyed men.

The dudes were treated like pale gods here in Korat. And they did tend to run amok. Some drank like fishes. They were pure death on the Thai waitresses, though no one ever remembered Hambleton — still smitten with Gwen — participating. And every so often they threw a party that required structural repair to the club itself.

Once, before Hambleton's time, a visiting American nurse at another

Thai base had been having dinner when she objected to all the drinking and carousing and loud hoo-hawing emanating from a group of eight Air Force dudes who were no doubt a few bottles into their evening. She was eating her dinner, for God's sake, and she demanded that the airmen quiet down and behave like officers and gentlemen. After she returned to her table, the boys looked at one another, stood up as a group, walked over to the nurse's table, scooped her into their arms, flipped her skirt up, slapped some green paint on her backside, and raised her with a great tribal bellow to the ceiling of the club, where they pressed her cheeks against the wood and left two fat green blotches there as a memento of the evening.

Everything was provided for at Korat. It was almost as if the Air Force were trying to make up for the fact that the war not only was stupendously unpopular back home but also, after seventeen years, had become deeply frustrating to fight. The troop withdrawals were continuing, and many airmen were hoping that their one-year tours would soon be cut short and they could return home. No one wanted to be the last man to die in Vietnam.

But there were still combat missions to be flown, and no one was deceived about what they were doing in the skies over Southeast Asia. It's not as if the service didn't try to warn you what could happen. Far from it. One aspiring jock remembered the moment during undergraduate pilot training when he was directed to the doctor's office and found a nurse bent over, laying eighteen-inch paper squares on the floor. She proceeded to ink up the soles of his feet and told him to stand on the squares. What the hell for? he wondered. The young man could make neither heads nor tails of the whole procedure until another candidate took him aside and explained that when you're piloting an F-4 Phantom II, say, and you crash through the forest canopy going 1,400 mph and smash into the earth while carrying several thousand pounds of aviation fuel, the only thing that tends to remain of your physical person are the bottoms of your feet sitting inside your jungle boots. So that's what the Air Force used to identify you.

(And what you must understand in order to fully enter into the mind of an Air Force combat pilot circa 1972 is that the inkblot thing wasn't a problem for most of them. It was *part of the attraction*. They weren't flying puddle jumpers or "buses"—transport planes—that lumbered through the sky like oversized bread boxes, things a man would be ashamed to be seen in, let alone fly. You were strapping yourself into the hottest, loudest, most violent machines on the face of the earth, machines so powerful they would not just zorch you across the open skies at Mach 1+ but could magically change you from a solid to a gas—or at least a loose assembly of particles suspended in a gas—in the blink of an eye. You had to admit it was intriguing.)

There were reminders at Korat, too, of the bad things. A large plaque hung on the wall of the briefing hut with the name of every squadron member who'd gone MIA or KIA in the war, and the men passed it every day on the way to learn about their next mission. And there was Roscoe, a big long-haired brown dog of no recognizable breed. Roscoe had the freedom of the base, attended briefings or didn't, according to his mood, ate in the kitchen of the Officers' Club, and toured the grounds by his own mysterious schedule. You could pet Roscoe all you wanted and offer him treats, which he'd accept, but if you tried to get him to become your dog—and many dudes did—you were shit out of luck. Because Roscoe had once belonged to a pilot who flew out of Korat, and that pilot had been shot down and never returned. That night, Roscoe had waited as usual by the man's hooch for him to land. When he failed to arrive, the dog refused to leave. He wouldn't eat. He wouldn't be comforted or coaxed away. He wouldn't, that is, forget.

The guys on the base absolutely adored Roscoe. They secretly hoped *any* living thing loved them as much as that goddamned dog loved that goddamned missing flyboy. And yet it was hard to look at Roscoe and not contemplate the fact that his master was at that moment hiding somewhere in the northern Vietnamese jungle or was boxed up in a prison being ravaged by dysentery and enduring periodic torture by the NVA. At best. Chances were the aviator had become "monkey meat," as the dudes said. That is, he was dead.

That afternoon, Hambleton reported for his crew briefing in the Operations Center. The building's interior walls were lined with high-resolution maps of target areas in Laos, Cambodia, South and North Vietnam, as well as overhead recon photographs, all laid out in precise order. Sometimes you would see pilots and their navigators stalking a slow path about six feet from the walls, staring intently at the photographs. From that distance, the pictures showed what you would see from your window at ten thousand feet up, so the two men would be "flying" the route in their minds, memorizing the landmarks as they crept along. The place was usually crawling with airmen, and today was no different.

When he checked in, Hambleton learned that two EB-66s — electronic countermeasures planes that kept the SAM missiles off the big bombers — were needed to accompany three B-52s to bomb an area below the DMZ, west of a town called Cam Lo. NVA battalions were attacking the South Vietnamese bases in the area and the B-52s were being sent to hit them as they advanced.

Hambleton was in charge of scheduling the squadron navigators, and he was in a fix. One of the planes was all set to go. But the navigator scheduled to fly in the other aircraft, a man named Thomas McKinney, wasn't on the base. The Red Cross had informed McKinney that doctors near his home in Boston had discovered a congenital defect in his three-year-old son's heart; McKinney had received emergency permission to travel stateside and was now somewhere in the air on his way to Massachusetts. Short a navigator, Hambleton had to make a decision, and he decided he would take the seat behind the pilot and fly the mission himself.

The briefing was fairly standard. The North Vietnamese hadn't launched an organized offensive in two full years; there was a sense, at least among the airmen, that the war was winding down. The aircraft would leave Korat in the afternoon and rendezvous with a tanker plane to refuel before heading toward the target point. The officer in charge mentioned the destination was in a hot zone, but that in itself wasn't unusual.

There were SAM sites in North Vietnam and reports of them as far south as the DMZ, but none had ever been spotted in South Vietnam. Hambleton's plane would spend only fifteen minutes over the target; if everything went according to plan, Hambleton and the B-52s would fly over, drop their bombs, turn around, and be back in Korat in time for a round of Manhattans and some good-time Air Force drinking.

Hambleton and his crew left the meeting and headed to the Life Support Shop. There they found everything they needed for the mission: survival vests, helmets with their black glass visors, oxygen masks, ejection harnesses. The men talked and joked as they suited up. "Our conversation usually runs to sharp banter and relentless kidding," said one Vietnam pilot. (Talking about the dangers of the mission was, of course, completely forbidden.) The men adjusted the harnesses, fit their oxygen masks to their helmets, and tucked away the requisite flight cards and maps in their flight suits. They removed anything from their pockets that would give away their rank or details of their mission, in case they were captured. Carrying their helmets in their bags, the six men filed out of the shop into the muggy heat.

On the aircraft parking ramp, the crew spotted their assigned aircraft, an EB-66C, painted in jungle camo, looking long and lean in the late morning light. The plane stretched seventy-five feet, weighed 42,000 pounds, and was capable of a top speed of 643 mph. Introduced in 1954, it had originally been designed as a light bomber, but now its hold was chock-full of state-of-the-art electronic equipment designed to locate and avoid enemy radar and missile sites. The mission of the plane and its crew was to help protect the B-52s on their bombing run.

The technology was fairly simple. When the enemy turned on its radar systems, the equipment onboard the EB-66C picked up the signal. The navigator, as well as the "crows"—the electronic warfare officers, or EWOs, in the back of the plane—would get an amber light on their monitors. When the SAM guidance system came online, they got a green light. When the missile lifted off, there was a flashing red light and the message "launch, launch, launch." Amber, then green, then red.

The Russian SAMs were needle-shaped missiles thirty-five feet long, twice the thickness of telephone poles, and topped with warheads wrapped in metal chain. By 1972, they'd become icons of the Cold War. It was a SAM that had shot down Francis Gary Powers in his spy plane over Russia in 1960—a major embarrassment to the Eisenhower administration, which initially lied to cover up the purpose of Powers's mission—and the appearance of SAM sites in Cuba that had alerted JFK to the presence of missiles there. The SAM was, even to the dudes of the USAF, who admitted to fearing nothing, something that motivated regular attendance at the base chapel. "I'll tell you one thing," Hambleton said. "A SAM coming up at you is a hell of a feeling."

The US government was intensely interested in the missile. The CIA had secretly bought a Fan Song radar from the Indonesians, the same model that guided the SAMs to their targets, just to study the system and try to game its flaws. But they quickly realized there was no way to shoot a SAM down once it had been launched. There were no antimissile missiles, no lasers that would intercept the SAM mid-flight. And so the Air Force had developed the technique known as "jinking."

It was a simple, if terrifying, process for an Air Force pilot. First, an electronic warning buzzer would blare in your headset, or your backseater would yell out the dreaded words *"SAM on scope!"* On hearing these warnings, you had to immediately snap your gaze earthward and search the sky below until you spotted the fat white contrail of a missile rocketing your way from the earth. Ideally, you would then maneuver your plane so that the SAM was coming up either on your right at two o'clock or on your left at ten o'clock. At the same time that you were positioning your aircraft for optimal vision, you'd increase your power and drop the nose for extra speed. Now came the difficult part, the part that would prove your blood ran colder than Antarctic ice melt and that you were not a disgrace to the holy name of Chuck Yeager. You had to sit quietly in your cockpit as a SAM carrying a ginormous load of TNT came rocketing toward you at Mach 3.5, its shape growing larger and larger with each passing second . . . and do nothing. Zero. Just sit there and count, *one thousand one, one thousand two, one thousand three,* like some eight-year-old boy playing hide-and-seek with his hand over his eyes back home in Indiana or Wyoming or wherever you were from. You knew you had precisely ten seconds from when the NVA operator launched the missile to the moment when the warhead ignited in a burst of super-hot gases. As you counted, you let your hand rest on the stick, inert, while the missile loomed up in your windscreen until it was close enough — but precisely *how* close was a matter of personal judgment, as this was all done by feeling, by a sense of internal timing — and then you "jinked," that is, snapped the stick left or right and dove toward and under the oncoming SAM. This was also called a "SAM break." You checked the

SAM to make sure it was following your descent. When it was fully committed, you pulled the nose up and hoped the missile didn't snap its nose back up and track you again.

Most pilots executed the break right after counting *one thousand five.* It had happened in the past that a pilot lost his nerve and broke too soon, turned the plane over on *one thousand three,* and discovered to his horror that the missile's guidance system had sensed the evasive maneuver, corrected for the new course, and found the escaping plane in its ninety-degree dive, following it right on down until it blew the pilot and his fellow crew members out of their seats and sent bits and pieces of them raining down over the Vietnamese rice fields. If you broke too late? Letting it hang out there till *one thousand eight,* perhaps? The same thing.

But if you held on until the missile was almost ready to detonate and then and only then did you snap your stick hand over all the way, the SAM would shoot harmlessly out into the cold ether. Instead of feeling the first wave of overpressure and seeing the bloom of the fireball as it expanded toward your windscreen, the rocket would either whisper past you to detonate with a satisfying *krrruummmp* in the distance or begin to roll and tumble, spraying various Soviet components all over the Vietnamese countryside in a gratifying display of American technological superiority.

It all came down to those ten seconds, whether you would make it or not. "Every day," said one airman, "was like going to the OK Corral."

4

THE BOYS IN THE BACK

ONE BY ONE, the crew members ducked under the tail of the plane, found the rectangular hatch cut into the fuselage, and stepped on the lowest rung of the drop-down stairs that led upward into the EB-66C, which carried the call sign Bat 21 for this mission. There was one pilot, Major Wayne Bolte, one navigator, and four crows. Hambleton climbed aboard and took the navigator's seat, just behind and to the right of Bolte, a blond, blue-eyed, square-jawed thirty-seven-year-old Oklahoman who looked for all the world like a pilot from an Air Force recruiting poster; the only things that were missing were a toothy smile and a vigorous thumbs-up. The four crows were behind and below Hambleton, in the belly of the plane.

As Bolte taxied out to the runway, Hambleton flicked on the radar switch. Once the monitor warmed up, he clicked it to high-power mode. Then he leaned back into his seat and lit a Lucky Strike. He was relaxed, calm. Years of experience, the ambient cockiness of the airmen around him, and the winking space-age equipment of the EB-66C all told him that he would be practically invulnerable during the flight. "There is no way a SAM could hit my airplane," he thought to himself.

Bat 21 taxied down the tarmac. At 3:20 p.m., it lifted into the air and joined the four other planes on their way north.

The crows sitting behind Hambleton, out of sight, were mostly mysteries to the navigator. Squadron dudes, just like him. Lieutenant Colonel Charles Levis was a thirty-nine-year-old Texan who'd gone to the

1955 Sugar Bowl as a member of the US Naval Academy football team and had become a favorite of the maids at Korat, passing them extra cash to help them through emergencies and even sitting on his bunk listening to them pour out their stories of errant husbands or ungrateful children. First Lieutenant Robin F. Gatwood was a dark-eyed twenty-five-year-old from Hickory, North Carolina, who'd left a young wife and a one-year-old son to fight. Born and raised in Louisiana, Major Henry M. Serex was a forty-year-old Naval Academy graduate known to his family as "Mick"; he had a wife and two young daughters at home waiting for him.

The men, by and large, had the support of their families and loved ones, if not the country they fought for. But the tension that the war had created back home was clearly traceable in the life of the crew's final member. Lieutenant Colonel Anthony Giannangeli was a forty-one-year-old math whiz, first-generation Italian American, Catholic, a funny, gregarious, meticulous man who loved nothing more than to go fishing with his sons. The memories of their trips would remain with his boys all their lives. Once, the airman took his sons out to a fast-flowing mountain stream in Colorado, hoping to catch some cutthroat trout. Giannangeli and his sons stood there hour after hour, waiting for the tip of the pole to bob up and down. Such was the force field of competitive desire that emanated from their father's body that afternoon that his oldest son, Robert, found himself praying for the line to jerk and for his father to bag a fish. "He wanted," Robert says, "to catch that fish *so bad*." In his mind, Robert pleaded with God to intervene in the natural world just this once and direct a good-sized trout to his father's hook so that the man's brow could unclench and he could be completely happy, at least for a moment. It wasn't just that Giannangeli loved fishing; it was more that these trips were so brief, squeezed in between military assignments, and he wanted them to be a success.

In 1972, Robert was sixteen. Secretly, without his father's knowledge, he'd become an ardent opponent of the Vietnam War. "My father would have been livid had he known," thought Robert. So he hid his feelings. The Giannangelis were living in Colorado Springs at the time, a military town that almost — but not quite — seemed cut off from the roiling mood of the rest of the country. One day, Robert got word that an antiwar march was going to be held the next day and the route would take it to the Air

Force base — actually, to the very building where his father worked. Robert decided to go.

The next afternoon he found himself striding toward the base, chanting antiwar slogans with other men and women of all ages and hoisting their signs decrying the bombings and the napalm runs and the deaths of innocent civilians. When they reached his father's building, Robert saw military snipers on the roof, watching the crowd and ducking to speak into their walkie-talkies. There were the disapproving faces of Air Force officers in the windows as well, but what Robert feared most was the heart-stopping possibility that a friend of his father's might spot him and tell the old man and he would learn that Robert despised what he was doing in the service of his country. Robert knew a confrontation between him and his dad was inevitable, but he could no longer countenance the burning hooches and dead children he saw on the *CBS Evening News*. And so he refused to stop what he was doing.

If Robert was hiding his true feelings from his father, so was Lieutenant Colonel Giannangeli hiding his role in the war from his sons and daughters. He'd implied to his children that his work wasn't that dangerous; in fact, he'd basically told them he had what amounted to a desk job. But Robert had intimations that all was not as it seemed. Months earlier, Giannangeli had gone to a rigorous jungle survival school in the Philippines that all airmen were required to complete, the same one that Gene Hambleton had gone through on his way to the war. When he returned home to Colorado Springs, Giannangeli brought back a knife, a sharptoothed, dangerous-looking thing. Robert had found the knife and he'd been fascinated, almost obsessed, by it ever since, especially the special hook that his dad informed him was to cut a parachute cord if you got hung up in a tree. One night Robert secretly went to his father's room and took the weapon and brought it back to his bedroom, where he hid it on a shelf in his closet, a totem of unspoken things. He'd felt guilty about it ever since. On April 1, Robert had a dream in which his father came to him and asked for the weapon back.

As the EB-66s flew north that afternoon, Lieutenant Colonel Giannangeli, who was deeply religious, may have said a prayer. Then he likely settled into his seat and caught some sleep, which was standard for crows on long missions. Rest was hard to come by, and you grabbed some whenever you could. Colorado was fourteen hours behind. Giannangeli's children were asleep, as was Gwen Hambleton.

The planes drew closer to the target, flying in the thin air of thirty thousand feet. They were joined by two jet fighters that would watch for approaching MiGs, along with two F-105G fighter-bombers with special missiles mounted on their wings designed to hit SAM sites on the ground. The nine aircraft now flew in a loose formation as the bright sunshine of afternoon softened and the first hints of dusk darkened the line of hills on the horizon.

It was quiet inside the plane; there was a feeling of seclusion. Hambleton's tight-fitting helmet and rubber earphones, along with the thick soundproofing on the EB-66C, blocked the hiss of air rushing past outside the metal skin of the airplane. Hambleton could hear his own breathing and the breathing of Bolte; occasionally the navigator chatted with the pilot, updating him on their course. When they were ten minutes from the target, Bolte called back to the EWOs. "You crows in back wake up. Crank up your jamming equipment . . . Stand by to dispense chaff." Hambleton heard a click in his headset, one of the crows acknowledging. He bent over his monitor, his reading glasses perched on his nose. It was about 4:50 p.m.

As they approached the DMZ, something unexpected happened. The monitors in front of the crows and Hambleton began blinking. Amber lights. Enemy radar sites were turning on and tracking the planes, and the amber lights in front of the crows were flashing. The B-52s started to jam the enemy radar, throwing an electronic smokescreen up around the formation.

As they got closer to their target, two Fan Song radar systems to the west came up on their screens. The green lights blinked on. The crows onboard the B-52s turned on their jamming equipment and waited for red.

Red signal. Four SAMs launched into the air.

The other EB-66 was closer to the launch sites, on the opposite side of the formation, and the SAMs locked on it. The pilot counted off *one thousand one, one thousand two* . . . When he reached *one thousand five,* he rolled and dove for the earth, spraying chaff as he went. The missiles couldn't turn with the craft and exploded harmlessly in midair.

Hambleton heard a voice on his UHF radio. It was the pilot aboard the other EB-66, Bat 22. "SAM uplink, vicinity of DMZ, Bat 22." Six more SAMs hissed into the air and the planes dove and turned to avoid the rockets. The missiles shot up through the formation and exploded, but the bursts of shrapnel missed the diving airplanes.

To the northwest, a North Vietnamese SAM unit — Detachment 62 — was in an "alert posture." The soldiers were expecting American aircraft to pass over them on the way to delivering airstrikes farther north. The telephone in the command post rang; an officer picked it up, listened, then announced that enemy airplanes were approaching from the southwest. "Avenge our murdered compatriots!" the commander cried. The men of Detachment 62 watched the skies for contrails.

The American planes had regained their altitude and were streaming toward the target area at about 530 mph. Tracer bullets arced up at them from antiaircraft artillery — AAA — batteries on the ground, leaving puffs of white smoke in hollowed-out circles drifting in the air. The F-105Gs spotted the missile sites and dove to bomb them.

One of the men from Detachment 62 spotted the American planes above. "Target acquired!" he shouted in Vietnamese. Bat 21, Hambleton's plane, was the farthest out on the northwest edge of the formation. It was now between Detachment 62 and the B-52s.

The sky was thick with the white contrails of newly launched missiles soaring toward the glints in the sky. "Oh shit," shouted the pilot of Bat 22. He jinked the aircraft away from the SAMs, which began exploding one after the other, the concussions sending pressure waves through the thin aluminum skins of the American planes.

Hambleton was studying his instruments and glancing at his maps. In the belly of the aircraft, the crows were bent over their equipment, tracking the SAM launches. The air was now filled with a collection of dodging aircraft, Soviet missiles, and heavy flak. With so many SAMs in the air, you could jink away from one and veer right into the path of another. But Hambleton's lights were still dark; no amber or green lights had come up, which meant that no radar had locked on to his plane and no SAM sites were tracking it.

The men of Detachment 62 had purposefully not turned on their radar or guidance systems. They'd decided on an optical-only launch, something that Hambleton and the other crews had never experienced before. When the American planes came into range, the Vietnamese commander yelled "Fire!" Three SAMs leapt off their launchpads in a boiling mist of orange smoke.

Aboard Bat 21, the amber and green lights remained dark.

The solid boosters pushed the missiles skyward, the SAMs quickly attaining Mach 3. The boosters cut out and the liquid fuel ignited, a red fuming nitric acid acting as the oxidizer to the pure kerosene fuel. The wings on the tail stabilized the missiles as they rocketed upward at 2,600 mph, while the fretted surfaces of their metal fins prevented them from rolling over and exploding.

One SAM soared toward Bat 21, flying thousands of feet above. The North Vietnamese controller on the ground guided the missile by sight alone, maneuvering it by radio signals sent to two sets of small antennas placed just ahead of the forward fins. As the nose of the missile cut through the warm air, just behind it lay the fragmentation warhead, lethal within a radius of 820 feet.

Finally, the controller switched on the guidance system. The missile "found" the American plane and darted toward it.

Red lights flashed inside Bat 21. *"SAM on scope!"* a voice shouted in Hambleton's earpiece. Hambleton was bewildered. What had happened to the amber and green? The red warning signal was beeping furiously. The pilot, Bolte, began counting to himself. *One thousand one, one thousand two, one thousand* . . . But his margin of error had been cut in half. "We were five seconds late," Hambleton recalled, "and we didn't know it."

"Move right!" one of the crows said on the interphone. Bolte whipped the plane to the right, toward where he thought the missile was. He would dive under it and the SAM would roll and explode. The EB-66 began to turn into the break.

Another voice broke in. "Negative, negative, negative, move left, move *left!*" One of the crows had calculated the path of the SAM and shouted out a new heading. Bolte jammed the stick left, losing time. As the plane began righting itself and Bolte started to tip the wing left, Hambleton glanced out his window and saw a white shape rising from behind the aircraft at astonishing speed. Bolte pushed the plane left and the shape disappeared.

At that moment, the warhead detonated beneath Bat 21, instantly transforming the heavy chain wrapped around its cone into a white-hot bloom of molten metal, which then radiated out at supersonic speed and struck the underbelly of the aircraft. Had Bolte stayed with the rightward jink, the missile would have made impact near the navigator's window and Hambleton would have been incinerated.

5

THE TIME OF USEFUL CONSCIOUSNESS

THINGS BEGAN HAPPENING very quickly inside the cockpit. Hambleton heard a "tremendous noise" and a flash turned the sky above him orange with fire. His windscreen melted away and bits of metal shrapnel shot through the now-open frame and smacked into the front of his flight suit. He looked down and saw that the metal floor between his feet had disappeared; clouds drifted by beneath his jungle boots.

Something was beeping in his ear. It was the bail-out signal, triggered by Bolte, and it sounded to Hambleton like "the impatient jangle of a doorbell." The navigator immediately reached down, gripped the D-ring on his ejection seat, and pulled it. The canopy above his head lifted away and the compressed-air cylinder beneath the seat shot Hambleton out the top of the plane with gut-wrenching force.

As he spun away from the airplane, Hambleton found himself looking back and down at Bolte as the pilot leaned forward in his seat. Bolte's gaze was fixed on the dark visor of Hambleton's helmet, and the two men stared at each other for a few milliseconds. *Why was Bolte leaning forward like that,* Hambleton thought. Perhaps he'd been wounded by shrapnel in his legs or stomach and was bent over in pain. Or perhaps—and this was in some ways a more disturbing thought—he was holding his D-ring trigger and waiting for Hambleton to clear the jet, in order to avoid a mid-air collision. It was the equivalent of a ship's captain being the last man to leave the vessel; there was a code of the sky as there was of the sea.

It was impossible for Hambleton to say. Because as he rotated away from the aircraft, another explosion — perhaps the aircraft's fuel tanks going up or the impact of a second SAM — shook his body with tremendous force. When he swung back around, Hambleton looked for the plane and saw nothing. "It's gone," he thought to himself, "it's completely gone."

The navigator began gyrating wildly in the air, whipping in a flat circle. The compressed-air cartridge was supposed to launch him into a stable descent; after several minutes, his parachute was supposed to open automatically at a comfortable fourteen thousand feet. But the force of the blast had pushed him into a hard horizontal spin, gasping for breath in air that no human was supposed to breathe. The temperature was thirty degrees below zero.

The first darts of panic needled Hambleton's brain. Something was wrong.

But he needed to find the plane before he fixed the problem. He scanned the horizon as it whipped past in dizzying circles. Around him he saw dark shapes, moving almost lazily through the air. He stared and stared at the objects before he recognized them as seat cushions and other materials blown out of the EB-66 and now drifting earthward. But where was the aircraft?

His mind was going black. Breathing hard, Hambleton wrenched his head left, then right. *There.* Thousands of feet beneath him, a tiny black shape against white clouds, the EB-66C was on fire, out of control and corkscrewing downward. Hambleton watched helplessly as the plane tumbled toward a bank of cumulus, then shot into the mist and disappeared.

Parachutes, then. He wanted to see parachutes. He scanned the sky for dots of green nylon against the miles of white beneath him. But the blue was clear of anything except a dusting of clouds far below. The day was innocent, soundless. In the west, he could see the soft orange and purple glow of the horizon. Dusk.

This meant that the four Americans who'd sat in the belly of the plane — Giannangeli, Serex, Gatwood, and Levis — were probably dead or about to die. Bolte, too. The shock of this thought numbed Hambleton's body. He tried to imagine that these men he'd been bullshitting with just minutes before had been torn apart by a Soviet missile or were at that moment strapped into their seats approaching their deaths as the aircraft tumbled the final few hundred yards toward the earth.

By this time, Hambleton had achieved terminal downward velocity of 122 mph. If he didn't slow his descent, he would slam into the earth, punching a crater into a Vietnamese rice paddy, which some farmer would most likely discover in the morning along with his mangled body. Hambleton was suffering the first stages of hypoxia; his brain was being starved of oxygen, causing him to grow increasingly disoriented. Something called the Time of Useful Consciousness was coming into play. At this height, he had between 60 and 120 seconds before his brain shut down and he fell to earth.

Hambleton thought back to the parachutists he'd watched jump out of Air Force planes during his mandatory training sessions. When they got locked into a spiral like the one he was in, they executed a series of maneuvers to get out of it. They would contort their bodies and, almost magically, the gyrating motion would stop. Now Hambleton tried to re-create the movements as he remembered them, one after the other, twisting his body this way and that to slow the whirling. But nothing worked; in fact, things only got worse. "Everything I did made me spin faster."

His vision was going dark; it was difficult to breathe. "I thought, I'm going to black out." He closed his eyes and saw pinpricks of light. Finally, the answer came to him. Hambleton reached up and pulled the ripcord on his harness. The parachute shot out above him with a silky *fffffftttt*, then snapped open. It immediately slowed his descent.

It's a remarkable and little-known fact that when you descend from five miles above the earth at the end of a parachute, you often experience no sense of falling. As you hang by the nylon straps in the wide blue vault of the sky, everything seems still and picture-like, as if you were pinned to a child's bulletin board waiting for him to return home from school. "My God," Hambleton thought after deploying the chute. "I'm going to hang here the rest of my life." The spinning had stopped, and his dizziness was replaced with a sense of disbelief. The wind ruffled his flight suit, but for all he could tell, he was dangling, perfectly still, in the middle of the darkening sky.

His vision was still blurry and his brain was going black. Hambleton clawed at his chute pack, his numbed fingertips feeling for the tip of the oxygen hose. He found it and pulled it free. He stuck the cold rubber between his lips and reached down to find the oxygen bottle knob, called "the green apple." He pulled it. Oxygen hissed through the hose and his thoughts bloomed back into deep color. He gulped the cold air and his vision slowly cleared.

The airman spotted something below him, a speck of gray that was gradually growing larger. It wasn't a cloud. It wasn't a stream or a rock formation on the ground. It couldn't be, but it was — an American aircraft, circling just *below* him. He recognized it as an O-2, a propeller-powered spotter plane flown by two forward air controllers — FACs. Hambleton reached into his vest and pulled out his survival radio from one of the pockets.

Inside the plane sat First Lieutenant Bill Jankowski and a second FAC. A few minutes before, Jankowski had spotted the SAM from Detachment 62 shooting upward from its mobile launching site into the sky. He'd seen the smoke from the explosion far above him and watched as, seconds later, the EB-66C came tumbling silently through the air, burning brightly and trailing a tail of thick black vapor. The plane had sliced through the blanket of clouds below, cutting a hole in the mist. Then, seconds later, a puff of gray smoke rose from the earth and filled in the hole.

Now Jankowski heard something on his radio: a loud beeping noise followed by what he thought was a voice identifying itself as "Bat 21 Alpha."

Alpha would be the pilot. "Beeper, beeper, come up voice!" Jankowski said. But there was no response from the pilot. Static.

About forty seconds later, another sound crackled on the radio. A voice calling, "This is Bat 21 Bravo." Bravo was code for the number-two man on any EB-66 flight, the navigator. Though Jankowski didn't know his name, it was Gene Hambleton.

The voice repeated the call sign. Jankowski was astonished. He found it hard to fathom that anyone had survived the explosion and the crash. "Do you see us?" he asked.

The voice came back. "Yes, I see you."

Jankowski stared down but couldn't make out the ground through the clouds. He rocked his wings, a standard recognition signal, and asked Bat 21 Bravo if he'd seen the maneuver. The voice confirmed. Now Jankowski was completely dumbfounded. He peered down at the landscape through his side window but could see only gauzy white below him. "You must have damn good eyes to spot me all the way from the ground," he said.

"Look up," Hambleton said. "I'm in the parachute at about twelve grand. Coming down in the middle of your orbit."

Jankowski rolled his aircraft and peered upward. He quickly spotted the olive-green chute above him. "It about blew my mind," Jankowski said. He gunned his engine and flew toward Hambleton, floating at the end of his nylon parachute, then circled around him.

It was an excellent thing that even a lone airman had survived the SAM attack, but Jankowski knew the situation was far worse than Hambleton could have imagined. The navigator wasn't falling toward anything that resembled a demilitarized zone. Three days before, the North Vietnamese had launched what the Americans would name the "Easter Offensive" and the Vietnamese would refer to as *mua he do lua,* the "red fiery summer." Thousands of feet below, hundreds of Soviet tanks, missile batteries, and heavy artillery threaded through the normally half-empty landscape of rice paddies and jungle roads as they rolled toward the cities and firebases of South Vietnam. Along with them were thirty thousand NVA troops. It was Hanoi's all-out push to demolish Richard Nixon's strategy of Vietnamization, humiliate the regime of Nguyen Van Thieu, and win the conflict once and for all. "The great opportunity to end the U. S. war of aggression has come!" read one bulletin handed out to all Vietcong troops just before they streamed across the Z. "Kill the enemy, annihilate tyrants, break the enemy's oppressive control." Hambleton was falling into the midst of the largest enemy invading force of the war.

It was an almost ludicrously awful place to be rescued from.

Jankowski was aware of what awaited the airman below. He had an idea: *What if I tried to grab him now?* If he slowed down, waited for Hambleton to descend to his altitude, then cruised by him and snagged the parachute on his wing, he might be able to save the navigator. Then he could open the O-2's cockpit door and pull Hambleton inside. Was it dangerous? Hell, yes, it was dangerous. Was it *more* dangerous than attempting to evade thousands of highly motivated NVA troops? Maybe not.

Jankowski and his co-pilot talked the maneuver over. They decided it just wasn't possible. Hambleton would have to take his chances on the ground.

The American airman dropped past Jankowski's plane. Below, the mist had cleared and the airman saw a bright landscape crossed by the shadows of small trees and hillocks in a countryside as indecently green as the fields of southern Ireland. Sounds began popping in his ears, startling after so many minutes of hissing near-silence. He recognized the sound of heavy mortars and above it the *tak-tak-tak* of AK-47s. Clearly, someone down there was shooting. With his green chute stark against the blue sky, Hambleton thought, there was a chance the enemy might kill him before he even landed.

Just then, the blue vault in front of Hambleton's eyes disappeared as if by a magician's trick and was replaced by a wall of white. He stared into it, realizing after a few seconds that he'd sunk into a bank of cumulus. In the cloud, he would be invisible to the gunners. It was a stroke of luck.

The navigator broke out below the clouds at sixty feet. "I could see troops all around me," he said. The ground rushed up at him and his boots slammed into a green field. Hambleton pitched forward, then steadied himself and released the chute. He looked around. He was crouched in a rice field. Tracers whined above his head, and he could hear the *crump* of heavy guns in the near distance. The enemy was out there in the deepening dusk.

As he crouched in the furrows of the rice paddy crossed by clouds of mist, scanning the nearby fields for the enemy, Hambleton found himself paralyzed by successive waves of fear and self-doubt. "I said to myself,

'Don't breathe, don't cough, don't move.' I was scared to death." Was he really, as he'd told himself for so many years, a brave man? Could he handle himself behind enemy lines? Was he even physically capable of surviving on the ground in the middle of a shooting war? He had known once. He didn't feel confident that he knew now.

6

ERNIE BANKS

Hambleton knew he couldn't stay in the middle of the rice field. In the flat landscape, he would be like a bug on a tablecloth. The navigator scanned the horizon and spotted what appeared to be a ditch at the edge of the field. A barrage of rifle fire clattered overhead. He ducked down, then began running, crouched low.

When he reached the ditch, he dove in and lay lengthwise. The shallow trench would hide him from anyone scanning the fields from a distance. He looked to his north and west and saw groups of NVA soldiers walking or milling around. They seemed to be everywhere; he estimated there were 150 to 200 enemy soldiers just in his immediate vicinity. If the soldiers moved closer, the ditch would be useless. He had to find better cover.

His heart was racing. It occurred to him then that despite training for World War II, fighting in Korea and Vietnam, and playing his part in the long, dread-filled wait for all-out nuclear war against the USSR, he'd never experienced actual combat, not once in all those years. "I'm sitting in an airplane six and a half miles up," he said, "far removed from all the dirt, screams, and hollering, mud and muck." Now he would surely see war, smell it, wallow in it. He would be required to survive among the people he'd been helping to strafe and bomb and quite honestly obliterate for the past seven months. The Air Force would drop over twice as much ordnance on Vietnam as the total used in World War II, and Hambleton was about to witness the results of that astonishing bombardment, and perhaps answer for it, too.

Capture is what he worried about most. If Hambleton was caught, he believed he would almost certainly be tortured to reveal his secrets. Every American airman in Vietnam had heard the stories that had filtered out from the prisons in the North. The hooks suspended from the ceiling of the Hanoi Hilton where prisoners were hung, their hands and feet tied together like butcher's samples until their limbs swelled to twice their normal size and turned the color of eggplant. The four-by-four-foot tiger cages, made of bamboo, where men were imprisoned for months, left to rot in their own excrement, unable to sit up or lie down. The beds where the legs of POWs were locked in irons, cutting into the tendons, where they lay for weeks and months, prey to rats and sadistic soldiers. The guards at the prison were often chosen from the families of those killed by American bombs; they took their revenge nightly.

The story of Captain Glenn Cobeil was particularly well known among the airmen. He'd been a pilot in an F-105 who'd been shot down in the Red River Delta and brought to the Hanoi Hilton. Loudspeakers blared propaganda in the cells at all hours and a single light bulb burned throughout the night. Cobeil was beaten mercilessly in sessions that lasted as long as fourteen hours; his interrogators carved an X in his back with a rusty nail and pounded his face with a fan belt until one eyeball popped out of its socket. The rumor was that Cobeil had lost his mind after months of such treatment.

For those most intimately involved in the wizards' war, the risks were even higher. One such electronic warfare officer, Captain Jay Jensen, found his F-105 targeted by a SAM in February 1967. The shootdown was considered a "most important victory" for the North Vietnamese, and the men who executed it were awarded the Combat Achievement Medal, First Class, a high honor. Jensen was almost immediately singled out for special attention. At the Hanoi Hilton, the camp commander entered his cell and informed the airman that, as Jensen later recalled, "I had information that they must know, so they would have to make me talk." He was told a firing squad would arrive in five minutes, then three men entered the cell and bound his hands and feet and screwed iron handcuffs into his flesh and veins. They tied a rope around his neck and choked him, then rotated his bound arms over his head until his joints creaked with the pressure. "The pain was unbearable," he said.

His captors brought in another interrogator; Jensen believed he was a Russian.

The Soviet Union had been deeply involved in the war since 1965. The Kremlin's leaders were determined to outmaneuver their Chinese rivals, who were providing arms and troops to North Vietnam, and they hoped to sway governments in Thailand, Malaysia, and the Philippines toward the communist camp. For the Kremlin, the road to Southeast Asia ran through Vietnam. The Russians supplied the North with iron ore, medical supplies, rockets, antiaircraft guns, trucks, tanks, and supersonic jet fighters. In 1968 alone, they sent half a billion dollars' worth of aid to their allies. Along with the supplies came thousands of advisers and trainers, some of whom actually fought and died on the battlefield. And every year, thousands of North Vietnamese officers flew north to attend military colleges in the Soviet Union. Leonid Brezhnev and his peers had entered the war with misgivings, but they were committed to fighting it as long and as fiercely as the Americans did, even as they tried to improve relations with Washington.

One of the returns that the USSR sought for its billions was information about top-secret American technology. The Soviets sent KGB agents to Hanoi to advise their North Vietnamese counterparts on interrogating Americans, though the relationship between the two intelligence services was often tetchy. Moscow also sent a team of specially trained operatives to scour the battlefield for armaments. These operatives scooped up parts of radar systems, missiles, and classified weapons from airplanes that had crashed, crated them up, and sent them back to government laboratories for further study. At one point they even located and recovered the intact cockpit of a downed USAF F-111 in the Vietnamese countryside, which they shipped back to the USSR for further examination. American experts soon spotted knockoffs of American weapons emerging from Soviet factories, including versions of the Sparrow-3 guided missile and highly advanced aircraft engines. The war booty had allowed the Russians to leap ahead years in their weapons development. They were using Vietnam not just as a proxy war to battle American aggression but as a way to steal secrets.

The man who entered Captain Jensen's cell began questioning the American about the electronic jammers and the SAM countermeasures. "How could we find and attack their SAM sites?" he asked the airman. "What electronic equipment did we have?" Jensen found that he was able to trick the Soviet interrogator by passing on information about a "multi-megacycle oscillator with a push-pull amplifier and a squirrel-caged motor," which was a piece of absurdity made up by his classmates in electronics school.

Though he was a navigator and not an EWO, Hambleton was a much more experienced officer than Jensen, with far more exposure to classified information, including "six or seven" generations of American radar systems. It was highly unlikely such nonsense answers would help in the navigator's case, and it was reasonable to think the Soviets would take a keen interest in him. The secrets Hambleton was keeping didn't just concern Vietnam; they could affect the Cold War itself.

The navigator raised his head and looked back at the rice field. His parachute lay spread over the furrowed ground. He briefly considered racing back out and gathering it up, but the thump of a heavy mortar sounded nearby. He decided to wait. There was no rush. Hambleton still had no idea that an invasion was unfolding around him. He fully expected to be rescued within the hour.

He began inspecting his body, checking for injuries. He found a deep cut on his right index finger; he must have caught it on an edge as he was being ejected from the plane. Hambleton rooted around in his survival vest until he found the first-aid kit. He spread some disinfectant on the wound, bandaged it up. He realized that he was still wearing his reading glasses, which had miraculously stayed perched on his nose throughout the violent ejection. He reached into the pockets of his flight suit and felt around to see what else had survived the descent. The things he'd carried with him when he left Korat—cigarettes, lighter, gum—were gone. Hambleton sighed. Some good Virginia tobacco would have soothed his nerves. Deciding the glasses were a good luck charm, he left them on.

The day was warm and humid. Above him, the fog hid the sun. Hambleton knew that was a bad omen. The big-bodied HH-53 helicopters that picked up downed aviators would have trouble making it through the thick clouds.

Jankowski, circling thousands of feet above him, now came back on the radio. He told Hambleton to switch from the "guard" channel, which was heavily trafficked, to a discrete frequency where they could communicate more clearly. Jankowski knew the NVA might be monitoring this new channel, but he needed to authenticate Hambleton's identity before initiating rescue operations. Once they'd made the switch, he asked Hambleton the first question: "What is your dog's name?"

Hambleton blinked in confusion, then remembered that he'd filled out a form with secret questions before coming to Vietnam. He gave the dog's name—Pierre—envisioning the headstrong little French poodle as he did it. Jankowski asked him to spell the name, then confirmed. Next was his favorite athlete. "Ernie Banks," Hambleton said. Jankowski confirmed.

Jankowski began executing runs across Hambleton's hiding place so as to pinpoint his location. As he dropped below the clouds, in full view of the enemy troops, the FAC watched while the earth below erupted with gunfire. Tracers swept up at him in long orange waves; Jankowski could actually hear the rounds cutting through the air. "It started to look like the Fourth of July," he recalled.

Down below, the parachute nagged at Hambleton's thoughts. It was practically a billboard advertising the presence of an American airman in the area. He decided to retrieve it. Hambleton stuck his head above the edge of the ditch, then came up in a running crouch. Suddenly, tracers cut across his path and he could hear the bullets snicking past. He stopped and reversed course. He didn't believe the fire was aimed his way, but he was too close to an active firefight to risk getting shot.

The navigator began searching for a better hiding spot for the night. Half a mile away, he made out what looked like a line of brush. Hambleton memorized the features of the landscape, trying to make out landmarks in the drifts of fog. He took a compass reading. Then he stretched out on his back and stared at the sky, waiting for full darkness.

7

BLUEGHOST 39

Orbiting above the American, Jankowski switched back to the "guard" channel and broadcast a call for help. The crew of an Army helicopter, call sign Blueghost 39, heard the emergency call and flew toward the rescue zone. The Huey was piloted by First Lieutenant Byron Kulland and Warrant Officer John Frink. The crew chief was Specialist Fifth Class Ronald Paschall, twenty-one years old, from a small town in Washington; he'd already been in Vietnam for three years. And manning the door gun was a handsome, wiry nineteen-year-old from San Diego, Specialist Fifth Class José Astorga.

Born in Tijuana, Mexico, Astorga had immigrated to the United States and grown up poor and fatherless; as a boy, he'd worked two paper routes to support his family. The United States had not exactly been a paradise for him and his family, and he hadn't enlisted in the Army strictly out of patriotism, though that was part of it. What Astorga really wanted was to be a mechanic, which he believed might lead to a better job when he left the service. Yet after training him as a mechanic on the Chinook helicopter, the Army informed him he was going to become a Huey door gunner, one of the most dangerous assignments in Vietnam. It was said that the NVA were content to capture pilots and the rest of the Huey crews, but they hated door gunners so much they shot them on sight.

Astorga wasn't even supposed to be on the flight that day. He was sleeping in his hooch that morning when Paschall — a good friend — had shaken him awake.

"What's-his-name's sick," Paschall told him, meaning the other gunner. "You wanna fly?"

"Sure," Astorga said. Then Hambleton went down, and the routine flight had turned into a rescue mission. They'd changed pilots — Kulland took over — and headed for the downed airman.

Byron Kulland was one of those small-town golden boys obsessed with flight who seemed to be everywhere in Vietnam. He'd grown up in rural northwestern North Dakota among the Scandinavian and German families who'd, in many cases, been there since pioneer times. His family was Norwegian; his grandfather had come later than the frontier people, arriving at Ellis Island with fifteen dollars to his name, and made his way out to the badlands of the Dakotas. He'd homesteaded there on the land that Byron grew up on.

Byron was gregarious, a touch more confident than his brothers and sisters. "We would walk down the street in New Town and he might see someone and say, 'Gee, that guy looks familiar,' " said his sister Karen. "*And he'd go right up and talk to them!* He really enjoyed people." He'd gotten an ear for music from his mother and formed his own band as a teenager, the Silver Daggers, which played sock hops and high school dances, with Byron on guitar and lead vocals. He had a temper, too, and was stubborn as a mule. "We used to wrestle," says his oldest brother, Harlan. The bigger and stronger Harlan could usually manage to pin Byron to the ground in fairly short order, "but I could never make him give up."

When he was sixteen, says his sister Karen, Byron began dating a girl named Leona "from across the Missouri." They stayed boyfriend and girlfriend even when he went away to North Dakota State for college and joined ROTC. They got married and Byron enlisted in the Army.

There wasn't much controversy about the war in North Dakota; people there trusted that the government knew what it was doing. "It was like it was out there somewhere," his sister says, "but it wasn't going to touch us." Byron had no hesitation when it came time to leave for Vietnam. "They were told, we have to do this to save democracy," Karen says. "I think he was proud to serve."

While Byron was in flight school at Fort Wolters, Texas, the Army was running a program that brought Vietnamese aviators over to become familiar with the aircraft they'd be flying. There were frequent misunderstandings. One instructor told the Vietnamese trainees that if they got sick in the plane, they should take off their helmet and vomit into that. This was standard operating procedure for nausea in the cockpit. One day, a Vietnamese pilot went up, executed his maneuvers, landed the plane, stepped out onto the tarmac, took off his helmet, and vomited into it. The look on that hard-assed instructor's sunburned face . . . It just killed Byron every time he thought of it.

Byron and Leona grew close to Hai, one of the Vietnamese aviators. The couple took him everywhere they went, giving him a firsthand introduction to the country: drive-in movies, BBQ restaurants, shopping plazas, you name it. Showing him the real America, away from the cities. "One day we had gone someplace after dark," says Leona. "And we were just driving down the road. Hai says, 'We couldn't do this in Vietnam.'" Byron asked the pilot what he meant, and he explained that you couldn't drive after nightfall because the VC might pop out of a thicket and kill you or your whole family. That stuck with Byron. Later that evening, he brought it up with Leona. "That makes it that much more important that I go to Vietnam," he told her, "so that they can enjoy what we can enjoy." He didn't care much for politics, but the idea that a man couldn't even drive down a road near his house out of fear of being stitched across the chest with Vietcong bullets, well, it got to him. That he could understand, and he held on to it.

In the early evening of April 2, Kulland in his Huey along with an AH-1 Cobra attack helicopter headed toward Hambleton's position, about half a mile north of the Mieu Giang River. Kulland was told he wasn't to go north of the river without fighter planes to protect him; the concentration of enemy firepower there was just too strong. The A-1s and F-4s were pounding away on the enemy gun emplacements as Kulland flew across the Mieu Giang. It was hoped that the fighter planes would eliminate enough of the guns so Kulland could get in and snatch the navigator.

The Huey came in low, Kulland keeping its skids just above treetop level. José Astorga stood at the open doorway with his Minigun, staring down at the flat, dark jungle speeding by. He was wearing a "chicken plate," a piece of ceramic body armor across his chest to guard against ground fire. One thousand feet behind the lightly armed Huey, the Cobra crew were watching the ground, ready to hit any gun that started firing.

The only sound in the Huey was the murmur of radio traffic and the thudding of the rotors above. The instrument lights from the cockpit cast a soft glow into the crew compartment. The chopper flew toward the glint of the Mieu Giang.

On the ground, Hambleton had the flares laid out next to him. He was anxious. Jankowski's voice called "Bat 21 B" on the radio. "Rescue choppers are airborne."

Hambleton confirmed. He felt a surge of jubilation. He'd spotted an open area nearby. When Kulland told him to move, he would run as fast as he could, lighting the flares as he went. The Huey would come down ahead of the spurting fire, and they would be off the ground in a matter of a minute or two, winging toward Da Nang Air Base, where he would stand his rescuers a round of drinks. Airman tradition.

He heard the faint *whup-whup-whup* of a helicopter. He got ready to make his dash. He reached out and turned up the volume on the radio so as not to miss the order.

Kulland's chopper crossed the Mieu Giang. As soon as it passed a line of huts built close to a tree line, guns opened up in what seemed like a single explosion of fire. Astorga gazed down in astonishment as thousands of tracers swam up at him in lazily drifting lines. "Worst I'd ever seen," he said later. Hambleton listened to the varying registers of AAA erupting from all directions: 23 mm, 37 mm, 57 mm, each one distinct in the deafening barrage. *What in the hell?* Hambleton wondered. Where had all these NVA come from? He thought the A-1s had wiped them out.

Inside the Cobra, the pilot could feel the bullets banging into the underside of the chopper. The windshield in front of him exploded in a burst of flying Plexiglas. Warning lights flashed on the instrument panel;

the gunfire was eating through the components that kept the chopper airborne, the ground fire so intense that the Cobra "was being rapidly converted into a piece of torn wreckage."

The Cobra pilot called to Kulland to turn back and told him that he was aborting. He began his turn and saw Kulland doing the same. Then the pilot spotted a stream of thin blue smoke billowing from just below the Huey's rotors. Blue smoke usually meant a hit to the engine.

Kulland struggled to keep the chopper aloft, but the Huey began to lose altitude. "Sir, there's a lot of smoke coming out of the engine," Astorga called out nervously from the back of the chopper. Kulland, his voice calm, said, "OK."

A bullet thudded into Astorga's ankle, then ricocheted up. It clipped his knee and smashed into his leg, snapping his femur before slamming into his ceramic chest plate, "nearly tearing my head off." He fought to keep his balance. Standing upright on his broken leg, he kept his finger on the Minigun trigger and poured fire down on the enemy gunners. He could feel Kulland start to pull the chopper up. "He wanted to get us out of there."

Then, without warning, the noise of whirring machinery stopped. There was perfect quiet inside the chopper. The engine had failed.

The gunner in the Cobra, looking back at the Huey, watched as the chopper suddenly pitched nose-up and made a violent ninety-degree turn, its airspeed so low that it was almost hanging midair. Pitching left, it sank toward a village about a mile to the north of the river. As the helicopter fell out of the sky, Kulland cried out that he'd lost the tail rotor. "I'm trying to control it with the pedals," he shouted.

The chopper fell toward the earth. "We were coming down like a rock," Astorga said.

The craft seemed to tilt, left to right. Kulland wrestled the Huey down, but the chopper was on the verge of being out of control. The wind roared in through the cargo door.

Astorga felt a flutter of panic. "We knew we were in trouble. We knew we were going down."

The chopper plummeted through the humid air. Astorga braced for the collision. "I heard a *boom*." Astorga slammed back onto the steel floor and quickly lost consciousness.

A minute or two later, he came to. The chopper was silent, resting in a field. The rotors had stopped turning.

"Is anyone alive?" Astorga shouted.

A voice, close by: "I'm alive. I'm trapped." It was the co-pilot, John Frink. Astorga crawled across the wreckage and into the cockpit. There he found Kulland still strapped in his seat, unmoving, his eyes closed. "The color of his skin was real pale." The pilot from North Dakota, the teenaged singer from the Silver Daggers, was dead.

In the co-pilot's seat, Frink, who'd just arrived in-country a few weeks before, was conscious and talking. Astorga pulled the release on the safety harness and got him out of his seat. Frink handed Astorga two survival vests and told him they might have to leave the other two men behind; enemy soldiers would be coming soon. Astorga crawled from the wreckage into the field, carrying the two vests. Frink followed.

Someone was screaming from inside the chopper. "I can't get out!" It was Astorga's buddy, Paschall. Astorga, his leg broken, stumbled toward the wreck and made his way to the crew chief. His leg was trapped under some debris. Astorga pulled at the metal, but it wouldn't give. "There was nothing I could do." He had to leave him for the moment. Astorga crawled back out of the chopper.

Frink turned back — Astorga believes he was going for the radio, to call for a rescue. Astorga heard a burst of gunfire from behind him. Someone — Paschall or Frink — shouted, "VC!" Astorga heard the *snipsnip* of bullets passing over his head and rocking the fuselage of the Huey. "Get out of there!" he called to the two men. The Huey had just been refueled before they made the rescue run.

As Astorga watched, a tracer struck one of the Huey's five fuel tanks, and it was as if the air around the chopper drew in its breath and then the Huey erupted in an enormous wall of flame. Astorga ducked down and the fire passed over him. "I felt the heat on my skin." When he looked up, Paschall and Frink had disappeared and flames were licking up toward the sky.

He stood up and tried to run, but his leg buckled under him. He would struggle up and take a step and then fall on his face; again and again, he tried to get away, but he was barely making any progress. He heard rotors cutting the air and looked up. A Cobra was hovering above him. He stood up and waved, but nobody onboard saw him. The pilot pulled away. Astorga turned to look at the terrain around him and saw figures running toward him.

Astorga was losing blood; he could feel the first wave of shock daze his nerves. A group of NVA soldiers ran closer to him. Their body postures, their movements . . . Astorga could tell the men were furious. "They weren't taking any prisoners," he said. "They wanted to kill me." A hand grabbed him roughly and shoved him into a hole in the rice paddy, perhaps a crater from an American bomb. Astorga tumbled in. From the muddy bottom, he looked up and saw the soldiers gathered a few feet from the lip of the hole, black silhouettes looking down, their guns outlined against the sky. Astorga knew the rumor about what happened to door gunners as well as anyone. He was sure he was going to die.

Something heavy landed next to him. Astorga turned his head and saw that an enemy soldier had jumped into the hole. The man stood there for a moment, then reached down and grabbed Astorga by the uniform and pulled him to his feet. The ends of the broken bone ground together; Astorga cried out. The other men reached down into the hole and pulled at his flight suit, lifting him up. The mud streaked his uniform as the men dragged him over the lip of the hole. He nearly fainted from the pain. The men pointed their AK-47s and gestured. They wanted him to march.

Astorga had no idea why the Vietnamese soldier had decided to save his life. He moved off. He could hear the breathing of the fire as it ate through the aviation fuel and the metal, but no voices.

Unaware that Blueghost 39 had crashed, Hambleton rose to a crouch and began walking quickly across the rice field toward the copse of trees. He hurried over the furrows, glancing left and right to see if he was being observed. The presence of the rice paddy told him he was near a settlement, a village of some sort, and there must be locals nearby. Any one of them would turn him in, or shoot him if they couldn't catch him.

The thick hedge loomed up. His heart beating fast, Hambleton dove for it and burrowed his way beneath the branches. He lay there for a moment, listening for pursuers, then sat up. He couldn't hear any footsteps or voices.

Convinced he'd made it to the trees undetected, Hambleton decided to take stock of what items he still had on him. He began going through his flight suit and taking out everything he found there, laying the items out neatly in front of him. The name tag he'd worn around Korat had been stripped off the flight suit, as was standard for every mission over Vietnam, but there was still a pair of silver leaves sewn into the shoulders, the mark of a lieutenant colonel. He briefly considered ripping them off but decided he would be rescued soon, and it wouldn't be worth it.

He placed his bulbous flying helmet on the ground first. Then he turned to his survival vest. It was astonishing how much the Air Force had packed into the countless pockets of the little vest: gadgets and weapons and survival paraphernalia of every kind. Hambleton went through the pockets one by one and sorted the items in his lap. After a few minutes, he inventoried his bounty: one tourniquet, one first-aid kit, two bulky survival radios, one set of spare batteries, a number of rescue flares, a water bag, now empty, a hunting knife, a .38 Smith & Wesson revolver, twenty bullets, a signaling mirror, an infrared strobe light, a mosquito net, a tiny compass, a can of insect repellent, and a two-foot rubber map of Vietnam.

Hambleton surveyed his haul, feeling a rush of pleasure. If the choppers couldn't get through tonight, it would be a relief to have some survival gear. He stuffed the items back into their respective pouches, leaving the .38 out so he could grab it if he heard an enemy soldier approach. He looked around him and crawled toward the thickest part of the bushes, then pulled the knife out of its scabbard and began digging a hole. He carefully scooped up the displaced dirt and spread it evenly around the roots of the bushes to disguise his work. He scavenged about and collected a pile of leaves and dead brush, which he piled near the hiding place. Then the navigator backed into the hole, pulling the leaves in after him. He was now completely invisible to anyone walking more than a few feet away.

As dusk deepened, Hambleton noticed a change in the register of the fire around him. The popping of the small-arms guns disappeared and was replaced by the full-throated reports of heavy artillery. "It was almost like the time for the shift change at General Motors," he thought. Mosquitoes found his hiding spot and began vectoring in. Hambleton pulled out his insect spray and applied it liberally.

Then, voices. Hambleton froze. They were speaking Vietnamese. He couldn't see through the thicket or the fog beyond it, but from their pace he guessed it was a patrol out searching for him. "They were looking and looking hard," said Hambleton. He held his breath, his heart beating so fast it was almost painful. The unseen soldiers passed by the thicket without stopping. He relaxed and closed his eyes, hoping to sleep. His flight helmet served as a hard pillow.

A few minutes later, another patrol approached. Hambleton could hear the soft footfalls of their feet on the muddy ground. The voices drew closer, then stopped ten feet from his hiding place. Hambleton felt a rush of panic. "It was dark as pitch but I could almost feel the dull silver of the leaves on my shoulders looming brightly." He was sure the soldiers would spot him. How could they not?

Something flared in the black. The soldiers had lit cigarettes, which moved in orange arcs to their lips as Hambleton watched. When the soldiers pulled on the cigarettes, "their faces would leap from the darkness in the brief light like grotesque masks on Halloween." Each cigarette rose in turn and revealed its holder. Hambleton studied the men's features. It was his first time seeing NVA soldiers up close; here they were, the enemy, with their high slanting cheekbones and dark brown eyes. After a few moments, he'd counted seven of them.

The glowing specks began to drop to the ground. The NVA soldiers crushed the butts beneath their boots. Hambleton could hear them pushing the branches aside with their hands and their rifles, searching for something. Finally, the sounds grew dimmer and the voices faded.

At Korat, an alert klaxon blared and the rescue teams on standby dashed for their aircraft. Major Dennis Constant was the aircraft commander of a "King" HC-130, a hulking search and rescue plane that could orbit over a downed airman for hours. "My crew and I ran out to the airplane," Constant said, "hit the starters, and blasted off."

Eighty minutes after the shootdown, Constant and his crew arrived over Hambleton and took up the role of airborne mission commander, orbiting southwest of Hambleton's position. The cloud ceiling was fifteen hundred feet — high enough that aircraft could operate — and it was raining lightly. Another airman raised Hambleton on the radio and got him talking; the crew wanted to be sure that the navigator hadn't been captured and that rescue forces weren't being led into a trap. Hambleton answered his questions by whispering into his survival radio. He reported his injuries and described the terrain around him. His voice was even and calm. "I was thinking this guy sounds cool as a cucumber down there," Constant said. "I'd have been scared silly."

Constant's crew called Saigon and asked if there were any friendly ground forces around the survivor. The Seventh Air Force controllers told them no, nothing unusual was happening in the sector near the Cam Lo bridge and there were no SAM sites nearby. But Hambleton was reporting "gomers" — North Vietnamese soldiers — all over the place, hundreds of them just in his immediate area. He could see flashlights in the near distance as searchers moved closer to him. It became abundantly clear to Constant that Saigon was feeding him wrong or outdated information, and he began to get upset about it. "I kept calling back to Saigon and saying, 'What the hell's going on? Where are all these people coming from?'" But intel insisted he was misinformed. Nothing remarkable was happening in the sector.

The commander decided to grab what assets he could. "This is King," he called on the emergency channel, using his code name. "I got a guy on the ground." Voices replied out of the ether, pilots identifying their aircraft and drawling their approximate position. Constant gave them his coordinates and asked them to get to him as fast as possible. He was calling in every piece of airborne equipment he could find in the skies over Southeast Asia. He wanted Hambleton off the ground before dawn.

Slowly, planes appeared out of the clouds and gathered above Hambleton, their navigation lights winking green and red in the dark sky. F-4s loaded with air-to-air missiles arrived to guard against North Vietnamese

MiG fighters; A-1 propeller-driven planes flown by pilots who were specialists in rescue operations swept in and assumed on-scene command. Fighter jets rocketed past, heavily laden with bombs hung on their wings; the big HH-53 Jolly Green rescue helicopters hovered out over the South China Sea, waiting to swoop in and gather up the airman; O-2 and OV-10 FACs buzzed in tight orbits. "It was the whole world out there," Constant said.

Bat 22 remained on station to guard the more vulnerable planes from the SAM sites. It had lost pressurization on account of a hydraulic failure; protocol dictated the plane return to base. But the pilot got on the radio and said they would remain. "We'll stay here," he told Constant, "till this damn thing falls out of the air."

The fighters began hitting the AAA batteries and SAM sites so that the choppers could come in and snatch Hambleton. The pilots of two A-1 attack planes heard the call. They were flying alongside two U.S. Army UH-1H "Huey" helicopters, their tops and sides painted in jungle camouflage, their bellies painted light blue so they'd blend in with the sky. The choppers hovered south of the city of Quang Tri while the A-1s roared north. The pilot of one of the A-1s, Captain Don Morse, anticipated an ordinary recovery without too much trouble. Hambleton was down in the DMZ, not up near Hanoi, where rescues were nearly impossible because of the high number of AAA guns that ringed the capital.

The two A-1s found Jankowski orbiting in his little spotter plane. He showed them Hambleton's hiding place, a small grove of trees. Jankowski now took off south, hoping to gather more aircraft for the rescue mission. Morse gazed down on the dark fields surrounding Hambleton and was taken aback. "I'd never seen so much ground fire in my whole life," he said. Thousands of tracers rose like embers from a burning forest. The noise was deafening, the sky streaked with flame. "Every hill looked like a Christmas tree," a reporter later wrote, "from the numerous sparkles of NVA machine-gun fire." Morse couldn't understand. Nobody was supposed to be down there except farmers and maybe some lightly armed VC. What was going on?

Rounds began crimping into the fuselage. Morse tried to dodge the streams of flak but found that they were so thick he couldn't avoid them.

He realized that he could only hope to take the hits where they did the least damage. Any one of the shells could strike a fuel line or another piece of vital machinery and send him corkscrewing into the jungle below.

Orbiting above, Constant watched as airstrike after airstrike hit the guns firing from the ground. The A-1s dove down and dropped their bombs, which sent balls of orange fire rolling up from the jungle canopy. As Constant watched, a plume of smoke erupted on the ground near Hambleton's position: a SAM where no SAMs were supposed to be. It was quickly followed by more. One OV-10 pilot, Captain Gary Ferentchak, found himself targeted by a swarm of missiles. He counted them as they whisked by. "I'd gotten five and couldn't see number six." He screamed at his backseater, "Where is it?" The answer came back: "Off your nose." Ferentchak swiveled his head and rolled the aircraft upside down, jettisoning his external fuel tanks and rocket pods. He searched the blackness, hoping to spot the SAM before it exploded. There it was, straight ahead, "just dead locked on." Ferentchak dove for the forest canopy in the darkness, waiting for number six to blow his plane apart.

When the missile detonated, "it looked like somebody took a strobe light and lit it off in your face." The explosion thumped the fuselage, blasting off the flare pads and spare fuel tanks, but the plane stayed aloft. As Ferentchak sped earthward, his finger pressed the "present position" button, which locked his altitude into the navigation system. Later, he checked and found he'd pulled out of the dive at 250 feet above the ground. "That put my heart in my throat." In the pitch darkness of the Vietnamese night, he'd been perhaps a second and a half away from smashing his plane into a rice paddy.

Constant, too, heard the blaring SAM warnings in his ear. He peered into the darkness and spotted what looked like five headlights speeding toward him above the cumulus. He was shaken. The massive HC-130 wasn't known for its maneuverability, and the missiles were streaking toward him at Mach 3. They came straight up, leveled off at about twenty thousand feet — the same altitude as Constant — and turned toward him. "I was like, 'Holy shit, man.' I figured I'd wait until they were about to hit me and do some kind of Hail Mary maneuver."

As the first SAM grew in his windscreen, Constant pulled the throttles back to idle, dumped his flaps, and did a wing-over, tumbling straight toward the ground. As the plane screamed earthward, completely inverted, Constant waited for the burst of overpressure. Waves buffeted the plane as the SAMS went off, "boom, boom, *boomboomboom*." One of his engines failed — he guessed it was because of a SAM — but he finally made it to the South China Sea, its lines of waves thin and pale in the moonlight.

Constant sensed something gathered around Hambleton's position that the intel officers had no idea was there. "We really came close to getting nailed," he said later. "It was grim."

Jankowski got on his radio. "Bat 21," the forward controller said. "Can you dig in for the night?" There would be no more rescue attempts that evening. Hambleton felt a wave of depression wash over him. He confirmed Jankowski's transmission, but the reply stuck in his throat. *Would he be a free man in the morning? Would he be alive?*

The flames from José Astorga's chopper burned out of sight of Hambleton's hiding place. He had no idea that three men were dead or that Astorga was a POW beginning his odyssey northward. The FAC orbiting above knew, but no one told the navigator, or at least Hambleton didn't remember being told. Perhaps he blocked out the deaths; perhaps he was kept in the dark to keep up his morale.

One by one, the planes that had swarmed the skies above Hambleton now turned and slipped back to their bases. The Cobra that accompanied the Huey on its run over the Mieu Giang had been shot to pieces and made it to a landing spot thanks only to a remarkable piece of flying by the pilot. It was abandoned on the tarmac, never to fly again. Captain Morse in his A-1 had spent three hours over the scene; by the time he broke off, his plane was barely flyable. He just managed to put it down at the airfield at Da Nang, climbed out, briefed the intel guys, then walked to his hooch to rest.

Morse lay on his cot and stared at the ceiling. Nothing in his training or in his previous flights over Southeast Asia had prepared him for what he'd seen just north of the Mieu Giang. "It was the worst night of my life," he said. "I was scared to death. It was just horrendous." He lay shaking in his bed, seeing again the long bursts of AAA floating up toward his wings, the fire that seemed to leave no room for an aircraft to fly through. He didn't sleep that night.

8

TUCSON

Gwen Hambleton was cleaning up after morning coffee with some friends in her suburban Tucson home. It was the afternoon of April 3. In another week she would be joining Gene for R&R, and she had a long list of things to accomplish.

Gwen was in a hurry but not in a rush. Supremely organized, she had a checklist of everything she had to do before she boarded her flight to Thailand. Cancel the newspaper; turn the ice maker off; ask the neighbors to water the plants. She also had to remember to bring her golf clubs on the trip. Gene, a self-confessed "golf nut," had scouted out a new course for them to play. She was looking forward to Thailand and the first sight of her handsome, mischievous husband.

Gwen, at forty-eight, was close to the Hellenic ideal of an Air Force wife. She dressed well, despite being fantastically thrifty, perhaps a result of her Depression childhood. She was highly sociable and joined one club after another. Gwen actually seemed to *enjoy* the coffee klatches, the committees, the blood drives, the dinners at the commanding officer's house, and all the rest of it.

Gwen was checking an item off her list when the doorbell rang. She went to the door and looked through the side window and saw her best friend, the base chaplain, and a nurse standing on her doorstep. Like any good Air Force wife, she understood immediately what the visit meant.

"Oh, Lord, not that," she thought.

. . .

In the hours that followed, old friends responded to a jangle on the Air Force gossip network, and called her, asking what they could do. But Gwen found it hard to be soothed. The thought of losing Gene was horrible. "There isn't anything that can comfort you," she said. "At the end I thought he would just disappear and I would never know what happened to him." She found the thought "terrifying, really."

She called the Casualty Center in San Antonio and spoke to an officer there. She talked on the phone with her mother, sisters, and brother, received her Air Force friends and made them coffee. All the women had been rehearsing the same routine in their minds ever since their husbands joined the service. With the Marines or the Army, it was unlikely that your husband would be killed stateside, but an Air Force wife whose man was flying knew that a gust of wind or a flock of birds could take him just as easily as a missile. The tension was constant, a gray tripwire waiting in the background of the ordinary suburban day.

That afternoon, word of the downing of Bat 21 and the crash of Blueghost 39 spread to other towns and cities across the country. A telegram arrived at the home of Ronald Paschall, the crew chief onboard the Huey. It read:

THE SECRETARY OF THE ARMY HAS ASKED ME TO INFORM YOU THAT YOUR SON, SPECIALIST FIVE RONALD P. PASCHALL, HAS BEEN REPORTED MISSING IN VIETNAM SINCE 2 APRIL 1972. HE WAS LAST SEEN WHILE THE CREWCHIEF OF A MILITARY AIRCRAFT ON A MILITARY MISSION WHEN THE AIRCRAFT WAS FIRED UPON BY A HOSTILE ACTOR, CRASHED BUT DID NOT BURN. SEARCH IS IN PROGRESS. YOU WILL BE PROMPTLY ADVISED AS ADDITIONAL INFORMATION IS RECEIVED . . . PLEASE ACCEPT MY DEEPEST SYMPATHY DURING THIS MOST TRYING PERIOD. VERNE L. BOWERS, MAJOR GENERAL USA.

The aviators who'd watched Blueghost 39 go down assumed that Paschall was dead. But it was the Army's informal policy to report their men missing in action. There were a number of reasons for this, but the simplest was that miraculous things often happened in war. One time near Hanoi, several airmen had watched a badly damaged F-105 fully engulfed in flames go cartwheeling over and over above the jungle foliage, until it dove and disappeared into the ground fog below them. Everyone who'd watched the crash agreed the pilot must be dead, but three hours later he was sitting in a hospital in South Vietnam, suffering only from two broken legs. He'd managed, somehow, to fly the aircraft out and bail out over the South China Sea.

And what if a man survived and was taken prisoner and spent years being brutalized by the North Vietnamese and then boarded a flight home with thoughts of the first embrace of his wife, only to find her living with his best friend or his insurance salesman, because his buddies had reported him dead? No one wanted that on his conscience. So first reports almost always eschewed the terms "presumed dead" or "killed in action." Soldiers, sailors, Marines, and airmen went "missing." And they often stayed that way until their remains could be positively identified.

During World War II, Ruth Paschall, Ronald's mother, had lost her brother in a bomber accident over the South Pacific. As a young girl, she'd watched her mother answer the doorbell one afternoon, observed the dumb show of chaplain and telegram and tears. Her brother had never come home from the war. But when she read *her* telegram, the one addressed to her and her husband, Mark, Ruth fixed on that one word: "missing." It gave her an immediate and completely unwarranted amount of hope.

Her husband later said that "99 percent of the family," after hearing the details of the crash, accepted that Ronald had been killed. But his mother did not. "Ruth," Mark said, "could never really let it go." If Ronald was missing, he could be found.

In the small Minnesota town of Wadena, Karen Wallgren—the sister of Byron Kulland, the one who'd been so amazed by how he'd go right up and talk to near-strangers—was at home doing laundry. She'd married and had moved away from North Dakota with her husband; she was pregnant with her third and last child.

The phone rang. It was Karen's father, who told her about the visit he'd just gotten from some Army personnel. They'd informed him that Byron was missing. Karen felt her heart skip a beat, but she tried to be positive, for her father's sake. "I said, 'Well, that doesn't mean they won't find him.'"

To take her mind off the news, Karen took the clothes from the washing machine and went outside. She walked to the clothesline and began pinning the shirts and children's dresses on it, but her thoughts quickly turned back to her brother. Karen sensed that Byron was dead, and she thought of the things that he'd wanted to do but that would never happen now. A ranch out west, "to go live where the cowboys are." Sheepherding by helicopter, a pipe dream of his. Children. Time.

The only consolation she could find was that Byron had been living his life as he saw fit. "He was flying a helicopter and he loved that. He was married to a woman he loved. And he had enough money and was able to pay cash for a car." Karen thought to herself that the men in her family went bald early and put on weight. But Byron? He was strong and lean. Handsome, too. He'd died a good-looking man.

She pinned more clothes on the line. The thought came to her that wherever her brother was lying at that moment, he could no longer feel the wind on his skin, the animal pleasure of being alive. "I thought, 'Oh, he might not ever see the blue sky again, just to enjoy being outside.'" She tried to dismiss the thought but was unable to. She put down the shirt she'd been trying to pin, brought her hand to her mouth, and wept.

In Colorado Springs, the younger Giannangeli children were preparing for their day at Catholic school. The airman's oldest son, Robert, was struggling to put on a tie. His friend had been riding his bike in the neighborhood days before when he was struck by a car and killed. Robert was dressing for the boy's funeral. He was feeling doubly unsettled, not just because of his friend's sudden passing but because of the dream he'd had two nights before, the one about his father's survival knife.

The doorbell rang. Robert gave up trying to fix his tie and went to answer it. Opening the door, he spotted in the driveway a blue Ford Falcon, which he immediately recognized as an Air Force base car. Standing on the porch of their ranch house was the base commander and a chaplain. Robert said hello to the men. They nodded and asked to speak to his mother. He went and got her and told her who was out front.

"I'll never forget that moment," he says. "The look on my mom's face."

The base commander handed his mother a yellow telegram saying that her husband had been shot down. His voice was subdued, soft; he was trying to avoid, apparently, having the children hear the news, but they gathered around the open doorway anyway and listened. The chaplain broke in to say that he was returning to his chapel to say a mass for Giannangeli. Their mother thanked the men and closed the door.

Mrs. Giannangeli was clearly upset, but the children couldn't tell how upset. They'd never seen their mother cry, and even now she maintained her composure. She told her second son, Dennis, that he was going to school that day; all the kids were. She made it clear that as soon as Dennis arrived at the school, he was to go to the principal's office and ask the people there to make an announcement saying that their father was missing. There was a certain way Air Force families did things at such times, and the Giannangelis were not going to deviate from it.

At the school, Dennis walked into the principal's office. One of the nuns who worked there spotted him. The visit by the base commander and the chaplain had thrown off the precisely calibrated timing of the Giannangelis' morning, so Dennis was a few minutes late. The nun glared at him and said, "What are *you* doing here?" Dennis tried to answer but found himself unable to speak; he began to sob. The nun's expression immediately changed. Colorado Springs was a military town, and the war was regularly claiming airmen; perhaps she guessed the truth. When he was able to tell her what had happened, the woman looked mortified by her harsh words. She told Dennis they would make the announcement.

The voice on the intercom was informing the school what had happened as Dennis walked into his homeroom class. "It was the strangest feeling," he said. "I was so distraught and everyone was looking at me." But no one spoke to him about the announcement or asked for details about his missing father. They spoke to him kindly but acted as if all that had been broadcast that morning on the intercom was the weather report and details of the school day. Dennis's track coach did come to the class and mentioned the news about his father but told him that it would be best if he took his mind off the incident by going to practice. Some wind sprints would be the best thing for him. Dennis passed through the day in a half-remembered fugue.

But he followed his coach's advice. For the next few months, Dennis would take refuge in sports, shooting hoops obsessively on the street in front of his house, where a streetlight lit the backboard all evening long. "I'd be out there in the middle of the night," he said. "I was angry about losing my dad, and about Gene Hambleton. *Why did* you *get to eject?* I thought. *Why did you get to go early?*"

9

BLOWTORCH JOCKEYS

Hambleton napped fitfully in his dugout, never sinking into deep sleep. It was full night now. The blackness was like a shroud over his head; he'd never experienced anything like it. "It was *dark* dark."

He woke and raised his head. He could hear the buzz of the orbiting plane above. The sound was a comfort to him. He thought of the FAC aboard as his personal guardian. "I felt he was mine. All mine."

The sky in the east began to show a thin line of light. Hambleton spotted lights across the fields from the south. One set to his east, one to the south, and one, farther away, between the two. Villages, clearly. He saw people emerging from their huts. "I could faintly hear people talk excitedly." The sound grew louder. Peasants from the three villages seemed to have come out of their homes and joined together in a single group. Among them, Hambleton spotted men dressed in the pea-green uniform of the NVA. It appeared that the army had organized some kind of meeting. Hambleton wondered if he was the subject of it.

The cluster broke up and the villagers began walking toward him. They reached the edge of the rice paddies and stopped there, apparently uncertain which way to go. The villagers had flashlights, and he could see them flashing this way and that.

Hambleton got on the radio and whispered a request for gravel mines. These were small hand-sized bomblets made up of camouflaged pouches stuffed with lead azide and thirty grams of ground glass, held apart by thin sheets of plastic. Soaked in liquid Freon, the bombs were dropped frozen. It took between three and eight minutes for them to thaw out, and then they shot out a web of tripwires that became "shock-sensitive." If your foot brushed against one of them as you walked, the little things would explode and take your arm or leg with them.

Hambleton listened to the sounds of the planes in the sky overhead, each identifiable by the pitch of its engines. He recognized the sound of a Douglas A-1 dive-bomber that dated from World War II. He could hear the buzz of the plane's big propellers. The A-1 swept overhead, dropping a load of gravel. The bomblets spread out in the air and fell to the earth. Hambleton was now sitting in a minefield with his hiding place at its center.

He watched as the villagers fanned out and headed into the rice paddies; the bobbing lights reminded him of a "field of fireflies." There was no doubt they were headed his way and eager to find him. "The urgency of their voices made me ill at ease," he said. Hambleton knew that if the villagers discovered him, his gun would be of little use.

He studied the villagers' movements. They would come over the furrows toward him, but when they arrived at a certain spot, near the middle of the rice paddy, they would stop and deliberate. Hambleton suspected they'd heard the A-1 flying low and guessed that the fields nearer him were littered with the gravel mines. A Vietnamese villager in 1972 would have been intimately acquainted with the weapon; it had left many men and women amputees or worse. The people feared coming any farther. After an hour, they turned back to their huts.

Dawn was approaching. The FAC had assured him that the choppers would take off at first light. He decided he had to save his energy for the burst of speed he might need to reach them when they landed. He might have to sprint for the doors before the NVA soldiers could zero in on him with their rifles.

He drifted off to sleep. About an hour later, a noise woke him. He glanced up and saw what looked like Roman candles exploding in the air above him. One would blaze to life in the inky murk with a *fffffffttttt*, then slowly die out.

They were flares. The villagers must be searching for him again.

But when he sat up and gazed toward the village, he saw people walking parallel to his position. Now he picked up the squeak of treads, along with the roar of trucks revving in the near distance. After listening intently for a few minutes, Hambleton realized that the NVA were moving vehicles down the road with their lights off to avoid American fighters. The flares were being used as navigational aids.

He radioed the FAC and told him about the lines of trucks and tanks making their way south. The voice rogered back. Soon Hambleton heard the scream of a plane cut through the humid air as it dove on the vehicles. Immediately, the noise of antiaircraft shells erupted from the fields around him. It was like an enormous kettledrum sounding continuously, an "overpowering rumble" that temporarily deafened him. A shell burst overhead. "Tiny pieces of pot metal, thick as BB shot, rained down on me." He dove for the ground and burrowed in.

Then, quiet. He could hear the far-off clanking and grinding of machinery coming from ground level. He peeked out between the branches in front of him. He couldn't see the trucks, but they were out there. What if they're friendlies? He had to find out.

Hambleton stood up and made his way down the hedgerow. There was no one out now in the fields. As he came closer to the noise, which seemed to grow in volume, he went down on his stomach and crawled through the undergrowth. When he saw light streaming through the leaves of the last bush, he reached out and pushed his hands through it, moving the branches to one side.

He caught his breath. Ten feet away was not a road but a highway, and it was lined with military vehicles of every type and description. There were the enormous Soviet T-54 battle tanks in jungle camo clanking along, followed by jeeps pulling howitzers, SAM missile batteries, transports filled with NVA soldiers. The invasion force was a modern Soviet-equipped mechanized corps. It looked like . . . *Stalingrad* or something, some World War II battle relocated to the rice fields of Vietnam.

Hambleton realized with a jolt that this must be Highway 561, a main north-south artery that he'd seen on his maps. But now it was thick with enemy. For the first time it began to dawn on the navigator that he had landed in the midst of a major invasion.

This was bad news, terrible news, for his rescue, but it did give him a chance to be useful. He was not just a man on the run; he was a soldier of a nation at war. While he waited to be rescued, he could act like one. He radioed the FAC above and started calling in what he was seeing.

Minutes later, he heard the sound of the O-2 growing louder above him. The enemy guns opened up. The pilot shot smoke rockets to mark the roadway. As soon as the rockets were away, the plane arced upward and the drone of its propeller faded. White smoke billowed over the highway yards from Hambleton, mixing in with the exhaust of the transports.

Hambleton could hear the engines of other planes above. The ground beneath his belly shook as nearby antiaircraft batteries opened up. Their muzzles flashed orange against the gray sky as they aimed streams of bullets and shells toward the descending fighters. Hambleton flicked his radio on and lowered the volume. He began listening in to the traffic of the pilots.

He heard a faint buzz that grew louder. An American fighter. Suddenly it was right above him. It released its bombs and the terrain in front of him erupted in rolling balls of orange fire. Explosions sent pressure waves through his body, "heaving, rocking, crashing" the earth around him. He gave up any thought of sleeping. A shock wave distorted the black-green landscape before him. The sound of the detonation was quickly overtaken by the whine of other aircraft, unseen in the night, and the concussions of bomb after bomb on the trail of vehicles.

Gas tanks went up in bright white flashes. Black smoke billowed upward. Hambleton keyed his radio button and called in more directions. A plane whipped in low with its 20 mm wing-loaded cannons spurting fire and smoke. The pilot raked the line of trucks and swept upward, its roar merging with the sound of the AAA guns.

Hambleton watched the tracers and tried to orient the guns in the half-dark landscape. His survival map was useless; there weren't enough details to give coordinates. He radioed the FAC. "Roger, Bat 21," the voice came back. Hambleton gave the coordinates of one of the emplacements. "I told them to make the same runs on the same IP, same heading, but to move over right fifty or sixty yards and hold the drop until two seconds later."

A new sound above him, a shrieking, wind-sucking howl. It was, he knew, the F-4 Phantom, the apex American fighter, able to fly at twice the speed of sound. He'd never seen one in combat, though he'd met plenty of the pilots in the Officers' Club back at Korat. "Blowtorch jockeys," he called them.

The sound grew and the Phantom came in, a "monstrous" black shape against a blacker sky. The position he'd just called in was lit up by an orange plume. Hambleton saw the silhouette of a heavy 100 mm artillery gun jump into the air and spin lazily against the flame. He reported a direct hit. The trucks still rolled forward; there was no backing up, nowhere to escape to. Hambleton called in strike after strike — "Next pass a hundred yards east of the last one" — and watched the shape of the trucks disintegrate in the fire.

Finally, the F-4s ran out of ordnance. He listened to one of the pilots call in to the FAC and then heard the massive twin engines cycling high as they flew off. The remaining AAA guns fell silent; there was quiet now. The excitement that had lifted him through the past hour or so dropped away; the adrenaline slipped out of his bloodstream.

As his ears acclimated, he picked up other sounds. There were fires crackling on the roadway as transport trucks burned out. Beneath that sound, he could hear soldiers screaming in the darkness, calling out in Vietnamese for a medic. Young men bellowed in pain. He could smell the sharp tang of cordite in the air, the nauseating stench of burning rubber and flesh.

The sky was growing lighter. Hambleton peered through the hedgerow and saw dead bodies thrown across the roadway. Limbs were scattered in the bushes and in the ditch at the side of the road, their green uniforms torn open, their faces cut by shrapnel. Some of the jackknifed figures were close enough that he could make out the features of the young men. It was his second time seeing the enemy soldiers up close, but these faces were slack and empty.

Hambleton found the amount of devastation hard to comprehend. His directions, which he'd relayed to the FAC above with such excitement, had left men torn apart and wriggling in the mud. The pilots who'd dropped the bombs were cruising back homeward, thinking of their first

Manhattans or of sleep, as he had, many times. But here he could almost reach out and touch the dying.

The navigator felt repulsed. He thought to himself that for thirty years his idea of war had "almost been a computer game — his electronic sophistication matched against that of the enemy in the crisp blue skies of the upper atmosphere." He'd imagined that winning glory would be somehow painless, almost mechanical. "Dropping a bomb from a plane is not an emotional experience," he said. "I got on the ground and found out what war was."

What was it? What had really been happening six miles below his plane as he dreamed of making his name as a warrior? "Turning healthy human beings," he said now, "into fertilizer."

Hambleton ran a hand across his face; his skin felt clammy. For a moment he thought he was going to be sick.

PART II

DARK KNIGHTS

10

JOKER

THE TAN SON NHUT AIR BASE outside Saigon, the South Vietnamese capital, had been built by the French in the 1920s, in the first lethal, romantic years of flight. It had been a tiny outpost then, with one crude runway and some low-slung buildings servicing the biplanes that carried French businessmen, military officers, and the odd colonial administrator to their new homes. At the time, Vietnam, along with the kingdom of Cambodia, was known as French Indochina, a profitable, restive colony that pumped millions of francs into the empire through the sale of opium and rice alcohol, while the French denied the Vietnamese any semblance of self-rule.

By 1972, Tan Son Nhut had been taken over in large part by the United States military; as they'd inherited the war, so had the Americans inherited the airfield. It had become a sprawling military base that housed, among other units, the Joint Rescue Coordination Center, radio call sign "Joker." Joker had been established early in the war to coordinate search and rescue of American service members caught behind enemy lines. Now that the quick snatch by Blueghost 39 had failed, the officers at Joker began to plan a fully mounted rescue mission to retrieve Gene Hambleton. In the humid air, Joker's office buzzed with voices.

Downed American airmen were a top priority for the US military. General Creighton Abrams, the commander of military operations in Vietnam, had made it clear that his men were to be brought back at any cost. "I had clear instructions," said Major General John Carley, Abrams's operations officer, "no matter what else was going on, that we would stop what we were doing . . . to recapture prisoners of war or to rescue our people. He left no doubt in my mind." The extraordinary nature of those words — *no matter what else was going on* — hadn't been fully reckoned with before the shootdown of Gene Hambleton.

Colonel Cecil Muirhead, Joker's commander, listened to the rolling reports of Hambleton's situation coming in over the radio. He ordered the FACs to stay above the navigator's position twenty-four hours a day and attack any enemy fortification or gun emplacement they could find. The firepower around Hambleton had to be degraded before more choppers could go in. Muirhead, rather astonishingly, hadn't been informed that the Easter Offensive was under way, but he was by now aware that the NVA forces around the navigator were formidable.

Master Sergeant Daryl Tincher was the noncommissioned officer in charge on the Joker desk that night, along with two radio operators, a weatherman, and a soldier manning the telephones to different command posts. Tincher had no ground troops to call on; the Army battalions and most of the Marines had left months ago. By 1972, the war was seemingly at a stalemate. The country was divided roughly at the 17th parallel, and neither side seemed able to deliver a decisive blow to the enemy. The ferocious 1968 Tet Offensive, in which the North Vietnamese attacked more than one hundred cities in the South, had shocked Americans and their allies and initiated a gradual drawdown of US forces. The following year, American paratroopers successfully retook Ap Bia Mountain from enemy forces in the Battle of Hamburger Hill but were later forced to abandon their position, dealing another blow to public support for the war. The secret peace negotiations between Henry Kissinger and his North Vietnamese counterpart, Le Duc Tho, had ground to a halt over the issue of removing the South Vietnamese president from power, which the Americans balked at, and the withdrawal of enemy forces from the South, which Hanoi refused to consider.

It was a different war for the Americans now, a war fought largely in the air. And the men fighting it suffered far less from the ills of the late sixties than their land-based brothers did. Gone were the tunnel rats, the fraggings of officers, the racial agita (for the most part), the troops dazed on smack in their miserable hooches, the seeming derangement of the American psyche on a foreign battlefield. What Neil Sheehan wrote about Army aviators was true for the Air Force servicemen as well: they "were the sole combat element . . . that did not come apart under the stress of the war in Vietnam . . . As the French parachutists became the paladins of that earlier war, so the . . . aviators became the dark knights of this one."

Now Tincher was busy calling in dozens and dozens of these dark knights to save one of their own. When an airman was down behind enemy lines, Joker's power expanded at a stupendous rate. "At my side, I had an Army liaison," said Tincher. "I had Air Force, I had Navy, I had Marines. We could call the Navy and say, 'We need some fast movers'"— that is, fighter planes — "and *boom*, they're in the air . . . When we had a rescue mission, everybody backed off. We had everything in Southeast Asia right there at our fingertips."

As well as assembling a veritable armada of aircraft, Tincher also ordered a no-fire zone established around the navigator. These were standard for all rescue missions; in order to clear the area for rescue teams to work, artillery batteries stood down, bombers and fighters weren't to bomb, and the Navy ships floating offshore in the South China Sea were ordered not to fire their guns into the zone without coordinating with the rescue forces first. The size of the no-fire area varied according to a number of variables: landscape features such as mountains or roads, enemy activity, the presence of friendly forces. A typical zone was a few miles in radius. But that morning, Tincher settled on a zone of sixteen miles' radius. That was much, much larger than usual.

The officers at Joker, unaware that the invasion was under way, were trying to give the pararescuemen and the Huey crews the widest possible area in which to work. But the zone covered much of the area that the NVA was pouring through in its massive attack on the South. Without knowing it, Joker had effectively decreed that a huge chunk of the available American firepower in this crucial zone would be dedicated to the rescue of Gene Hambleton and not to countering the North Vietnamese offensive.

The idea of "leave no man behind" is ancient, going back at least as far as the Greeks, who wrote lyrics about young men who ventured behind enemy lines to save their fellow soldiers. On the American continent, a unit called Rogers' Rangers—frontiersmen and woodsmen fighting for the British during the French and Indian War of the 1750s and 1760s—refused to leave their brothers in the hands of the Native American warriors they considered to be savages. "This has been part of American society," says the historian Paul Springer, "before there was an American society." The oath is even encoded in the USAF's Airmen's Creed, which every airman recites when entering the service. "I am an American airman," it reads. "Wingman, leader, warrior. I will never leave a fellow airman behind."

But the truth was that airmen and Marines and sailors had been left behind in World War II and Korea and long before that, when circumstances made their rescue too costly or dangerous. Had Hambleton been caught far behind enemy lines at the Battle of Belleau Wood in 1918 or during the invasion of Sicily in 1943, there is every chance he would have stayed there until he was captured. A rescue operation as large as the one launched in 1972 would have been almost inconceivable to the military commanders of those times. And it wasn't just the technology—the choppers that could drop in and pick up a lost aviator in a matter of minutes—that was different.

Joker was aware of Hambleton's top-secret background. "We knew who he was," said Tincher. "We knew he had a lot of highly classified material." But the pilots and the navigators and the FACs working the rescue didn't know who Hambleton was, and it wouldn't have mattered if they had. Hambleton could have been some pogue lieutenant or a dumb-ass private who'd fallen out of a Jolly Green and they would still have gone out to save him.

Why? What motivated these men to throw themselves at defenses so ferocious that many had never seen anything to compare them to? It wasn't just esprit de corps and three hundred years of tradition. It was the nature of the war in Southeast Asia.

Many of the officers and airmen who were being called in to save Hambleton were on their second or third tours in Vietnam. When some of them had returned home between deployments, they'd encountered the ferocious gauntlet of antiwar sentiment. Some had been shouted at, spat on, and called "mercenaries." If you parked your car with its Air Force base sticker on an American street, even in a military-friendly town, it might be egged or keyed by the time you got back. In the late sixties, some Army soldiers had bought long-haired wigs to cover up their military haircuts. Not all that much had changed since then.

About their allies the Americans were, for the most part, unenthusiastic. There were brave, good men fighting on the South Vietnamese side, but there had been too many instances when their allies had melted away during battle or shirked what the Americans saw as their duty. One nickname for the South Vietnamese Air Force, the VNAF, was "the Very Nice Air Force," based on its pilots' habit of hauling ass for base whenever challenged by the enemy. When one airman arrived in-country early in 1972 the first thing his squadron commander told him was "There is nothing over here worth an American life."

In this environment, the rescue of a fellow American acquired an urgency that raised it above almost every other thing. One OV-10 pilot who flew the Hambleton mission found only one thing that gave his service meaning, and it wasn't Vietnamese democracy. It was rescuing his brothers from behind enemy lines. "I would have ripped that country up from all sides," he said, "to get our POWs back." This was a widespread sentiment within the USAF. "The feeling when you get those guys out must be like winning the Super Bowl," said one Air Force commander. "You just get this tremendous high."

The men at Da Nang that spring would have loved to fight for values like freedom and liberty on behalf of a grateful republic. But as it was, their leaders were feckless, their country had forgotten them, and their allies rarely felt like allies. It wasn't 1944, and this wasn't France. All they had, many airmen felt, was their unbreakable bond to one another.

As Hambleton waited to be rescued, Joker's order for a sixteen-mile no-fire zone on all sides around his position went out to the different commands in Vietnam. It quickly reached the American officers who were embedded with the South Vietnamese units in the Dong Ha area, the men who coordinated US Navy gunfire and airstrikes for the troops fighting the war on the ground. These officers knew about the Easter Offensive. It was all around them.

American helicopter pilots flying south of the DMZ saw waves of NVA troops running toward the firebases below them, hundreds and hundreds at a time. The enemy soldiers would sweep through the jungle, disappearing for a moment under the dark green of the tree canopy, then reemerge, firing their rifles. They would climb over the dead bodies that were caught in the barbed wire and charge toward the guns shooting at them. For the pilots, it was a bewitching sight, almost beautiful, these flowing rows of men silently rushing forward over long expanses of pitted earth. For the men on the ground, it was terrifying. One crew flying a nighttime mission approached a firebase that had been under attack for many hours. They dropped flares to illuminate the terrain below, which was hidden by night fog. When the flares finally penetrated through the mist, the crewmen saw lit up in the orange-colored gloom dozens of bodies lying on the ground in postures that showed they'd died under intense fire. The pilots realized that there was no one at the firebase left alive, and pulled away.

At the Ai Tu Combat Base in Quang Tri, headquarters of the Third ARVN Division, the Vietnamese soldiers were engaged in one of the fiercest ground battles since World War II. Major David Brookbank, the Air Force air liaison adviser, was in a command bunker as artillery shells thudded into the concrete structure. He could hear the cries of men being shot. "We were in full-scale war," he said. Firebases were falling one after the other; soldiers were surrendering and dying by the hundreds.

It was in this atmosphere that the no-fire order was handed to Brookbank. He took the piece of paper and began to read. The sixteen-mile zone where airstrikes and artillery were now forbidden encompassed the entire battlefield in front of him. Brookbank went back and looked at the words again. "He read the message carefully," wrote one military historian, "but could not believe what he was being told." At this crucial moment, when North Vietnam was invading South Vietnam in an attempt to annihilate its army and win the war, he was being instructed not to fire at the enemy. The battle against the invading forces was to take a backseat to the rescue of a single man.

It isn't true, Brookbank thought to himself. It couldn't possibly be true. You couldn't ask *the war* to take a backseat.

But the order was clear. Brookbank brought it to another American on the base, Lieutenant Colonel Jerry Turley, a tough-minded Marine who had just arrived in Vietnam. "You've got to shut it down," Brookbank told him. Turley looked at the directive and he, too, was taken aback. "We were deeply involved in a war," Turley said. "I had tanks on a [nearby] bridge and I had a massive three-division attack coming at me. Total chaos." Turley took a sketch of the sixteen-mile radius and laid it over a map. He realized he wouldn't even be able to fire artillery in self-defense.

Word quickly got out to the Vietnamese soldiers. "My god, my god!" Brookbank heard someone cry out. One Vietnamese commander found the adviser and asked him, "Where are the American planes? . . . If they don't come to our aid, we're lost." The bridge at Cam Lo, just two miles from Hambleton's position, was a special concern. Another bridge farther upriver, the one at Dong Ha, had been destroyed by US Marine adviser John Ripley, who, in the face of withering enemy fire, had swung out on the beams beneath the structure carrying explosives and detonators and blown the overpass into the water. It was an act of almost lunatic bravery that saved many hundreds of South Vietnamese lives.

But NVA tanks had been redirected and were now rolling across the bridge at Cam Lo, close to Hambleton's position, and heading straight toward the ARVN's firebases. Could Brookbank get an airstrike on it, the South Vietnamese asked him, or a naval gun to target it? "People were just begging for artillery."

Panic engulfed the towns just south of the DMZ as villagers streamed onto the roads by the thousands. The North Vietnamese dropped mortars on the escape routes and people fell unmoving to the ground, turning the roads bloody and littering them with severed limbs. The terrified Vietnamese villagers stepped over the dead who piled up on the roads; corpses were pushed into the ditches so that the flood of people could press on. "Mass hysteria," Turley remembered. "It was the worst thing I'd ever seen."

The commander of a South Vietnamese Marine regiment overheard a heated discussion between Brookbank and Turley and asked what was going on. The Americans explained there was an Air Force navigator down north of the Mieu Giang and the military was diverting all airstrikes to the rescue mission. The commander, seeking to understand, held up his index finger. "One?" he said. "Just *one* man?" In the first week of the invasion, the South Vietnamese would lose five thousand soldiers to death or surrender. The commander, like so many others that day, had trouble comprehending what he was being told.

As more shells came in, shrieking and then going silent before impact, Turley made a decision. He would disobey the order. "I said, Screw you, I'm not going to do it. We're going to keep shooting." The guns at Ai Tu never stopped firing at the human waves of NVA pouring down from the North.

But the Air Force controlled the airstrikes, and many were diverted to the search and rescue effort. As the battle continued to rage — some firebases later reported eleven thousand shells being fired at them in a single day — Brookbank got on the radio and called the USAF controllers. There was no answer; his fellow Americans wouldn't respond. "This was the attitude — this is our war, we've got something going on, don't bother us," Brookbank said. Desperate to save his men, he found himself shouting into the radio: *"This is important. Can't you understand how important this is?!"*

Ensconced in their base near Saigon, more than six hundred miles to the south of the DMZ, the intelligence officers of the Seventh Air Force still hadn't confirmed that an invasion was under way. They had approved channels that provided them with raw intelligence; Marine officers at forward bases weren't one of them. If they had known the long-awaited attack had launched, they might have pushed back against the no-fire order. But they didn't know, just as Joker didn't know.

Brookbank's disbelief gave way to bitterness. He felt powerless, abandoned. There were Marine commanders who, if you told them you were canceling their air support in the middle of a major firefight, would have taken out their sidearm and executed you. "They would have killed you," Brookbank said. "Then the general would have gone to the president and said, 'This is asinine.'" But it was happening and Brookbank was unable to stop it. "They were running their own war for one guy. It was the most devastating thing I could ever imagine."

In fact, the Air Force *was* hitting some of the targets that Brookbank wanted hit; it was just that they were doing it to save Gene Hambleton. The two missions occasionally overlapped. The problem for Brookbank and the ARVN was that the units being hit were a day or two behind the lead elements of the invasion. The South Vietnamese and their American advisers wanted the enemy soldiers *directly in front of them,* the ones coming through the wire and attacking their positions, killed first. That wasn't being done.

Fierce arguments rang out up and down the chain of command, across service lines, in person and over radio links. Another Marine officer, Lieutenant Colonel D'Wayne Gray, read the order, found it "obscene," and flew into a rage. "I was absolutely up the wall." Gray approached an Air Force brigadier general who happened to be visiting his posting and confronted him about the no-fire zone. During the conversation, it became clear that the brigadier general thought there were two airmen down, not one. Gray, trying to maintain his composure, pointed out that their allies were being killed by the hundreds and that the enemy was forging a breakthrough that could lead to defeat.

The brigadier general was unmoved. "I would rather lose two ARVN divisions," the man told Gray, "than those two US Air Force crewmen."

As a highly decorated Marine who'd fought in Korea before being assigned to Vietnam, Gray wasn't easily shocked. But the general's statement took his breath away. Two ARVN divisions totaled twenty thousand men.

It's not an exaggeration to say that, on that day in April, some Marines and Air Force officers came to the conclusion that the US leadership in Vietnam had lost its collective mind.

11

YESTERDAY'S FRAT BOY

At about one in the morning of April 3, at the Nakhon Phanom Air Base in Thailand, an airman shook Bill Henderson awake. The man told Henderson there was an American down and that he was needed to fly on the rescue. The pilot dressed quickly in his hooch and hurried to the briefing.

Tall, mustached, and handsome, Henderson was a prototypical Air Force pilot, a species that one pilot described as "yesterday's college frat boy with a ten to one ratio of impulse to common sense." The son of a World War II flight engineer, Henderson grew up athletic and highly competitive, a swimmer who, by the time he was fourteen, had risen to number three in the nation in the freestyle for his age group. There were people in Milwaukee who were even beginning to talk about the Olympics.

His father was his swimming coach. One day, the elder Henderson told him to skip practice; he wanted to take his son sailing instead. Bill eagerly agreed. They headed to Pewaukee Lake, a half-hour ride from Milwaukee, and sailed five miles from the west end to the east end, slipping across the dark blue water with bright sunshine overhead. Bill was enjoying the trip. About this time, his father caught his eye and said, "Get out." Bill inquired what his father was talking about and what he got back was: "Not much of a wind. You'll get your workout here." So Bill took off his shirt and dove in the water and began swimming, and after two and a half hours he'd covered most of the length of the lake again, back the other way, with his dad leading him in the sailboat. That was how it was for Bill Henderson growing up.

Bill went to Dartmouth and became a music major. It was the late sixties by then, and the campus was pulsing with an anti-Vietnam vibe; at times it seemed the majority of the student body was at war with the country's future military officers. Bill, however, was otherwise occupied. His girlfriend had become pregnant before his senior year; he'd married her, and so he was now a student, a husband, and a father all at once. He possessed neither the free time, the money, nor the psychological makeup to get involved with the anti-war movement. Instead, he became the campus sandwich man, selling ham and cheese or liverwurst on wheat to leftists with deeper pockets than his.

After graduation, Henderson found himself without prospects. Nobody was hiring music majors in 1968. What to do? His dad, the former military flight engineer, had taught him that flying was something almost inexplicably special. The Air Force was hungry for young, vigorous bodies. Why not go along for the ride? It was his patriotic duty, and besides, he needed a job. Bill Henderson was a pragmatist down to the soles of his feet.

His young wife objected. She worried that he was going to end up in Vietnam and get himself killed. But even then, in his early twenties, Henderson was an unusually confident person, possessed of an unshakable belief that he could outthink almost any human being you cared to stand up against him. "I said, 'Listen, my dear, I'm brilliant and you're not. Let me tell you how it's going to be.'" It was late 1968 and Richard Nixon had been elected on a promise to get America out of the war. Henderson took him at his word and did the math in his head. He would have to go to three months of officer training school, then a year of pilot training, then advanced training (which he did, in the gorgeous F-100 Super Sabre) for another six months. "I figured after two years, the frickin' war's going to be over. Shit, what the hell, I was a Dartmouth grad. I knew everything." It would be many months before he realized how wrong he was.

Bill Henderson wasn't a John Bircher. He didn't hate the Vietnamese. He wasn't particularly bloodthirsty. But he'd discovered the second great love of his life and he wished to pursue it in the defense of his country. "I found flying," says Henderson, "was better than an orgasm."

At the rescue mission briefing, Henderson learned he would fly over to Vietnam and join the ongoing effort to save Hambleton. In the vicinity of Dong Ha, he would connect with two long-range Sikorsky HH-53 Jolly Greens and at least two Douglas A-1 Skyraider attack aircraft that were about to take off from Da Nang. (The big choppers always traveled in pairs, as a precaution: the "low" bird retrieved the downed American; the "high" bird waited a mile or so back in the event of a crash, in which case it would swoop in and rescue the crew members.) Henderson would fill the role of spotter for the mission, diving beneath the clouds in his OV-10 aircraft to "zot"—slang for mark—Hambleton's location with his LORAN laser beam so that the choppers could come in and pick the airman up. He would also draw the first rounds of fire and give the other guys an idea of how hot the zone was.

It wasn't anything new for Henderson. On previous missions he'd flown escort for the 21st Special Operations Squadron—they were called the Knives—who went behind enemy lines to assassinate North Vietnamese mayors. "Every time the North killed one of ours, we killed one up there." The insertions could be gnarly, and the passengers were something else. Assassins, real-life American killers who didn't say much as they came and went. "*Craaaaaaaaazy* people," Henderson said. After that, rescue missions were not something that made him unduly nervous.

Despite the Knives, Bill Henderson was having a fabulous war. "I killed guns," he said, referring to North Vietnamese AAA, "and I killed a lot of 'em." Henderson loved flying the OV-10 and sending a five-hundred-pound bomb rocketing toward the AAA sites, loved the moment the bombs hit in a bloom of smoke and fire, loved the Thais and their sweet-natured laughter, loved the action. Flying above Vietnam at night was magical: the meandering silver glint of the rivers, the black foothills folded back on one another in serried, ghostly rows gripped by thin fingers of mist. The country was lush even in darkness. The only signs of war from this distance were the innumerable bomb craters, now filled up with rainwater. The pilots looking down would see them flash with moonlight as they flew over.

Henderson hitched his six-foot frame into the cockpit of his OV-10, call sign Nail 38, and set to work. It was still pitch-black. Behind him, he could hear his navigator, First Lieutenant Mark Clark, settling in.

As he drew near Hambleton's position that morning, Bill Henderson studied the cloud cover. It topped out at about two thousand feet, with a bottom of about seven hundred. Those numbers would usually be problematic. But this was a rescue mission and Henderson thought he could find a way in.

He knew Hambleton was surrounded by guns. The pilot of the previous OV-10 that had flown over the downed airman had been startled at what he'd seen: a beehive of tanks, transports, artillery positions, and troop carriers, crisscrossing the area around Hambleton. The number of vehicles was so unexpected that the pilot checked his map coordinates, thinking he'd somehow gotten lost and was looking at a massive camp deep in South Vietnam. But then he spotted red stars — the symbol of the NVA — on the doors of the trucks and, soon after that, a wall of flak rose up to greet him. *Where had all these troops come from?* he wondered. Headquarters still had not briefed the rescuers that they were going into an invasion zone. As he departed the area, the pilot relayed the information, along with the navigator's coordinates, to Bill Henderson.

As he arrived over the rescue zone, Henderson contacted the A-1 pilots and Jolly Green crews to coordinate their efforts. "OK, guys, we might be able to pull this off," he told them. "Here's what we're going to do. I have the coordinates, so get on my wing. I'll get you within a quarter mile of him. Stay on my wing." The plan was that Henderson would break through the clouds at the head of the set, angle downward toward Hambleton, and get the rescue choppers positioned above him. The A-1s would rip the shit out of any enemy guns that were targeting the choppers. The lead helicopter, flown by a Coast Guard pilot, Lieutenant Commander Jay Crowe, would then buzz in behind him with fighter cover. The high Jolly, flown by Lieutenant Colonel Bill Harris, would hover a mile south, ready to move in if trouble developed. If the approach could be made, Crowe would touch down, grab Hambleton, and get back up in the air as fast as possible, and they'd all turn around and haul ass back to base.

Henderson pushed the stick down and the plane's nose dipped. His windscreen was covered by streams of wet gray mist as the seconds passed. At seven hundred feet, the plane broke out of the cloud bank. There was Vietnam below them. A second or two later, "the whole fucking world lit up." The sky seemed alive with pulsing fire and puffs of dark smoke. Tracers streaked across his windshield; Henderson had never seen anything like it. "Flak *everywhere.*"

Henderson zotted Hambleton's position, then jinked and climbed to get out of the AAA. Behind him, an A-1 headed straight toward Hambleton, followed by the low bird, its engine whining at high speed. As the crew of the Jolly Green looked on in amazement, it seemed that everyone on the ground—NVA troops, tank gunners, truck drivers—turned their guns and began shooting. Bullets chopped their way through the nose of the helicopter and splintered the instrument panel. A round slammed into the flight instrument gyro, knocking out the navigation. Warning lights lit up all over the cockpit. Lieutenant Commander Crowe jumped on the radio and called out that he was taking heavy fire. "Break it off, break it off!" the on-scene commander shouted on the radio. "Get out, Jolly Green, get out." Crowe pulled back on the stick and the chopper climbed upward, but the controls had gone sluggish. Perhaps a hydraulic line had been cut or a component smashed by a bullet.

Crowe experimented with the speed to see if the chopper could land. When he dropped the Jolly Green below 120 knots, it began to veer out of control. But he needed to get it down to 105 before he could lower the landing gear. The pararescuemen in back had chutes; if the bird was high enough, they could bail out. But Crowe's altimeter had been shot out; he had no idea what his altitude was. Watching Crowe struggle to keep the chopper in the air, Harris, the pilot of the high bird, was incredulous. "How he managed to fly that bird is beyond my comprehension."

The escorting A-1 pilots called the control tower at the Hue airfield and requested an emergency landing. The air controller came back to him; he was *not* to attempt to bring the bird in. The airport was under rocket attack, and they were too busy to deal with some shot-up helicopter. As they argued, the A-1 pilot jumped into the traffic and told the controller in no uncertain terms that the Jolly Green was coming apart and he was either going to land at Hue or crash into the jungle. The officer relented.

Crowe spotted the runway and came in at 105 knots. The chopper touched down and whipped along the tarmac. Crowe shut off both engines to slow it, but ahead of him he could see a deep hole in the runway where a rocket had blown out the asphalt. If he hit that, the chopper would wreck itself. He did a quick cycling flare and the chopper lifted a few feet into the air, just managing to clear the crater. The Jolly Green touched back down and slid to a juddering halt.

A fire touched off in the back of the crew compartment. Tendrils of acrid smoke seeped forward. Crowe shouted for his men to get out. Rockets were thudding into the ground as the crew ran down the runway toward a waiting base vehicle. They climbed in and the transport sped off.

With Crowe out of action, the pilot of the high bird, Bill Harris, decided he would try to grab Hambleton with a run-in from north of Dong Ha. He made a beeline for the copse of trees where the navigator was hiding and got within a hundred yards. Hambleton popped his smoke. But rounds were *thwock*ing into Harris's aircraft one after the other. "Extreme, intense fire," he remembered. "Big orange balls of fire coming through the rotor blades, right at us." The on-scene commander called for him to break off. Reluctantly, seconds away from getting Hambleton out, Harris aborted and turned away. "We were *that close.*"

Hambleton had listened to the choppers approach and heard the roar of the AAA guns opening up. "Where in God's name had those guns come from?" he thought as the din pounded in his ears. He believed that the F-4s and A-1s had killed almost every enemy soldier within a large radius.

The navigator crawled forward to take a look at the roadway that had been decimated hours before. To his shock, a revivifying miracle had taken place. "Like a busy anthill that had its top kicked off, the whole area was swarming with parties of soldiers." The blackened wrecks of the tanks and the transport trucks were already being hauled to the side of the road and abandoned in the bushes so new transports could get through. The wounded and dead were being loaded into trucks, some of them still moaning from their untreated injuries. Fresh camouflaged trucks, with youthful faces staring out at the carnage, roared by, headed south. Hambleton could hear the orders of officers in clipped Vietnamese. In a few minutes, it was as if nothing had happened here at all.

Hambleton felt hollowed out. How could the Air Force save him when the NVA sprang back to life every time you destroyed it, sprouting new soldiers and new equipment like some unkillable golem? How could they do it if every chopper that approached his little grove was shot to pieces?

The navigator turned back to his hole, crawled in, took off his holster that carried the .38, pulled the mosquito netting over his body, and stewed about his situation. Through the brambles and leaves, he watched fog begin to steal across the rice fields, "like some melancholy emblem of his own sinking spirits."

12

"THEIR GLOWING TRAJECTORIES"

In the capital of north vietnam, the sounds of Radio Hanoi were a familiar presence in shops and schools and on the heavily trafficked streets. Every day, the station's announcers would read news accounts of the previous day's battles, of American planes shot down by stalwart communist youths and stunning NVA ambushes in the jungle, along with reams of propaganda and promises of the coming victory. Even in the Hanoi Hilton, American POWs confined in their tiny cells, sweltering on the concrete slabs that served as beds, were forced to listen to the reports. There was one propagandist the men called Hanoi Hannah—her real name was Trinh Thi Ngo—a Vietnamese woman who spoke slangy English in a high, seductive voice. Hannah would read off the names of Americans killed during the previous month, play tapes sent to her by antiwar activists in the States, including Jane Fonda, and drop the needle on American pop songs. Elvis was a particular favorite.

North Vietnamese diplomats in capitals around the world sent copies of *Time, Newsweek,* and *Stars and Stripes* back home so that Hannah and the station's other announcers could broadcast the accounts of antiwar protests and capitalist depravities. The "reports" were often ridiculous, with descriptions of hundreds of American planes being shot down at once. But in early April, Radio Hanoi announced a great victory that was fleshed out by a good deal of detail: "Fliers used every trick to confuse ground detection ... [T]hey could not cheat the radar observers of Detachment 62 ... [T]he men quickly fixed the enemy on their screens ... The whole battleground shook in the deafening burst of the missiles streaking up into the clouds in their glowing trajectories. One of the B-52s was hit, burst into flame and exploded. Its debris were scattered over a wide area. The rest of the eight-engine craft together with their escort jet fighters fled in disorder."

The NVA had mistaken the type of plane they'd downed. They believed they'd hit a B-52 when it was really Hambleton's EB-66C. Nevertheless, the shootdown was announced in "triumphant" tones. For the North Vietnamese, shooting down one of the most advanced American aircraft wasn't just a victory of arms; it was an unmistakable sign of progress. The leaders in Hanoi clearly regarded it as an event that would strike fear into the hearts of the enemy.

Magazines and newspapers around the world noted the downing of Hambleton's aircraft, along with its disturbing implications. "The loss of the EB-66C dramatically underscored the new sophistication of North Vietnam's air defense system," reported *Newsweek*. "The shock waves that rippled through Saigon and Washington could not have been greater if the lost plane had, in fact, been a B-52." One American official expressed a fresh anxiety over the incident. "We're supposedly fighting a primitive enemy," he told the magazine. "But the way things are going, that just isn't so anymore." With the NVA's new tactics, the missiles that had brought down Hambleton's plane could change the war, or future, larger wars.

The *Times* of London struck a similar tone, while noting that one of the plane's crew had survived. "The EB-66C contains highly secret electronic equipment designed to jam the radar guidance devices of North Vietnamese missiles," the paper reported. "The fact that it was shot down at all sent shock waves through the Pentagon. The Americans were determined that its navigator should not fall into enemy hands." Losing an EB-66C was a serious matter for the military, but the plane's equipment was likely to have been destroyed when it crashed into the earth from thirty thousand feet. Losing Hambleton would be worse.

• • •

Bill Henderson continued orbiting above the clouds until his fuel ran low, then headed back to Da Nang. While his OV-10 was being fueled up, the on-scene commander raised Henderson on the radio. They were going to try again. Was he willing to come back?

Henderson thought about it. "My arrogance at the time told me I knew how to dance around that crap," Henderson said, meaning the AAA. "So I said yes." He and Clark finished refueling, got a quick intelligence update, and flew back to Hambleton's position.

It was now about 3 p.m. Henderson raised the navigator on the radio. "We're coming in again," he said. "When the time comes, we'll ask you to pop some smoke."

The radio crackled. "Roger," Hambleton answered from down below.

The ground beneath the OV-10 was still cloaked in low-hanging clouds. Henderson arrived over the position, synced up with the other aircraft, gritted his teeth, and dove into the cumulus again, and when he emerged from the bottom of the clouds, what seemed like a significant portion of the North Vietnamese Army opened up on him and Clark.

Almost immediately, a SAM warning sounded in Henderson's ear. At that moment the missile appeared and arced over a nearby plane — the pilot watched it swoop past him — dove under his wingman's belly, and headed directly at Henderson's OV-10. Henderson was just about to execute his SAM break when the missile smashed into his right wing at the engine joint and exploded.

The wing snapped in half. The plane shuddered and then began to fall earthward. The canopy vaporized, just went away; the shock wave destroyed the metal and plastic sheathing that protected Henderson and Clark. A fireball blew forward and engulfed the two airmen, burning off Henderson's mustache; only the sturdy ejection seats protected the two men from being incinerated. A chunk of glass tore through Henderson's flight suit and ripped the flesh away, leaving his breastbone exposed.

What was left of the plane turned over and lost speed rapidly. Henderson found himself upside down. The wings had snapped off, the tail was now debris sailing away from him in all directions. The molten metal from the warhead had burned off the rest of the airplane.

In the backseat, Mark Clark pulled the ejection seat D-ring and the hard *whoomp* of the ejection seat rocketed him out of the craft. Henderson had no intention of following; his number-three-swimmer-in-his-age-group-cum-Dartmouth-grad-cum-fighter-pilot brain told him that as long as he was strapped into an airplane, he was damn well going to fly it out of there. But just as Clark went shooting out from behind him, Henderson heard a voice, deep and commanding, "a very powerful voice that brooked no hesitation." It said simply: "Pull the D-ring." It took something approximating the voice of God to get Bill Henderson out of the plane at that moment. Humbled, he reached down, pulled the D-ring, and ejected straight toward the earth.

The pilot rotated upright and popped his chute. As it opened above him, he looked down. He was close to the ground, perhaps two thousand feet, and could hear the snap of AK-47s beneath him. A backseater in another OV-10 circling above watched the chutes pop and silently said good-bye to Henderson and Clark. "We didn't think they were coming back."

Henderson drifted down for thirty of forty seconds before landing softly in a wheat field. The plane had been traveling at 130 mph, and the fraction of a second between their ejections had determined the airmen's respective fates: Clark floated toward the south side of the Mieu Giang and Henderson to the north. Clark felt horribly exposed as he descended. "There were a lot of people on the roads," he remembered, "and they seemed to be looking at me." He jettisoned his seat pack and saw that he was coming down in thick jungle. As the ground came rushing up at him, he lifted his feet, slammed into the branches, and surfed across the treetops. He cleared the trees, pulled back on his risers, and made a soft landing on open terrain. The airman quickly began running and found a barbed wire fence secured to the ground by two crossed posts. He pulled some vegetation back from the posts and crawled underneath. It was an excellent hiding place.

Henderson landed in a field in the thick of the enemy offensive, just over a mile away from Hambleton. He released his chute and ducked behind a nearby rock pile, surveying the fields around him. Almost at once, something caught his eye. An old Vietnamese peasant was ambling toward him, moving at a stately pace despite the small-arms fire that was popping off everywhere. Henderson watched as the man strolled along until he reached the parachute, now ruffling gently against the soil. He bent down, picked up the edge, and calmly began rolling up the nylon. It took a while. When he was done, the villager turned and walked back toward his hut, carrying the chute under his arm. It had been a hypnotizing, disdainful performance. Clearly, the old man had seen his share of war.

When the villager turned away, Henderson took the opportunity to go "screaming to the nearest hedge line." He raced toward the underbrush and pushed his way through the branches. Once inside, he set about burying himself in bamboo leaves. Within a few minutes of landing, he was completely hidden from view. Though he'd expected no less of himself, Henderson was satisfied that he'd executed the USAF post-shootdown checklist with flawless aplomb.

Henderson got on the radio, and the voice on the other end told him to sit tight, a Cobra was on the way. The Cobra was a shark-nosed attack helicopter studded with nasty weaponry, including 70 mm rockets and Miniguns that could fire up to four thousand rounds a minute. If you were down behind enemy lines, a Cobra was what you wanted coming for you.

One did arrive almost immediately. Captain Tim Sprouse was heading toward Henderson when he heard a voice on his headset: "SAM, SAM, vicinity of Khe Sanh!" He was too low for the SAM to operate, or at least he thought he was, so he kept his course. Then the A-1 above him called out, "Here it comes guys — hit the deck!" Sprouse pushed the stick and dove for the ground as the SAM streaked above his rotors. The dive nearly put the chopper into the treetops, but Sprouse managed to pull out just before impact. The Cobra aborted the mission.

A Huey pilot, Warrant Officer Ben Nielsen, flying with the Cobra, turned to go after all the downed airmen in succession: first Clark, then Henderson, then Hambleton. Three quick hops and it would be done. As the Huey dropped down on its approach, rounds pinged off the fuselage. Then "something really big" sounded below. Nielsen could hear heavy things — artillery shells of some kind — cutting through the air around him. The Plexiglas in front of him shattered and pieces sprayed over his flight suit. A shell blew the right cargo door off the helicopter and sent it spinning down to the rice fields below. The Huey aborted.

Henderson had watched the whole thing with awe. "The shit lit up. The Cobra didn't have a chance." The choppers turned south, the chirring sound of their rotors fading slowly. Quiet returned.

At the same time that Henderson was watching the helicopter depart, Jay Crowe, the commander of the Jolly Green that had nearly crashed at Hue, was riding in a jeep speeding away from a barrage of mortars. He needed to speak to someone, urgently. His Jolly Green had been practically dismantled in the air by something that wasn't supposed to be there. What was this mystery force? Why hadn't he been told about it? Something big and menacing was hunkered down in the area around Hambleton and it had opened the eyes of the men going after the navigator. "The 'war is over' syndrome was rapidly evaporating," Crowe said.

Lieutenant Commander Crowe was a big, genial, buttoned-up officer, a Coast Guard man who'd requested transfer to Vietnam from a "cush gig" flying C-130s in Hawaii because he'd become bored with the dullness of it. He'd grown up the son of a Massachusetts educator and violin teacher, a man with exacting standards when it came to established knowledge. The trait had been passed down, in spades. Crowe was a voracious reader, "big into researching things," said his son Ty. "He knew something about everything, almost to an obnoxious degree." What had happened to his aircraft above Cam Lo shouldn't have happened. And Jay Crowe wanted to know why.

When he jumped out of the jeep, Crowe buttonholed a few officers from US Army intelligence. They told him what they knew. There was a full-blown invasion under way and Hambleton was sitting in the middle of it. Crowe was taken aback. Why hadn't he been told this? Why hadn't anyone trying to rescue Hambleton been told this?

The pilot grabbed a ride aboard the Jolly Green piloted by Bill Harris and flew to Da Nang. At the sprawling base, he sought out some of the Air Force intelligence officers who were generating intel for the rescue mission and told them what he'd seen: armored cars, command vehicles, massive numbers of troops, SAMs where no SAMs were supposed to be, all of it. A couple of A-1 pilots had even spotted what they thought was the pride of the Soviet arms industry, the highly advanced SA-7 missile — shoulder-launched, heat-seeking — coming up at them from the rice paddies. With those things, a single soldier could take down a $3 million plane in the blink of an eye.

Crowe unloaded all this on the intel guys. And after he'd finished giving his report, he lingered, listening in, eager to know how the rescue briefings would change. But it soon became clear that his hot scoop — *by the way, it's fucking Vietnamese D-Day out there, boys! Might want to pass it on* — hadn't set the officers on fire. The men carried on with their day, talking about this target and that target and not bothering to get on the radio and inform the rescue teams what was down there waiting for them. When Crowe, confused by the lack of action, asked about one part of his report, the sighting of SA-7 missiles, the intel guy looked at him. "There aren't any SA-7s in-country," he said.

The military often acts slowly, as commanders struggle to absorb chaotic bits of information arriving in real time. Crowe understood that. But he wasn't repeating some flyboy gossip he'd overheard at the Officers' Club. He'd been right over the area in question; he'd seen this stuff with his own eyes. More Americans were going after Hambleton, and intel was letting them think it was just another day over the Mieu Giang. It wasn't.

Crowe found it infuriating.

13

TINY TIM

ON THE GROUND, Hambleton heard the FAC above revving its engine. It was his signal to call in. "An OV-10 has been hit by antiaircraft and is down," the FAC reported, referring to Bill Henderson's plane. "The No. 2 man is down also. No word from the pilot." Hambleton absorbed the news, his mood sinking.

Henderson and Clark were safe for the moment, but the rescue scenarios had just become much more complicated. "The entire picture changed," Hambleton said. The rescuers would have to coordinate three pickups instead of one, and in a fantastically hostile environment. But not today. The FAC informed Hambleton that no more choppers were on the way until further notice.

He kept to his hiding place as the hours passed. By that afternoon, Hambleton found he was growing increasingly hungry and decided to go scouting for food. He knew from his jungle survival training that Vietnamese families sometimes grew vegetables and fruit—corn, pineapple, watermelon, red pepper—in small plots near their homes. Some watermelon or pineapple would give him an energy boost. He wouldn't be able to venture out from his hiding place until darkness came, but he could find possible targets to return to later that night.

The navigator got on the radio and told the FAC circling above of his plans. There was a delay. "Roger, Bat. I'll alert the A-1s . . . Any trouble, click your transmitter at three-second intervals."

Hambleton confirmed.

"And, Bat? Be careful. Make like Tiny Tim."

The FAC was aware that the enemy were probably listening in, so this was obviously some kind of code. But what the hell did Tiny Tim mean? Hambleton thought back to *The Tonight Show* with Johnny Carson, which had occasionally featured a hairy oddball character by that name, strumming his mandolin and singing a song. What was the song? *"Tiptoe . . . through the tulips."* The gravel mines, of course. Had to be.

First he studied the little copse where he was hiding. The trees themselves were about ten feet high and threw the whole area into deep shade. The waist-high undergrowth was thick and tangled; as he looked around, he could see no paths cutting through it. That meant that villagers didn't come through it very often. "I would defy anyone to be able to see a person hiding," Hambleton said. "The only chance to be discovered was to be stepped on."

Hambleton removed the survival vest, which would only slow him down. He took his knife and the radio and left the other items in his hiding place, with leaves and branches covering them. Studying his compass, he set out eastward, pushing slowly through the undergrowth. He listened carefully for any human voices, counting his steps as he went. He moved through the brush until he reached the outer edge. He measured the little grove as he went and determined it was only about fifty yards wide, though looking back and ahead, he figured it stretched as much as two miles north and south.

Hambleton lay down and peered out at the fields simmering in the strong afternoon glare. He was struck immediately by how the landscape in front of him resembled the rural parts of Illinois and Indiana. This was real farm country, with hills covered by green fields and dotted with small villages. Instead of cornfields, there were long rows of rice paddies, bordered by ditches for irrigation. Between the paddies and the ditches were narrow paths about one and a half feet wide that the farmers presumably used to reach their fields.

Beyond the paddies Hambleton spotted a village, perhaps a mile and a half away, the huts strung out in a narrow line instead of clumped together. He couldn't see beyond the village but imagined there were more rice paddies on the other side. Looking south, he saw another, smaller hamlet, with fewer huts. But what caught Hambleton's attention was a small garden next to the rice paddy a short distance away.

With the eye of a born midwesterner, he studied the garden closely. There was a big plot of corn, as well as what looked like watermelon, taro — a starchy tuber — pineapple, and red pepper. He looked for the bright reds and yellows of ripe fruit and vegetables, but everything in the garden appeared to be green. Clearly it was the wrong time of year to go foraging in South Vietnam.

Hambleton squinted at the tall stalks of corn, studying the tassels that moved lazily in the light breeze. It looked to him as if the strands of silk that fluttered below the tops of the plants were just starting to turn brown, which meant they were beginning to ripen. He thought of the taste of young corn. He memorized the position of three ears that seemed the ripest and decided to return tonight and take just those.

Closer to him, he saw spotted something red. Berries, they looked like, hanging in the branches of several bushes in one of the paddies. His mouth was painfully dry and his stomach was rumbling; he decided to risk it. Hambleton stood up, took a deep breath, and dashed out into the paddy. When he reached the first bush, he plucked a piece of the fruit — it looked like a raspberry — and popped it in his mouth. Sweet. The Negritos who ran the survival school in the Philippines had taught him that sweet meant safe to eat. Usually. Hambleton wanted to grab handfuls of the fruit, but he was worried that someone would look up and spot him. Reluctantly he turned and ran back to the trees and from there made his way toward his hiding place.

After a few minutes of walking, he stopped, looking around in confusion. Where *was* his hiding place? The trees all looked the same to him, and he hadn't dared mark his shelter, in case a villager stumbled across it. By running off without leaving a trace of where his stuff was, he'd managed to outsmart himself. The navigator felt panic rise up. Without the flares, the rescue would be much harder to pull off, and he needed the .38 to fight off any pursuers.

Hambleton took several slow breaths, telling himself to calm down. He marked the spot where he was standing, then began to walk in concentric circles. It took him three minutes, but after a few circuits his boot slipped into the hole. He let out a breath and crawled in.

When dusk fell, he emerged from his hole and walked to the edge of the undergrowth, pausing several minutes to make sure no villagers were walking nearby. Then he stepped nervously out of the dark grove onto the trail and headed straight for the garden. He plucked three ears of corn, along with some berries and a pineapple, and headed back to his hiding place.

When he'd made it, Hambleton lay down in the dugout hole and brought out his take. He popped berry after berry into his mouth. They were unlikely to keep off the vine for long, so he decided to eat all of them. Delicious. The juice relieved the raspy dryness of his throat; he thought he'd never tasted anything so refreshing. Then he moved on to an ear of corn. He slowly stripped away the husk and the wisps of silk covering the ripe kernels, then dug a small hole in the ground with his knife and placed the discards in it. Once he covered that up with dirt, he held the ear in both hands and took his first bite of the yellow kernels. God, they were tasty — ripe and filled with a sweet milk. He savored the ear, biting into one kernel at a time until he'd finished the whole thing. Then he took the cob and bit off a chunk, grinding the stuff between his molars before swallowing. The pineapple came out next. It was hard as a piece of granite. Hambleton spent a few minutes turning it this way and that, trying to penetrate its husk with his teeth, but gave up and tucked it away for the future.

For the moment, he was satisfied.

While this was going on, Bill Henderson, hiding about a mile from his fellow American, took time to examine his injuries. The explosion of the SAM had messed him up a bit. His eyebrows and mustache had been burned off by the fireball; he had a deep cut across his cheek — which he immediately began to hope might produce a facsimile of one of those German dueling scars — and that gaping hole in his chest through which you could see the white of his sternum. But, all in all, he was in good spirits.

He thought of the voice that had sounded in his ears and told him to eject. He was shaken by it, and comforted. He believed he'd heard, in his moment of extremity, nothing less than an angel.

The pilot settled deeper into his hedgerow, confident that in the morning "we'd get reinforcements and they'd blow the shit out of 'em and they'd pull me out and God bless." But at around 8 p.m. he heard the sound of voices. An enemy patrol approached, beating the thickets looking for the downed airmen. "They came in there and they're chitter-chattering away." The squad of twelve soldiers began to dig twenty yards from where Henderson sat. The men chunked their shovels into the earth and threw the dirt into the nearby underbrush.

It dawned on Henderson what all the digging was about: the NVA soldiers were building a machine-gun pit. But why do that in the middle of nowhere? The South Vietnamese hadn't been here in many months; the front line was now miles away. After thinking for a few moments, Henderson decided there was only one possible answer: he had unwittingly become part of an ambush. Knowing an American was somewhere in the area, the NVA soldiers were planning to build the pit, pop a 12.7 mm machine gun into it, cover the gun with branches and leaves, then wait around until his rescuers arrived in their helicopters. Then they would kill as many as they could.

Once he understood what the enemy was doing, Henderson decided he wasn't going to become a piece of bait. That was beyond the pale. Combat pilots in Vietnam had a motto: "Better dead than a fuckup." This situation fell under the moral clause of the adage. Anyone who allowed the NVA to grind up his friends with a hidden machine gun was not acting in accordance with the brotherhood's core values.

But if he wasn't going to stay in this bamboo, where could he go? He began thinking of what he'd seen in those thirty or forty seconds he was descending on his parachute. He remembered the blue glint of water. It had to be a river. Henderson, the former swimming champion, mulled that over. What if he left his hiding place and made his way over the nearby fields to the water, then swam through enemy lines to friendly territory? Sure, the plan would expose him to the battalions of NVA hidden in the nearby fields, but it might save his fellow airmen. "I wasn't going to set up my guys to run against that," he said. "I'll swim to Quang Tri, I don't give a shit." Quang Tri was at least ten miles from his present location, but he decided that was not going to be an issue.

Just as Henderson readied himself to try the solo run for the river, the NVA squad returned. He could hear them moving through the brush; it seemed they were coming straight toward him. As the sounds drew closer, Henderson watched in horror as a hand appeared and began to pull away the leaves that he'd piled on top of his flight suit. A face appeared. "He looked at me and almost did a backflip. I scared the living shit out of the guy."

The soldier screamed. In the seconds afterward Henderson heard the distinct sound of a dozen rifles being cocked. He held a five-shot .38 in his right hand; the twelve soldiers, he guessed, each had an AK-47, with thirty rounds apiece.

Even for Bill Henderson, Dartmouth grad and shit-hot combat pilot, those were daunting odds. He raised his arms in the air and walked slowly out of the brush.

14

FUTILITY

By APRIL 4, the Hambleton operation had become a behemoth, drawing in the U.S. Coast Guard, the Army, the Navy, the Air Force, and the Marines. Hundreds of officers and airmen were involved and millions of dollars were being spent — and lost, in the form of damaged and destroyed aircraft — in what was becoming the biggest rescue mission in Air Force history and the largest of the Vietnam War. Three young Americans had died, two POWs — Henderson and Astorga — were being marched north, and another American, Mark Clark, was stranded behind enemy lines.

One note of sanity was introduced: the no-fire zone around Hambleton had been gradually reduced until it stood at a radius of about a mile and a half. But Major Brookbank, the US Air Force adviser who'd begged controllers to send planes to his beleaguered men, believed the order had already done enormous damage. "In my opinion, this gave the enemy an opportunity unprecedented in the annals of warfare to advance at will," said Brookbank. It was an exaggeration. But lives, Vietnamese and American, military and civilian, had certainly been sacrificed to save Gene Hambleton.

The operation remained highly classified. There were no reports on network television, no footage of the frantic activity at Joker. Even the massive invasion of South Vietnam was not a major news story; America had grown tired of the war.

One news consumer, however, was very interested in the bulletins about the "red fiery summer": the president of the United States. Richard Nixon and his national security adviser, Henry Kissinger, had been awaiting news of a North Vietnamese attack, half in fear and half in eagerness, for months. "In early 1972," Nixon wrote, "we expected a major Communist offensive that would decide the outcome of the war . . . If it succeeded, South Vietnam would be swept off the map. If it failed, North Vietnam would be forced to negotiate an end to the war."

The invasion came at a tense, febrile time for Nixon. Just over a month earlier, he'd completed his visit to China, beginning the process of normalizing relations between the two countries. A summit with the Soviet leader, Leonid Brezhnev, to discuss a new strategic arms limitation treaty was planned for May. Kissinger was scheduled to go to Moscow to arrange the details, but the invasion — and the American response to it — could, the two men believed, derail the meeting and endanger the warming relationship with the Soviets. A historic chance might be missed.

Nixon believed that if he could win victories on the battlefield of Vietnam while at the same time opening up communist China to American influence, he could force the Soviets to the negotiating table on terms favorable to the United States. There they would discuss, among other things, a nuclear weapons treaty that would lead to a massive reduction in the number of ICBMs each country possessed. But if the US military failed to stop the North Vietnamese divisions, Brezhnev might sense weakness. He might walk away from the negotiations and adopt a more aggressive posture in theaters far outside Southeast Asia. "That's one determination I've made," Nixon said that February about Vietnam. "We're not going to lose out there . . . Even with the election facing us, even with the diplomatic initiatives we have, we have to win it. We have to be sure we don't lose here for reasons that affect China. They affect Russia. They affect the Mideast. They affect Europe. That's what this is all about."

The first reports of the invasion had come in on March 30; ironically, the White House, nine thousand miles away from the invasion, would remain much better informed about its progress than many of the soldiers who were in the midst of it. Kissinger went to the Oval Office to inform the president the offensive had begun. The sound-activated tape machine that had been installed in the Oval Office the previous year recorded the conversation:

> KISSINGER: It looks as if they are attacking in Vietnam.
> NIXON: The battle has begun?
> KISSINGER: Yeah, the DMZ. And the sons of bitches [Kissinger was referring to the American military leaders in Vietnam] ... Of course, the weather is too bad for us to bomb.
> NIXON: Hmm.
> KISSINGER: We must have the world's worst air force.

Weather did hamper the early counterattacks. But by the evening of April 2, it wasn't just cloud cover that was hindering the counterattack. It was also the mission to save Gene Hambleton.

Nixon was unaware that a mammoth rescue operation was under way; such operational details almost never reached his desk. He was solely concerned with the larger strategic and geopolitical picture. The president wanted the Air Force to hit the invading North Vietnamese regiments — their tanks, personnel carriers, transport trucks, SAM sites — and obliterate them. On April 3, when he read reports of the modest Air Force response to the invasion, Nixon was furious, "only barely able to control his temper." The president brought the chairman of the Joint Chiefs of Staff, Admiral Thomas Moorer, into the Oval Office and grilled him. "I ordered the use of strikes," Nixon told him. "Five hundred sorties could have been flown."

Moorer replied that the USAF had managed to execute 138 sorties the day before. What he didn't mention was that a large number of *other* attacks had been flown in support of the Hambleton mission. It's likely Moorer had no idea who Gene Hambleton was or that he was down behind enemy lines, but there was a clear omission in the information he was giving Nixon, and it would continue for days.

Nixon fumed at what he saw as the Air Force's underwhelming response, and he directed that anger at General Creighton Abrams, the American commander in Vietnam. "What is his job out there?" the president asked on April 3. "Is it his job to try and see this kind of offensive is stopped?" He ordered a more vigorous response: B-52 runs, naval bombardments, a "massive use of all our assets . . . I want everything that can fly, flying in that area . . . Good God! In the Battle of the Bulge they were able to fly even in a snowstorm!" The president had been reading World War II history, and Eisenhower's relentless 1944 counterattack in eastern Belgium and northeastern France was on his mind.

On April 4, with the Air Force still unable to mount a counterattack that pleased the president, Kissinger relayed the substance of a conversation he'd had with Alexander Haig, the former Army general who was serving as an adviser to the administration. "Haig says, correctly," Kissinger told Nixon, "if he were out there he'd be flying over the battlefield and throw[ing] monkey wrenches out of the plane, on the theory that it would hit somebody." A few moments later, he reassured the frustrated president that the North Vietnamese would be beaten back. "This is the last gasp, Mr. President," he said. "But . . . we have to act ferociously."

Nixon agreed. He ordered the Joint Chiefs of Staff to bring more firepower to bear on the North Vietnamese. "I want to see the *Kitty Hawk*," he'd previously told Kissinger, talking about the Navy's massive supercarrier. "We want to see more B-52s, we want to see A-1s, anything that you think." Now he ordered the ships and planes into Southeast Asia. On April 4, Nixon directed that B-52 bombers be allowed to strike all the way up to the 18th parallel, far above the DMZ. The Joint Chiefs of Staff green-lighted an F-105G electronic countermeasures squadron to head to Korat from their base in Kansas, along with six entire F-4 squadrons. The aircraft carriers USS *Kitty Hawk* and USS *Constellation* — each carrying approximately sixty aircraft in their holds and on their decks — began steaming toward the South China Sea. A fleet of B-52s, fifty-four in all, were redeployed to Vietnam. It was, wrote one historian, "a rapid global mobility response unlike any in the history of warfare up to that time."

The escalation unnerved some observers in the States. The country had believed the war was winding down, but now Nixon was increasing the bombing and even expanding the target area into North Vietnam.

Many journalists and members of Congress believed that the president had just destroyed any possibility of a Moscow summit. One senator called the expansion "reckless and wrong," while a second suggested that Nixon had "lost touch with the real world." A congressman went so far to say that the president "has thrown down the gauntlet of nuclear war to a billion people in the Soviet Union and China . . . Armageddon may be only hours away." He was hyperventilating, but his words expressed the outer edge of the American mood.

Nixon apparently never learned about the Hambleton mission while in office. Had he been informed during the early days of April that the Air Force was devoting an average of ninety sorties a day to the rescue of an obscure lieutenant colonel, his reaction most likely would have been sheer incredulity, then rage. For Nixon, this was a world-historical moment.

Orders continued to fly from Washington to Saigon. The president pressured Abrams, who was being considered for Army chief of staff, to stop the North Vietnamese or face losing the promotion. "I want Abrams braced hard," he told his subordinates. "He's not going to screw this one up. Is that clear?" Reports filtered into the Oval Office that the general hadn't left his headquarters once since the offensive started; Kissinger and others took this as another sign of the general's timidity. "If this isn't fought more aggressively . . . by early next week," Kissinger told the president, "you might want to consider relieving Abrams." Nixon didn't argue the point. "He's had it," he replied. "He's fat, he's drinking too much, and he's not able to do the job."

Despite the unrelenting pressure, Abrams didn't call off the Hambleton mission; he kept to his pledge to retrieve every American airman whenever possible. But it was clear even by April 4 that the operation was becoming controversial. If it kept eating up airmen and aircraft at its current rate, the counterattack against the North Vietnamese would inevitably suffer. "It was my understanding," said Colonel Cecil Muirhead, chief of Joker, "that General Abrams was unhappy we were using so many of our resources to get one guy out. They wanted to know: How much longer is this going to go on?"

Gene Hambleton grew up in small-town Illinois wanting to fly planes but eventually found his calling as an Air Force navigator. *Courtesy of Jim Flessner, Mary Ann Anderson, and Donna Cutsinger*

Gil Hambleton (left) flew B-17 missions in Europe during World War II, but his older brother Gene had to wait until the Korean War to see combat. *Courtesy of Jim Flessner, Mary Ann Anderson, and Donna Cutsinger*

Thoughts of Hambleton's beloved wife, Gwen, sustained him throughout the grueling eleven-day rescue. "We always thought of her as a movie star," says Gene's niece. *Courtesy of Jim Flessner, Mary Ann Anderson, and Donna Cutsinger*

Jim Alley, a motion picture photographer (or "mopic"), joined the mission to rescue Hambleton ten days before his flight back to the States. Where others toted M16s, Alley brought along a camera. *Courtesy of William Van Der Ven*

Marine Corps Captain Larry Potts, a straight-arrow soldier from Smyrna, Delaware, was lost while on a spotting mission for the Hambleton rescue operation. *Courtesy of Trent Wicks*

Air Force Lieutenant Bruce Walker was flying an OV-10 when he was shot down during the Hambleton rescue operation, setting off a separate, unsuccessful mission to bring him back. *Courtesy of Martha L. Walker*

Army First Lieutenant Byron Kulland, who grew up on a North Dakota farm, was one of the first to join the rescue mission. He's pictured here with his wife, Leona. *Courtesy of Monica Lee*

Kulland piloted a Bell UH-1 Iroquois helicopter, better known as a Huey. These were multipurpose workhorses throughout the Vietnam era. *Bell Helicopter*

Air Force Captain Bill Henderson (left), pictured here with his escort officer, was held prisoner by the North Vietnamese after his shootdown. *Courtesy of William J. Henderson*

Hambleton was aboard a Douglas EB-66C Destroyer similar to this one when a surface-to-air missile struck the aircraft. *United States Air Force photo*

Air Force Lieutenant Anthony Giannangeli, the forty-one-year-old electronic warfare officer who flew with Hambleton that fateful day. The miniature planes in this photo were made by his fellow cadets. *Courtesy of Robert Giannangeli*

With his flight home approaching
within a matter of days, Air Force
Captain Peter Hayden Chapman
insisted on flying the Jolly Green
to pick up Hambleton. The
navigator recounted, "I can't say
enough about what Chapman was
doing. I owe my life to him and all
the other people involved."
Courtesy of Dorothy E. Murphy

A Sikorsky MH-53, better known as a Jolly Green Giant. Choppers like these were deployed
in the early stages of the rescue effort. *United States Air Force photo*

When two other commandos abandoned the mission, Petty Officer Nguyen Van Kiet (left) volunteered to go upriver with Navy Lieutenant Tom Norris. Kiet was awarded the Navy Cross for his efforts, the military's highest honor given to non-American service members. *United States Navy photo*

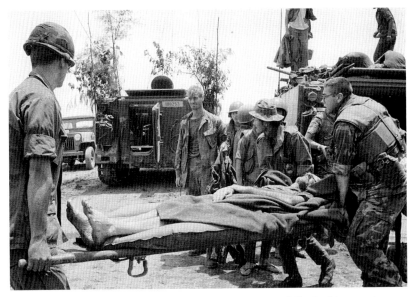

An emaciated Hambleton is transported to a hospital in Da Nang following his rescue by a commando team led by Norris (center), April 13, 1972. *Nick Ut for AP*

Hambleton and his wife, Gwen, reunited with Nguyen Van Kiet and his wife, Thuy, at Nellis Air Force Base in Arizona, in 1999, twenty-seven years after the Bat 21 mission.
Courtesy of Jim Flessner, Mary Ann Anderson, and Donna Cutsinger

Tom Norris wearing his Medal of Honor, awarded to him in 1976 by President Gerald Ford.
Courtesy of the Congressional Medal of Honor Society

15

"I KNOW WE'RE GOING TO DIE"

LIKE MANY AIRMEN DEPLOYED TO VIETNAM, Gene Hambleton had considered the possibility of being shot down before even setting foot in-country. Months before, he'd come to a decision. If he was stranded in enemy territory and couldn't be rescued, he would not be taken alive. "[If] my military friends couldn't get me, no one else would either," he said. "I WOULD NOT go to Hanoi. I DID NOT want to be a guest at the Hanoi Hilton."

What did that mean, exactly? Was he going to resist capture to the point of death, or did he actually contemplate killing himself rather than be taken? Hambleton never said. His motives were equally murky. Perhaps Hambleton, who'd felt belittled by his father throughout his childhood, refused to reenter a world where he would be humiliated again, and where his humiliation would now be combined with episodes of great pain. Or perhaps, at fifty-three, he simply thought he wouldn't survive extended torture sessions. But by the spring of 1972, he'd made up his mind that he would not be captured under any circumstances.

On April 5, the planners at Joker called in more resources from around Southeast Asia. A young Air Force photographer, Sergeant Jim Alley, was onboard a Jolly Green flying from Nakhon Phanom Royal Air Force Base in Thailand to Da Nang to reinforce the rescue squadron there. Time was running short. The next day, if the weather cooperated, Joker wanted to make a big push to get Hambleton back.

News of the mission was filtering out across US bases in Southeast Asia. It was acquiring a dark reputation; few could remember so many guys being lost so quickly during a search and rescue. "Fear is nibbling at your gut," said one airman. "You're meeting far more resistance than you have before. You know that people are dying out there."

Jim Alley was from Plantation, Florida, a sprinter, lean and short — five foot six — a quiet, shy, serious-minded kid with a hank of brown hair hanging over his watchful eyes. He was a gearhead, his bedroom packed with model cars he'd built himself as a teenager. Before his draft notice arrived, Alley had worked in his father's auto shop, degunking transmissions. When evening came, he'd wash up, put on some fresh clothes, and meet his equally gas-brained friends and go cruising around Plantation and the nearby towns. "On any given night in Fort Lauderdale," said a high school friend, "we'd be racing in the streets. Harbor Beach, US 1, anywhere we could find open road."

Jim wasn't really a racer, to be honest. He'd never had the car for it. He drove a '57 Chevy that just didn't have the horsepower to go up against the modern big-block Corvettes and the hellcat Z/28s. Jim's friends sensed he would have liked a serious hot rod, but his parents were quiet people and they probably didn't want him getting in trouble with the Plantation cops or, God forbid, putting his ride into an overpass and splattering himself all over the dashboard.

There were the usual teenage incidents around Plantation. One time, some football players from a rival high school blocked Jim's car in a parking lot and tried to goad him into a fight. He wanted no part of it. In the melee that followed, one of the boys pulled a knife and slashed Jim on his arm, cutting right through his shirt. Alley didn't lose his composure or try to beat the guy into the asphalt. Instead, he walked away.

In the late sixties, even peaceable kids like Jim Alley got their military notices. Jim had a moral issue with going into combat, and so the letter set off a crisis in his teenaged life. "He was drafted in the Army, but he said he could not kill," his mother wrote later. "He didn't want a gun." Eventually, Jim figured out a way to serve without carrying an M16. He entered the Air Force as a motion-picture cameraman. He would be an observer of battle, silent behind the lens, in the war but not of it.

When he was getting ready to leave, his father surprised Jim with his dream car, a canary yellow '67 Camaro. And his dad didn't go for the more run-of-the-mill motor; no, Jim Alley was finally going to get the boss racer he'd so ardently desired for most of his eighteen years. His dad splurged for the big 327-cubic-inch engine, the V-8 with the standard four-speed manual transmission that rumbled and then screamed when you stomped on the accelerator like some howling primordial beast. *That* would get their attention on Harbor Beach.

Despite this, Jim had a premonition. As he prepared for his deployment, he made an odd request of his parents. If he didn't make it back, he told them, he wanted them to adopt a baby. And not just any baby; he specified that they find an infant boy to take in. "I think he thought they would be lonely if he didn't come back," said his brother Tim.

The Alleys agreed and Jim went off to 'Nam.

Sitting in the back of the chopper with Alley were two pararescuemen (PJs), Louisiana-born Sergeant Doug Brinson and a tough, undersized Texan, Airman First Class Mike Vogel. It was dark, with just the low lights from the cockpit illuminating their faces. As the helicopter hurried southeast to Da Nang, the men occasionally got up and walked around, fighting boredom, their bodies casting shadows in the half dark. The thrum of the blades vibrated the air and shook the metal behind the men's backs as they talked. Idle chatter, really. Vogel and Brinson weren't particularly worried about the mission. The only reason you became a PJ in the first place was to get as much action as humanly possible.

Alley sat across from Brinson and Vogel, his big eyes visible through the clear visor of the helicopter helmet. It was well into the flight when he changed the course of the conversation. "I know we're going to die," he said.

The other men went silent. Talking about dying on a mission was verboten for pararescuemen. "You wouldn't hear a PJ say that if he was going to die in the next sixty seconds," said Brinson. And here was Alley, who wasn't just new to combat but a *photographer* who was hauling a camera instead of an M16 and would never leave the chopper, while the PJs could possibly be down there among the enemy, getting their asses shot at. "To the general public, that is not a remarkable statement," Brinson said, "but among us very gung-ho, brash PJs, it was horribly out of place."

The two men didn't react. They could see that Alley wasn't just fearful; he was transfixed by the idea of his own death. They felt sorry for him.

But he kept on with it. "I'm going to die," he said again and again. It was as if he couldn't help himself. Finally, the fourth or fifth time, Vogel snapped. "Will you shut up?" he yelled at Alley.

Seeing the terror on the twenty-three-year-old's face, Vogel softened a bit. "You're *not* gonna die," he said. Vogel explained to Alley that the Air Force only needed to use the Jolly Greens they were flying in on. "We won't even get in the action. They just want our choppers."

Alley went silent. He said nothing else for the rest of the flight.

They arrived at Da Nang in the early hours of April 6.

The morning broke clear. The pilots, navigators, forward air controllers, and other airmen who'd converged at the base were ordered to a briefing. A final decision on whether to go after Hambleton had to be made.

Before the gathering, an A-1 was sent out "to juke around and draw fire" to see what was out there on the ground. To the amazement of the Joker commanders and everyone else involved in the rescue, the pilot came back with a plane untouched by enemy bullets. He'd glided over the rice paddies and the village that had spouted lethal fire as recently as the day before, and it was like taking a scenic tour over the Grand Canyon. Not a single shell had been fired at him. No AAA. No SAMs. It was as if the NVA had melted away into the jungle and left Hambleton alone in his grove of trees.

The men in the room knew that the silence could signal a trap. It was a well-known technique of the NVA to go quiet, coaxing potential rescuers to a landing zone where gunners would then open up on them. The NVA had even instructed its soldiers on exactly how to do this. "When conditions are right, the pilot's radio transmitter and signal flares can be used to lure enemy aircraft into the ambush sites," read one of its training manuals. "The element on the outer perimeter fires at the A-1s. The one on the inner perimeter must conceal itself and suddenly open fire when the [helicopter] hovers and drops its rope ladder to rescue the pilot!"

But the test flight had been clear. It could be a trap but it could also *not* be a trap. After the A-1 pilot gave his report, the commanders announced that the environment around Hambleton was workable and the mission was a go.

Some of the airmen remained skeptical. "I was like, 'Oh, really?'" said Doug Brinson, the pararescueman who'd flown to Da Nang the night before. "So where did the thirty thousand NVA troops go in the last few hours? I'm not an idiot." He didn't say it, but he thought it; many of the men that morning probably did. "We all knew this was a fool's mission," said Brinson.

But the weather was perfect. The ground fire had vanished. The men in the room wanted to believe a rescue was possible.

As the meeting was wrapping up, an airman spoke out. Doug Brinson remembered turning to see who the man was and realizing it was the photographer from the night before, Jim Alley. The words he spoke were almost grotesque to Brinson and the others. What Alley said was: "I'm not going."

The faces of the other airmen registered shock. If the refusal to go on a mission had become an occasional occurrence among Army soldiers during the ground war, it was practically unheard of among airmen involved in a rescue mission. The statement hung in the humid air. The pilots and navigators couldn't believe that someone, especially this short, mild-mannered-looking dude, had the balls to say it.

It was, of course, perfectly reasonable to be terrified of going after Hambleton. There were thirty thousand NVA down there waiting to kill Americans. Everyone in the room was, on some level of his psyche, terrified. But no one was going to *say* that.

Alley did have a point when you considered his particular role in the mission. For years, rescue operations had been carried out without a photographer on board, but now the Air Force was sending him into the hottest zone many of the airmen had ever seen. He wasn't a pararescueman or a navigator or a door gunner. He was a short-timer, just ten days away from getting on the "freedom bird" and flying back to Florida. And now he was being asked to risk his life in a mission that had already killed three men and sent two others to prison camps, to *make a movie*. It's not as if Alley was going to reach down and pluck Gene Hambleton off a rice paddy.

The commander looked at the photographer. "You're either going to get on the chopper," he said, "or you're never going to fly again."

The threat was laughable. Alley was leaving the country in just over a week. If he never flew again, it would be fine. Who really cared? He wasn't a pilot. He wasn't career Air Force. He had no stake in the service to protect. The commander had threatened something that mattered not at all to Jim Alley.

The airman said nothing. The meeting broke up.

Hambleton was awake early the next morning. He took his flight suit off the bushes, where he'd laid them to dry after a downpour, and dressed quickly. The clothes were only slightly damp by now. Sunlight was beginning to penetrate the foliage. There were some clouds high up, but the sky was clear. It was a perfect day for a rescue.

He heard voices. The villagers to his east were out, going about their ordinary routines. He could smell the food they were cooking on their fires, but he wasn't tempted; he would soon be feasting on seafood and steaks at an American hospital or mess hall. "Today," he believed, "was the day of his deliverance."

16

LOW BIRD

THE HELICOPTER CODE-NAMED JOLLY GREEN 67 was chosen to pick up Hambleton; it was next in the rotation. The squadron commander, Lieutenant Colonel Bill Harris, was scheduled to pilot the chopper, but thirty-two-year-old Hayden Chapman, the young man from Centerburg, Ohio, who'd fallen in love with the B-17s flying over his father's farm when he was a boy, stepped forward and asked to fly the mission.

It was unusual for the rotation to be broken, not something Harris would ordinarily have allowed. He knew Chapman well; the two had carpooled when they were serving at Eglin Air Force Base in Florida. Over many mornings, they'd become close friends. Still, Harris refused the request. "It was my turn," he said. "I insisted." But Chapman was adamant. "I want to go," he told Harris.

Why did the younger pilot want the run so badly? Harris knew; the others in the squadron most likely did as well. Not long before, Chapman had been the low chopper on the rescue of some infantrymen. He'd brought the Jolly Green down to treetop level and was hovering there while the soldiers below — there were six or seven of them — waited for him to land. There was a firefight raging; tracers streaked through the jungle and upward at the chopper; the soldiers were in imminent danger of being overrun. As Chapman lowered the Jolly Green down to the landing zone, he felt the helicopter vibrate with what might have been small-arms fire. If one of the bullets hit a hydraulic line or a rotor, he could easily lose control and the Jolly Green would crash. Chapman made a split-second decision: he pulled up and flew the Jolly Green over the treetops and away from the firefight.

But then something unusual happened. Though he knew the landing zone was hot, the pilot of the high bird decided to make a pass. He brought his aircraft down on the LZ and immediately started taking rounds to his fuselage. The pilot kept the chopper steady while the soldiers poured into the cabin, turning to fire their automatic weapons at the enemy. When the last soldier was in, the pilot got the chopper above the trees and flew the men out.

That mission had stayed with Hayden Chapman. When he'd returned to base, he'd found to his horror that there were no bullet holes in his fuselage. Chapman was heartsick; he felt he'd aborted too early. And so he apparently decided to take the next mission, no matter what it was.

Like Jim Alley, on April 6 Chapman was about ten days from boarding a plane back to the States. His tour was up and he'd received orders to fly for the Eighty-ninth Military Wing out of Andrews Air Force Base in Maryland, the fabled "Special Air Mission" that piloted the president, vice president, members of Congress, and foreign dignitaries on trips all over the world. It didn't mean that Chapman would be flying President Nixon right away — he would probably begin with senators and the like — but still, it was one of the golden summits of all flyboy life. Before he went, though, the pilot felt a need to atone, to leave Vietnam with his conscience clear.

Harris gave him the mission.

Lieutenant Commander Crowe, who'd miraculously landed his chewed-up Jolly Green days before, briefed the men. The primary mission, as he understood it, was to resupply Hambleton with a Madden kit, a rescue package containing food, water, and fresh batteries dropped by one of the escort A-1s. It was not to save him. "I briefed the crew that they should not make an attempt on this mission," Crowe said. "I thought we should wait a couple of days." He made it abundantly clear to Chapman that it "would take an extraordinary combination of circumstances" to make a rescue feasible.

Early that afternoon, the teams gathered and began boarding their aircraft. Doug Brinson, the pararescueman, was slated to fly in the third helicopter, which would trail behind the low and high birds going in first. As he walked toward the aircraft, he spotted Jolly Green 67 sitting on the tarmac.

The standard crew for the rescue helicopter was five men. But as he moved to his aircraft, Brinson spotted a sixth figure waiting to board Jolly Green 67. The man had his flight helmet on and the visor pulled down, but Brinson recognized him. It was Jim Alley. The photographer stepped up into the open cargo door and disappeared into the darkness inside. In the short time between the meeting and loading, Alley had somehow overcome the premonitions that had haunted him since he'd left Plantation five years before.

The aircraft headed to a point southeast of Quang Tri. The two Jolly Greens, low and high, and two of the A-1s executed slow loops above the jungle from the target as the other A-1s flew to Hambleton's position to survey the terrain. The mission's on-scene commander, Captain Fred Boli, would decide if the rescue was a go. The two aircraft flew over the rice paddies and villages for half an hour, firing the 7.62 Miniguns mounted under their wings at any gun emplacements Boli spotted.

The response was spooky. The villages and fields remained placid. The American pilots streaked over them again and again and they stayed quiet, almost sleepy.

On the ground, Hambleton was watching for the planes. The weather was clear; he could see much farther into the countryside, past the village, which hadn't been possible before. "The good Lord was showing His favor," he thought. The radio was popping with the voices of men in the different aircraft. All told, there were about forty aircraft in the air preparing to rescue him and Mark Clark. Forty aircraft for two airmen; it might take your breath away if you thought about it.

Boli arrived over Hambleton's hiding spot. He hit the release for the Madden kit packed with food and water, but it failed to drop (something Boli would learn only when he returned to base). He probed more enemy emplacements with his guns and ordered his fellow A-1 to unload cluster bombs on the positions. The bombs erupted and orange fire burned through the trees, but no AAA arced up from the ground. Where was the enemy, Boli wondered? Why had the NVA suddenly gone silent?

Boli called out the plan on the radio. Everyone involved — including Clark and Hambleton — listened. An A-1 would go first, laying down smoke rockets leading to Hambleton's position, while another fired white phosphorus to create a smokescreen, behind which the helicopter could hide during its run-in to the survivor. Following close behind him, and guarded by two additional A-1s, Jolly Green 67 would rush in and grab Hambleton. If the ground fire remained light, the helicopter would then head east toward Clark's position and retrieve him. If 67 couldn't make the second snatch, Jolly Green 60, waiting a mile back, would swoop in and complete the mission.

With everything in readiness, Boli decided to fly a final pass. The artillery fire halted and Boli swept down, close to tree level, above Clark and Hambleton. He slowed the plane to just above stalling speed, fired rockets near Hambleton's position, then pulled up. The target was now marked.

The second A-1 dropped white phosphorus, which bloomed out in chalky clouds, obscuring the rice paddies. One pilot orbiting above pulled out a personal camera he'd brought along. He thought that the Hambleton mission would be remembered long after this day had ended and wanted to record the moment when the navigator was pulled into the helicopter. As Jolly Green 67 came in over the treetops, the pilot brought the camera up and began snapping photos.

Jolly Green 67 swept forward, headed toward Hambleton, who finally picked it out of the sky. One of the pilots raised him on the radio, asking about the terrain they would be landing on. Hambleton replied that there were rice paddies to the east and west and he could make it to either quickly.

At the base, Lieutenant Commander Crowe, who'd briefed the crews expecting they would only try to resupply Hambleton, was monitoring the radio traffic. He heard Jolly Green 67 commencing its run. "I was just stunned," he said. He hadn't expressly *ordered* Chapman not to attempt a rescue, but he'd made it clear it would take an almost perfect situation on the ground for one to be warranted. He listened in as the chopper made its approach.

As the planes swept toward the Mieu Giang, the fields south of the river looked serene in the afternoon sun. The calm that had so mystified the pilots that morning held. But as soon as the helicopter passed the far, northern bank of the river, the ground in front of Chapman's windshield erupted. The chopper was immediately raked by a wave of gunfire, the bullets hitting with the sound of a hammer slamming into sheet metal. It was clear within seconds that the lack of ground fire had been a trap. The NVA had been lying in wait for the rescue choppers.

Sheets of AAA fire and machine-gun bullets came up at the Jolly Green from the rice paddies and brush. Bullets were hitting everywhere as the gunners furiously fired their Miniguns. Hambleton was getting ready to pop his smoke when he heard a voice shouting on the radio: "I'm hit! They got a fuel line." It was Jolly Green 67. Brinson—two miles behind—could hear someone in on 67 yelling, *"We're taking hits, we're taking hits!"* The voice sounded panicked as it repeated the same words over and over.

Down below, Hambleton was listening in. The voices of the men watching Jolly Green 67 were "frantic." Despite the order, he decided not to light his flare. "I knew right then we were in deep trouble."

Jolly Green 67 was being whipsawed by ground fire. Boli had briefed the men that if they received damaging fire, they were to pull out and head southeast. Now, as bullets banged into the fuselage, the helicopter began to turn to the east. Other pilots were shouting on the radio, "Turn south, Jolly, turn *right*." Chapman and his crew needed to pick up speed and get out of the shooting zone. The other A-1s dove in to hit the gun emplacements firing at the stricken helicopter.

But something had gone wrong. Jolly Green 67 was flying east instead of southeast, which put it directly in line with the emplacements where the NVA guns were dug in. The radio traffic was chaotic. Someone in the craft was keying down the "transmit" button on the radio; the pilots in 67 couldn't hear the instructions.

"Stay away from that village!" a voice cried out on the radio.

An A-1 pilot was watching the chopper from above. Suddenly, "something big" hit the craft and it erupted in flame. The fireball lit up the afternoon sky as the chopper lumbered over the huts, losing altitude. The pilots kept the bird turning; it was now pointed southwest.

Fire spurted out of the helicopter. Pieces of the engine shot out and hit the main rotor, which started coming apart. The chopper began to roll. It was fully engulfed in flames now as, leaning left, it sank rapidly and smashed into the ground. A huge orb of bright flame leapt up from the green field.

"Jolly's down, Jolly's down!" Boli shouted on the radio. The men hovering above could see a ball of black smoke unfurling from the landscape. The urge to vomit rose up in Boli's throat. He began to cry.

Voices on the radio were calling over and over, "Jolly Green 67, come in. Jolly Green 67 . . ." No survivors emerged from the chopper. The aviation fuel was feeding brightly burning flames. Jim Alley was dead. Hayden Chapman was dead, along with his crew: Roy Prater, Allen Avery, William Roy Pearson, and John Henry Call.

Hambleton watched as the black smoke corkscrewed up, so tall and thick that it obscured the village behind it. He knew that the chances of a crewmember having bailed out of the helicopter were minimal. "Anyone getting out would be the result of a miracle."

He began to weep. "I hate to see a grown man cry," he said, "but I cried." *Five men,* he thought to himself. *Five good men lost.* Actually, counting the unexpected addition of Jim Alley, it was six.

The night before, he'd considered abandoning his hiding place and striking out on his own. During the internal debate, he admitted, "I felt it necessary to talk it over with someone I knew." The face of his squadron commander had appeared to him and Hambleton asked, "What do you think of the idea?" (The squadron commander said nothing.) Gwen materialized, and then the faces of some golfing friends. To each of them he said, "Shall I walk home and join you on the course?" He'd received no answer.

Now he felt he couldn't afford such indulgences. "You are by yourself," he thought. "Don't go off the deep end." He banished the dead from his mind. From now on, he was going to think only about surviving. It was as much a sign of his increasing fragility as it was of strength.

In his hiding place, the survivor Mark Clark had seen the stricken chopper trying to exit the battle zone. He'd heard the crump of the helicopter crashing into the field from his position across the river. He was distraught. "I really cocked this up," he said to himself. "Six more guys dying because I fucked up." He wondered if there was an antiaircraft site in his range of vision that he'd failed to spot, costing the men their lives.

The toll of the rescue attempt had reached nine, plus another man on the ground and two taken prisoner of war. It was a disaster with little precedent. There had never been a rescue mission in Vietnam, or in the history of the Air Force for that matter, in which so many lives had been lost going after a single soldier. When General Abrams was informed of the crash, he immediately ordered that there would be no further attempts to rescue the men by helicopter. His order was clear: "No more rescue attempts by helicopter." The effort to save Hambleton and Clark was, for the moment, over.

17

THE DIVISION

Many of the airmen who'd seen the crash of Jolly Green 67 couldn't sleep that night; the image of the aircraft bursting into flame in midair had imprinted itself on their memories with a Zapruder-like intensity. One of the FACs, Captain Harold Icke, sat in his hooch and taped a message to his wife, as he did every so often. "It's been a bad two days," he said. "A lot's happened. I've seen things that I hope I never see happen again. We've lost more people. I'm sure we're going to lose more today." The mood at Da Nang was grim, bewildered. "We now had two survivors," said Lieutenant Commander Jay Crowe, "and no new ideas." The airborne operation had failed, and it was not going to be resumed.

What about the South Vietnamese? There were ground units not too far from Clark's position. A call had previously been put in to the Second ARVN Regiment, which was holding ground south of the Mieu Giang River, asking if they could send an armored personnel carrier to retrieve him. The commander responded that they would "not move out of Cam Lo because they are afraid of the VC." This caused some bitterness among the Americans, but the truth was the Second, like many South Vietnamese units, was fighting for its life and had few resources to spare for a lone American.

Some officers believed that Hambleton and Clark couldn't, in fact, be rescued at all. They should be left right where they were until the South Vietnamese beat back the invasion and pushed the enemy north. When the American allies reclaimed the ground around Cam Lo, they would find the two survivors. But that could take months, if it ever happened at all, and it was an open question whether Hambleton and Clark could evade capture, or even survive, that long—especially Hambleton, who had no access to fresh water. For their part, Crowe and his fellow rescuemen refused to entertain the idea. "[We] found this impossible to accept after so much sacrifice," he said.

There was, the men knew, one final way, a simple rescue method that had been practiced for centuries: sending a team of soldiers overland into hostile territory to get the survivors out. And there existed a team of operatives in Saigon that specialized in exactly these kinds of missions. They were known as the Military Assistance Command, Vietnam—Studies and Observation Group (MACVSOG), and they did just about everything relating to lost airmen: they went behind enemy lines and reconnoitered enemy camps, scouted troop movements along the Ho Chi Minh Trail, studied raw intel for information on downed Americans, and dropped millions of leaflets promising rewards to Vietnamese who helped locate them. On occasion, the unit's recovery unit—known as the Recovery Studies Division, which made it seem like a Harvard think tank—even went after Americans who'd been taken prisoner by the enemy or were on the run from them. When traditional methods failed, the Division was the last resort.

But the group, like many ground-based outfits, was being phased out. In fact, its commander, USMC Lieutenant Colonel Andy Andersen, a "short, stocky, fiery" Marine officer who was about as gung-ho as they came, was in the process of closing up his office. And besides that, the Division's track record was nothing short of horrible. In six years, it had gone on dozens and dozens of missions and had managed to recover 492 South Vietnamese soldiers, as well as the remains of 101 dead American pilots and navigators and return them home to their families in the States. But when it came to living, breathing Americans, the Division had experienced one disaster after another. Its operatives would chopper in to a location deep in Laos where an American was reportedly being tortured and find an empty hut, or they would burst into a remote village in North Vietnam looking for a hidden pilot and find only hungry peasants. "Informants" regularly conned the Americans out of money. It drove Andersen crazy.

If the airborne effort to get Hambleton out had been a costly failure so far, the Division's track record looked much, much worse. In many months of trying, it hadn't managed to save a single American airman.

As he closed up his operation, Andersen had been quietly monitoring the message traffic on the Hambleton and Clark situation as part of the unit's normal operations. The Marine, however, had done more than listen; he'd ordered his second-in-command to gather intel for a possible rescue try and asked other members of the Division for ideas on how it might go down. If the choppers failed, how could they get Hambleton out? Slated to return stateside in a matter of weeks, Andersen was deeply distressed at the Division's long list of failures. "He burned to rescue a fellow American from the clutches of the communists," wrote one historian. But even if he did somehow persuade his superiors to give him the mission, which seemed highly unlikely, he would still need a specially trained operative to lead it. And that he didn't have.

PART III

THE SWANEE

18

THE REAL JOHN WAYNE

APRIL 7 BROUGHT NO RELIEF to Hambleton or the men attempting to save him. Down in his patch of foliage, Hambleton heard on his radio that yet another OV-10 had been shot down that afternoon. The FAC, First Lieutenant Bruce Walker, and his Marine Corps spotter, Captain Larry Potts, had been flying about five miles northeast of his position when they were hit by a SAM and bailed out of their OV-10. The two men were now on the ground and Walker was actively evading the enemy; Potts hadn't been heard from since the missile hit.

Hambleton's thoughts darkened. His rescue had become this endlessly unfolding, man-killing nightmare that seemed to repeat itself day after day. His depression deepened when the FAC called down that afternoon. "We won't baby sit you tonight," the voice said. "Adios."

The navigator felt a twitch of paranoia. "Was that my Air Force's way of saying 'Adios' to me, too? Were things that bad? Were more troops coming from the north?" The closeness he'd felt with the observers melted away; the mistrust that every soldier feels for the military brass seeped in. Had the generals in Saigon written him off as too expensive to recover?

To add to his worries, Hambleton was growing concerned about his physical condition. For the past couple of days, he'd found he could barely lift his head above the edge of his little hole in the ground. His neck muscles couldn't support the weight. Hambleton was forced to reach back and push his head up and hold it in position so he could look out over the fields. Were his muscles beginning to atrophy? Or was something wrong with his spine?

He heard a rumbling in the sky. "It sounded," Hambleton said, "like two freight trains running 400 mph," but as he listened he recognized the pitch of those particular engines: B-52s. The enormous bombers released their loads and the countryside around him erupted in fire and sound. Hambleton ricocheted off the walls of his hiding place, tumbling as if he were in a washing machine. "The goddamn ground actually moved," he said. He had a flash of empathy for the Vietnamese peasants. "I don't understand how those guys stood it for ten years."

When the rumbling stopped, Hambleton lay gasping in his hiding place. He thought he was doomed. Nixon had clearly resumed the bombing of the North, which meant that his little situation was going to be a footnote to the resumption of the Vietnam War in its full ferocity. "I thought hell, it's all over." But in fact, the B-52s weren't part of the president's counter-strike against North Vietnam; they'd been sent specifically to hit positions around Hambleton, both to support his rescue and to destroy those forces attacking to the south. It was the first time the bombers had been used in a search and rescue in the history of the USAF. It was also a sign that the Air Force had not completely given up on the idea of saving the navigator.

The bombs shook the branches of the trees around Hambleton. "The earth crawled and humped like some huge, writhing cobra." Hambleton had no idea what was happening. He began debating with himself, going over and over his remaining options now that the air rescue had failed. As he saw it, there were two things he could do: *Stick with the plan . . . Or run.* Should he try to make his way to friendlier lines? Or should he trust the Air Force? He went back and forth between the options until his brain ached.

The planes departed and he tried to sleep but couldn't. He was too distraught. "I never felt so lost and orphaned before in my life." It seemed to him the motto of "Leave no man behind" had found its exception. He was going to be left behind.

In Saigon, Lieutenant Colonel Andy Andersen was also engaged in a passionate internal debate. The Marine officer badly wanted to volunteer the Division for the Hambleton mission. But Andersen sensed that if he asked his commanding officer to give him a shot at the navigator (and Clark and Walker and Potts, who'd just been shot down), the answer would be a hard no. What had his men done in six futile years to make anyone believe they had the capability to retrieve the lost airmen?

The thought of leaving Vietnam without saving a single one of his brothers pained Andersen to his core. He *had to have* the mission. Andersen "had a fire burning in his belly," said one intel officer. "He saw this as a last chance."

As Andersen sat in his office, the phone rang. It was Major Winton W. Marshall, the vice commander of the Seventh Air Force, who was desperately looking for new ideas on how to save Gene Hambleton. If Andersen took the call, he'd be going outside of his chain of command and would surely face his commander's wrath for violating one of the most basic rules of the American military. But the fiery Marine ruminated for only a few seconds before coming to "a bold and perhaps dangerous decision" — dangerous not only to his men but to his future prospects in the Marine Corps. He took the call.

When he picked up the phone, Marshall asked for a meeting. Andersen agreed. He quickly gathered up all the intel that his men had been collecting, along with all the maps and other aids he would need for the meeting. He would have one shot at convincing the general.

Marshall was at least willing to listen, but other commanders had turned decisively against the rescue mission. Perhaps it was the pressure from the White House, perhaps it was the unprecedented scale of the operation, but there was palpable disappointment, even anger, over the Hambleton affair. The commanders at MACV, the joint command that ran the war in Vietnam, vehemently opposed using any more of its men or hardware to save the navigator. One major who planned to go with Lieutenant Colonel Andersen to the Marshall meeting was even told that if he so much as stepped outside of headquarters, he'd be court-martialed.

The next morning, April 8, Andersen arrived at Marshall's office at Tan Son Nhut Air Base. The Air Force men had been shaken, even stunned, by their defeats in the field; the mood in Marshall's office was chastened. But when the fire-breathing Andersen walked in the room, it was like a jolt of adrenaline. "It couldn't have been better," said Jay Crowe, "if it had been the real John Wayne."

After the men had been introduced, Captain Boli, who'd been the leader of the Jolly Green 67 attempt, laid out the latest intel. Everyone in the room agreed that any further attempts by helicopter were not up for consideration; the area around Hambleton was still bristling with enemy hardware. The airborne rescue phase was over. Marshall then turned the meeting over to Andersen.

The Marine officer stood up and unfurled the maps he'd brought with him. He pointed to Hambleton's and Clark's locations and estimated their distance to the Mieu Giang River. What he was proposing was this: a team of commandos trained in "water work" would proceed to a forward operating base on the Mieu Giang. At the same time, the survivors would be directed to make their way to the river and then swim down it to the east, traveling only at night, when the risk of capture was lowest. The commandos would then cross the front lines into enemy territory and be poised on the banks of the river to bring the survivors in.

Andersen ended his presentation with a flourish. He would travel to the forward operating base, he said, to lead the operation personally. If this was going to be the Division's last shot, he was willing to put his life on the line to make sure it succeeded. Major General Marshall, impressed with the Marine's commitment, agreed to the plan on the spot.

An energized Andersen left to begin prepping the mission. Marshall personally briefed General Abrams, a longtime friend. He laid out Andersen's plan. Abrams repeated his concerns about the tremendous expenditure of men and materiel that had already occurred at a critical time in the war. Every man sent after the navigator was another potential casualty or prisoner of war. But Marshall persuaded him to let the ground team take one last shot. Abrams restated his ban on any helicopters but agreed to the rest of Andersen's proposal.

The first phase of the operation had involved five services, dozens of different personnel types, and hundreds of men. For the second phase, the rescue planners decided to "do it black." The mission was to be not only secret but also secretive. No longer was everyone from Da Nang to Saigon going to be following the mission's progress as if it were the seventh game of the World Series. No one even announced a team was going in. "It was, 'we're going to do something *special,*'" said one intelligence officer involved in the planning.

The number of men privy to information about the unfolding operation was radically reduced. Personnel, especially forward air controllers, were individually selected to fit the mission. "It became a close cadre of FACs," the intelligence officer said. "You kind of knew, these were *the guys.*" Once they'd been chosen, the FACs began looking for intel on the terrain and conditions around Hambleton and the other men. But they were cagey; they refused to pinpoint which areas they were interested in. One experienced intel officer found himself getting annoyed — "Just tell me what you need to know!" he wanted to yell — but after the loss of Jolly Green 67, it was a different kind of game.

The intel officer brought the FACs over to a new kind of map that had arrived at Da Nang only three weeks before. It was a large-scale, fine-detail overhead photograph with a grid of map coordinates laid over it. The men clustered around the thing and studied the important landmarks: hills, valleys, and rivers. Finally, they all agreed on Hambleton's position inside a tree line, and they marked it. The same with Clark's. Those would be the starting points for the operation.

Meanwhile, Andersen was calling the Navy and Seventh Air Force controllers; they agreed to provide artillery and airstrikes for his last-ditch effort. But he still didn't have a tactical leader. All his highly trained operatives were slated to head stateside in three days. The operation might take longer than that, and Andersen couldn't risk his point man being pulled out in the middle of everything. He had the mission he wanted but no one to execute it.

What he was looking for was a particular kind of soldier. He had to be near-impervious to cold, as the spring runoff now flooding the Mieu Giang was sure to be frigid, and the team might have to wade through the river to reach the men. He had to have experience leading South Vietnamese soldiers, as they would form the bulk of the rescue team. He had to follow orders to the last period and comma, because his every move would be coordinated with preplanned artillery strikes. And he had to be highly amenable to risk.

Andersen wanted a hunter-killer with the mind of a Boy Scout, and there were very few Americans like that left in Vietnam. Almost all of the Army Rangers, Green Berets, and Navy SEALs had departed months before. The Marine officer picked up the phone, hoping to get lucky.

19

THE HURRICANE LOVER

ON APRIL 9, Tommy Norris was sitting in an office at the Tan Son Nhut Air Base, dressed in jungle greens, briefing his new commanding officer, Lieutenant Commander Craig Dorman, who'd just arrived in-country. The phone rang and Dorman picked it up. Norris sat back in his chair, bored but polite, and waited for his CO to finish his conversation. As he listened in, however, he realized that Dorman was discussing something interesting. Two phrases got Norris's attention: "downed pilot rescue" and "behind enemy lines." Norris leaned in to hear more.

Dorman looked at the SEAL and, still speaking into the phone, said, "Well, it just so happens, he's sitting right here in my office."

The officer hung up. He'd just learned from Andersen that a team was being put together to extract two airmen in an overland mission. (Bruce Walker, who was still on the run, would be snatched up afterward; Larry Potts still had not been heard from.) The operation needed a leader, and Norris — who had previously met Andersen during operations in the Mekong Delta — was the lead candidate. In fact, he was just about the only candidate. As far as men with combat experience, time in with Vietnamese commandos, and a background in "water work," Norris was someone who checked all the boxes.

Dorman was in a bind. He had just arrived in Vietnam and he needed this young SEAL to guide him through the complex bureaucratic and operational issues he faced. Technically speaking, Dorman could deny

Norris permission to join the mission. But the thought of telling that to Norris, who sat across from him looking like a mongoose that had just spotted a brown water snake, was exhausting. "Tom," Dorman recalled, "was chomping at the bit."

Dorman gave the Navy SEAL the details of the mission. Before he'd even finished speaking, Norris knew he wanted it.

Now that they had a team leader, the next thing the rescue planners had to figure out was how to get an emaciated, fifty-three-year-old man across land overrun with thirty thousand enemy troops and to the Mieu Giang River. They would have to guide him around the obstacles — gun emplacements, natural barriers, NVA positions — over an open radio channel. How could they accomplish that without giving away his route?

To get the navigator to his pickup zone, the Air Force had to find a language only he and they could speak, an entirely private and unbreakable code that would be inscrutable to the North Vietnamese. And so the officers of the Seventh Air Force began considering the minutiae of Gene Hambleton's existence. The men started calling Hambleton's friends and family scattered across the globe. They talked to his squadron mates in Thailand, phoned the Pentagon, and spoke to Air Force buddies spread out across bases in the United States and abroad. They got Gwen out of her bed in Arizona in the middle of the night. They spoke to guys who'd flown with him in Korea and served under him at Davis-Monthan Air Force Base in Arizona. They were trying to find something — a hobby, a favorite book, perhaps — to work with. They asked each of these people about Gene's pastimes, his enthusiasms and obsessions. It was as if they were collecting material for his biography.

The answers trickled in. The planners learned that Hambleton was from Illinois. That had possibilities. The exact deliberations that the rescue commanders went through were never written down, but it's likely they thought about the state itself as a code source: it contained landmarks and distances, and those could be molded into a numerical cipher. But it took only a minute of thinking to realize that the scale was too large; the planners were going to move Hambleton to the river in segments that were perhaps a few hundred yards long. The geography of Illinois was simply too big to be helpful.

They might have narrowed the search to Wenona itself. Would Hambleton remember the distance and direction between his house and, say, Main Street? The idea had potential. But for it to work, they'd have to get someone to go out to Wenona and measure off the distance from Hambleton's boyhood home to the road. There was no time for that. And even if they had gone with a Wenona cipher, who knew if Hambleton — though his memory was excellent — would recall the exact size of things? To a boy, houses appear bigger and streets longer than they are in real life. The planners couldn't depend on childhood memories; they needed precise figures.

The men kept phoning. They learned that Hambleton had a fondness for pranks; that he liked to drink whiskey cocktails; that his dog was named Pierre; that he was a regular churchgoer; that his church was of the Lutheran denomination; that he was careful with his money; and that he loved his wife. All of it was perfectly, utterly useless. One topic, however, did keep coming up. A significant percentage of the men and women who were woken out of their sleep mentioned the same thing when asked about his hobbies: Gene Hambleton was a stone lunatic for the game of golf.

Golf! Officers in Saigon managed to rustle up an atlas of North Vietnam and checked the country for signs of a course. There weren't any. The officers realized that the game was as foreign to the enemy as polo or the novels of Booth Tarkington. But how could the planners turn the suburban American pastime into a unique military code?

Golf is a game of numbers. Many obsessive duffers — and it soon became clear that Hambleton was about as obsessive as they got — knew how far a famous hole was from its tee. That meant the planners could map out his first walk toward the river, measure the distance, then match it up with the distance of a hole that Hambleton knew. The first tee at Tucson, his home course, was 430 yards. They could begin with a walk of that same length and then move on.

The river was about a mile and a half from the navigator's hiding place.

Taking in the various detours they would have to work into the plan, nine holes should get him to the water. It seemed perfect.

But a complication quickly arose. Hambleton couldn't get to the Mieu Giang by the shortest route possible. There were villages and minefields and NVA positions along that route that would have been suicidal for him to approach. So he would have to go indirectly, in precise, short walks that skirted the dangerous terrain but still kept him on a general course toward the water. His journey might look like the handle of the Big Dipper or the Grim Reaper's curved scythe. So the code would have to contain both distances *and* directions.

This presented a new dilemma. How could you convey to Hambleton whether he should head north or south on each leg of the escape route? The calculations on Hambleton's end could be done: he had a compass on him, and he was a kind of savant of cardinal direction. But how to broadcast which way he should head across a radio channel without giving the game away? The NVA knew approximately where Hambleton was. Once he emerged out of his protective circle of gravel, if you got on the radio and mentioned a course heading — "play the fourth at Augusta, heading northeast" — the enemy would be able to intercept the American as he crept through the furrows at night.

It was a seemingly insurmountable problem. There were good pop culture references for things like "west," for example: one might get on the radio and say, "Go this way, young man," and hope Hambleton had paid attention in his grade-school history lessons about the opening of the frontier. But for the directions they'd actually be using, such as "southwest" or "northeast," there were few, if any, hints that would work.

In their phone calls, the officers probed further into the recollections of his friends and family. And here they learned something remarkable: not only could Hambleton recall the shape of every hole he'd played, where the weeds were thickest, and how many traps it had, but also he could tell you whether it was laid out northeast or southwest. This applied to dozens of courses across America as well as in Europe; the navigator had even played St. Andrews, the Scottish birthplace of golf. It turned out, merely by coincidence, that there was a long list of numbers and directions stored in Gene Hambleton's head that he could access at will.

Perhaps one in a thousand golfers knows which way number 6 at Augusta plays. That statistic isn't even published in the course's manuals or its scorecards. But Hambleton was that golfer. He knew.

What if, the planners thought, they overlaid those links onto the map of central Vietnam and used Hambleton's memory and geeky skill set to get him to the river? His commanders decided it was worth a try. They collected details on the various greens that the navigator had played over the decades and soon had nine holes that would, if Hambleton executed them correctly and an NVA patrol didn't catch up with him en route, put him on the banks of the Mieu Giang.

With that, they were ready to begin.

20

WHEN THE MOON GOES
OVER THE MOUNTAIN

On the night of april 9, Tommy Norris headed to Da Nang to meet with Andy Andersen. Creighton Abrams had grounded the choppers, and the rescue operation was now in the hands of a tiny, secretive group, but it became clear to Norris that Hambleton was still a priority for the US military, because when he made it to the airfield to fly to Da Nang, he found a general's plane — a gorgeous T-39 Sabreliner — sitting on the tarmac waiting for him. It was the military equivalent of a Learjet, and Norris found he was the only passenger. "I felt like a corporate exec," he said. The young SEAL sank back into the leather seats as the twin turbines spun and lifted the Sabreliner into the night sky.

Norris was impressed by the commitment to get Hambleton. He understood the stakes. "This guy knows something that they want back," he thought. There was little question that "they," the leaders of the US military, were concerned about Hambleton being taken to Hanoi. But Norris didn't care about the navigator's background one bit. "That's my fellow American out there," he said. "I'm gonna bring him back."

He arrived at Da Nang at around 8 p.m. and immediately sought out Andersen. He'd met the Marine a couple of times before and knew him as "a short, cocky guy . . . very passionate and very professional." When the two sat down together at the sprawling base, Andersen started laying out the mission. He'd already arranged for a team of five South Vietnamese sea commandos — led by a "superb, hard-charging" officer, a

Lieutenant Tho—to accompany Norris on the mission. But Andersen had run into problems with other aspects of the operation: the existing maps of the area were sketchy, for example, and the intel on NVA units in the rescue area was thin and constantly changing. Andersen had no idea where the enemy was going to be when the rescue team went in. The mission would have been a risky proposition even in normal times, but during a large-scale invasion, with the NVA present in huge numbers and on alert, it was even more so. This type of rescue was called "E & E"—escape and evade—and it had never been used in this area of Vietnam before.

As he went into the details of the operation, Andersen briefly mentioned that Norris and his team would be restricted to a five-hundred-meter area outside their base. He didn't want them going any farther: too many NVA moving around out there. The last thing the military wanted was to lose more men getting Hambleton back.

The word "restricted" got Norris's attention. In fact, it bothered him. And the more he thought about it, the more it bothered him. "My concern was, well, suppose we don't get him within that five hundred meters, do we go beyond that?" He knew what his answer was: of course you go beyond that. You go as far as it takes. But Andersen made it clear: under no circumstances were any of his men to proceed beyond his clearly defined perimeter. This was not what Tommy Norris wanted to hear. "I would have liked to have him say, 'What are your feelings, how would you approach this, what do you think would be the best method to recover these people?'" But that wasn't Andersen's style. Marines, in general, don't ask. They tell.

It was an old story. There is the US military way of doing things and there is the SEAL way. The military likes plans, procedures, timetables. It is the Organization Man going to war. It prefers to go into battle with superior numbers; the concept dates back to Napoleon and beyond, and Army and Marine officers probably mumble it in their sleep. But within the American military, a Navy SEAL is a countercultural figure. He is trained to think for himself. He doesn't salute, shaves only if he feels like it, wears whatever suits the mission. He operates in teams of seven or fourteen men. He revels in uncertainty. And he makes his living by going up against numerically superior forces. "We function much different than they [the Navy] do," Norris said. "We were renegades of the Navy as well as everybody else."

So he nodded along at Andersen's briefing and didn't make too much of a fuss, but privately, Norris had already made his decision: when he got out in the field, he was going to run the operation exactly as he saw fit. The perimeter was a figment of the Marine's imagination. "What Andersen said didn't affect me," Norris said. Behind the Boy Scout smile, he was already planning a rebellion.

At the end of the briefing, Norris went over the mission in his head. He liked the plan that Andersen had drawn up, but the difficulty of what he was proposing was slowly dawning on the young SEAL: infiltrating an area full of thirty thousand enemy soldiers to save two men, overland, at night. Just reverse the situation in your head. Imagine a squad of NVA soldiers sneaking past the American lines in, say, 1968, grabbing three of their men, and then walking them out through patrols of Marines and Army soldiers. What were the odds of success? One in three? One in four? Whatever numbers you came up with, they weren't good. "I don't mind saying," Norris recalled, "that I was beginning to wonder just what I'd gotten myself into."

But Hambleton and Clark weren't just Americans. They were American *airmen,* the very thing that Norris had wanted to be before he became a SEAL. He would have signed on if the dudes had been kitchen attendants, but the aviator thing added a personal connection. He felt obligated to get the men back. "Nothing else really mattered."

That afternoon, Norris and Andersen, along with their South Vietnamese team, jumped on a helicopter and flew to Ai Tu Combat Base. They landed in the middle of a firefight; the North Vietnamese invasion had pushed ten miles south of the Mieu Giang, and shells were impacting the airfield and the base buildings. The two Americans ran from the chopper, took cover from the artillery barrage, then went to see General Vu Van Giai, the South Vietnamese commander for the area. Giai, understandably, had only a few minutes to spare for the Americans. After he listened to Andersen outline the mission, the South Vietnamese general told them he could give them transport up to the forward operating base, where a unit of Vietnamese rangers would support them. But his artillery couldn't reach the area where the operation would unfold. Norris wouldn't be able to count on their guns, even if he got into serious trouble.

As the meeting ended, General Giai mentioned one more thing. "He . . . told us, directly in his broken English, that he thought we were crazy and that our mission had little chance for success," remembered Norris. The South Vietnamese, with artillery, heavy machine guns, and thousands of troops, were barely hanging on in the face of the enemy onslaught. The Americans were going to send a few lightly armed soldiers into that onslaught and try to bring out two men. To Giai, it wasn't just foolish. It was inexplicable.

Undaunted, Norris and Andersen thanked the general and raced off to their next set of briefings, which stretched into the afternoon. Then they and their team headed to Dong Ha, where they met with the commander of the First Armor Brigade, exchanged radio frequencies, and finalized their plans.

Andersen had put the mission together with dazzling speed, but in his determination to save Hambleton, he'd left some rancor trailing in his wake. In the eyes of his superiors, the Marine was off the reservation. Perhaps fearing that he'd find a way to scuttle the mission, Andersen hadn't notified his commanding officer that he was leaving for the Mieu Giang; in fact, he'd failed to tell anyone at all in his chain of command the first thing about this daring and perilous operation he was going to lead behind enemy lines. Instead, he "kind of disappeared," in the words of his second-in-command, Major Gerald Bauknight. Unable to find Andersen anywhere, one Colonel Frank Zerbe summoned Bauknight to his office to express his deep displeasure at recent developments. "They didn't know what was happening," Bauknight remembers. "And partly out of frustration, Zerbe just gave me a really terrible dressing down. He said, 'You goddamn son of a bitch. If anything goes wrong with that operation, you guys are gonna be hung out to dry. We're not gonna protect you in any way.'"

• • •

The next morning, Hambleton heard a buzzing in the air; it was one of the FACs, revving his engine. Hambleton got on the radio, and the two joked about what each had had for breakfast. The FAC said he'd feasted on bacon and eggs, while Hambleton pretended to seethe about his meal of cold corn. Actually, the kernels had partially frozen overnight and the milky liquid inside was cold and refreshing. Most of all, he was happy to have an American above him again.

Around four o'clock, the FAC raised him once more on the radio. "We are going to have to do something different," he said.

Hambleton nodded. "Roger."

The FAC asked if Hambleton knew his exact position. Hambleton confirmed. "All right," the FAC said, "the high command has decided that you are going to have to act like Esther Williams and Charlie the Tuna."

Hambleton froze. What on earth was the guy talking about? He vaguely remembered the second name — it was the plummy-voiced cartoon character from the seafood commercials on TV — and clearly the FAC was employing some kind of code. But what did it mean?

He called up the FAC. "What have you been smoking?" he asked.

The FAC said again that he was to make like Esther Williams and Charlie the Tuna. Hambleton was still stumped. It was "the damnedest thing I had ever heard," he said. Esther Williams he understood. She'd been a competitive swimmer who'd starred in a series of "aquamusicals," where women in one-piece suits executed elaborate numbers, synchronized to perfection. She was known as "the million dollar mermaid." Everyone knew Esther Williams.

It meant he was going to swim. Clearly. But why Charlie the Tuna? He asked the FAC to elaborate. "Because nobody ever catches Charlie the Tuna," the man finally said.

Hambleton smiled. "I think I've got your message."

"Good. What we are going to do is this . . . You've got to get to the Swanee."

There was a real river, actually spelled Suwannee, in Georgia, but what the Air Force expected Hambleton to remember was the minstrel song "Old Folks at Home," written by Stephen Foster in 1851. "Way down upon the Swanee River," it went, "far, far away." Many Americans of Hambleton's generation knew the song, and the navigator recognized the reference immediately. "I've got it now," he said. It was the Mieu Giang River; had to be.

The FAC, or those directing him, were clearly choosing pop culture references that would be inscrutable to the NVA intelligence officers listening in. If he'd said "the Amazon" or "the Mekong," the meaning would have been immediately clear. Not once during the long and complex journey that faced Hambleton would the word "river" be uttered over the radio.

"This is a decision that is going to be entirely up to you," the FAC said. "You don't have to do this. You can stay where you are and we will make every effort to get you out of there but it will be faster if we can get you where we want to pick you up."

Hambleton rogered that.

"Now remember what is out there on both sides of you. It is going to be very dangerous."

"I realize that," Hambleton said.

The FAC again repeated that this was Hambleton's decision. The navigator asked for some time to think it over.

In Washington, President Nixon and National Security Advisor Kissinger watched the developments in Vietnam with growing alarm. The NVA were sweeping through the northern provinces toward the provincial capital of Quang Tri; firebases and towns were falling to the enemy one after the other. The president was incensed about Moscow's role in the offensive. He knew the North Vietnamese leaders kept the Soviet leadership informed about major initiatives on the battlefield, so they must have known the attack was coming. Had they done anything to prevent it? The world press was decrying Nixon's massive buildup, but Nixon regarded the Soviets as the true aggressors. "If this succeeds," Kissinger told the president that morning, "Soviet arms will have overturned the balance on the Indian subcontinent and run us out of Southeast Asia." Nixon agreed with this bleak assessment.

The afternoon of the tenth, Nixon attended a diplomatic gathering. The long-serving Soviet ambassador Anatoly Dobrynin was present in the crowd as Nixon rose to say a few words. "Every great power must follow the principle," the president said to the assembled guests, "that it should not encourage directly or indirectly any other nation to use force or armed aggression against one of its neighbors." It was a shot across the Soviets' bow. Dobrynin was said to have remained "stone-faced" throughout the speech.

Events in Vietnam were threatening to destroy many months of work that the president hoped would fundamentally reset the balance of power in the world. He was worried that the massive buildup he'd ordered to stop the NVA invasion would give Brezhnev a reason to cancel their historic meeting. It was possible Nixon could lose both the Moscow summit *and* the war in the coming weeks. He simply didn't know what was going on in the Kremlin. Were the Soviets ready to deepen the Cold War or were they eager for peace?

In Moscow, Dobrynin's superiors were equally disturbed by what was happening in Vietnam. Ever since Kissinger's trip to Beijing the year before, the Soviets had been eager for a summit. A reconciliation between China and the United States could leave the USSR isolated and weakened, and Brezhnev badly wanted the Nixon meeting to advance their own relationship with Washington and to end the nuclear arms race that was draining much-needed cash from the Soviet economy. But the North Vietnamese had thrown a wrench in the Kremlin's plans by launching the Easter Offensive. Months before the tanks started rolling, Hanoi had sent envoys to both Beijing and Moscow to inform them of the coming attack, hoping to combine their triumph on the battlefield with a united communist front against any American counterattack. Moscow reacted badly. "The Vietnamese risk too much," one Soviet diplomat wrote after hearing Hanoi's plans. Soviet leaders pressed their allies to work for a solution at the negotiating table in Paris instead of launching the blitzkrieg-style attack, but the North Vietnamese were adamant. They wanted to gamble on a victory in the field.

It was a game of four-cornered chess being played out in three world capitals and one third-world capital. And neither Brezhnev, Nixon, Mao, nor Le Duan in Hanoi had a very good understanding of what the others were thinking or how far their adversaries were willing to go.

In the early hours of April 10, Norris and Andersen, having made all the arrangements for the operation, rolled up Route 9 in an M113 armored personnel carrier. The North Vietnamese held the town of Cam Lo and the surrounding territory; the Americans were traveling toward the front line, just east of where the enemy units patrolled, on the south bank of the Mieu Giang River.

What Andersen's thoughts were on that journey have remained private, but he had to know that his reputation and his military career now turned on getting Hambleton out. "If the mission had failed," one officer later heard an Army colonel say, "I was going to be the first one in line to court-martial his ass." But the Marine was adamant. "I want to know some success," Andersen told fellow soldiers, "before we stand down."

The personnel carrier rocked its way over the rugged roads toward the forward base. When it arrived, Andersen and Norris found an old circular French bunker perched on a small hill offering a clear view of the river. The bunker was squat and thick walled, and it was flanked by three South Vietnamese tanks. The tank's crews and about twenty hungry, sleep-deprived South Vietnamese rangers manned the position. To get off on the right foot with the rangers, Andersen began handing out extra rations he'd brought along, while Norris greeted the men in Vietnamese. The rangers nodded and addressed him as *Dai Yu,* or "Captain."

As he talked to the men, Norris grew concerned. The officer in charge was a young second lieutenant, and Norris could tell just by looking at the guy that he didn't want the Americans there. Perhaps he believed the mission would draw the enemy to the bunker, endangering his men, or maybe he thought it was just a waste of time. In any case, Norris felt a dark vibe.

There were other things that bothered the SEAL as he checked out the forward base. Three tanks was a significant amount of firepower, but Norris discovered the crews had only a few shells for each main gun. Once those were expended, the soldiers would have to use the 50 caliber machine guns exclusively. The NVA were close, just across the river. If they attacked his team as they returned from the mission, the tanks would offer little protection.

The five South Vietnamese sea commandos who would go upriver with Norris were milling around the base. In Norris's experience, some of the South Vietnamese commandos were very, very good and the rest were barely adequate. Many, for instance, couldn't function long in cold water, especially in a heavy current. That would be a problem, as the Mieu Giang was likely to be near freezing. Norris was worried about the commandos' fitness for water work; he was anxious to get down to the river and test the current and temperature.

Among the commandos was a short, serious-looking sailor, Petty Officer Nguyen Van Kiet, who'd had a somewhat checkered career in the sea commandos. "In the early years, I felt free," Kiet later recalled, "and when we got our salary, we would drink and play around all night long and we didn't care about the rules. I got thrown in the monkey house [jail] for a few days because they considered me and my friends bad guys." Kiet was as rugged as he was wild. When a subordinate refused to obey his orders, Kiet wouldn't report him; his leadership style was more direct than that. The two men would take off the insignia that denoted their rank, and then they would fight until Kiet prevailed. "After, we shook hands," he said. "Man to man, you know." Kiet had calmed down since then, but he was still a tough, disciplined sailor.

After giving out his rations, Andersen, who spoke fluent Vietnamese, gathered up the South Vietnamese rangers and explained what they were going to do. The reception to the plan was frosty. The second lieutenant refused point-blank to take part in the operation; any foray into enemy territory could only call down bad things — such as enemy artillery — on his position. Andersen countered that, if trouble developed, the South Vietnamese troops and the rescue team would have as much air power as they wanted. That didn't seem to impress the lieutenant or the rangers, so Andersen pulled out his trump card: he announced he would shoot anyone who abandoned his post. The men listened silently. The briefing broke up with the threat still hanging in the air.

Afterward, Norris watched the rangers. They were sitting around the little base, grilling their food and joking with one another. The enemy was close, but the men seemed to feel no sense of danger. And despite Andersen's threat, they made it clear that their dedication to the rescue was conditional. "It was understood amongst them that if we feel insecure," he said, "we're outta here and you guys are on your own." Norris realized that if he was pinned down with one of the downed men a hundred yards from the base and called on the radio for help, the South Vietnamese might come, or they might not.

That afternoon, Hambleton sat in his little grove, thinking. Despite the FAC's insistence that it was his choice what would happen next, it was clear that the Air Force wanted him to move. He knew why: the exorbitant cost of his seemingly cursed rescue. "I thought of the . . . men who had been lost trying to get me," he said. "I thought of the many aircraft I had been tying up." He also factored in his dwindling supplies of food and water. He knew he was growing weaker and that his deterioration was likely to accelerate.

The grove was quiet as he contemplated the FAC's words. Birds chattered in the brush, but there were no sounds of guns or villagers calling out to one another. He had to decide quickly. The plan was not ideal; in fact, it was "goddamn grim" in his opinion. But he couldn't think of a better one. Unaware of General Abrams's orders forbidding any further helicopter rescues, he calculated that staying where he was would put more chopper crews and more aircraft in danger. It was also entirely possible that he could pass on the idea, remain in the grove or trees, and slowly sink into unconsciousness as his strength ran out. That would not end well.

Hambleton made his decision. He picked up the radio and called the FAC. "I'll go with the plan," he said. "Tell me exactly what you want me to do."

At that moment, Mark Clark, the backseater from Bill Henderson's plane, was still in hiding close to the river. The airman from Idaho was thoroughly miserable. He felt terrible guilt at the loss of the men who'd tried to save him, and this guilt preyed on his mind in the many empty hours of the day. He'd also found it difficult to get any rest. He could hear "tremendous numbers" of people — perhaps refugees from the American airstrikes—tramping by his hiding place. And every so often the sound of villagers moving down to the river to get water came to him through the brush. They passed within fifteen feet of him as he "scrunched himself up," praying they didn't stumble on his position.

After only two days on the ground, he'd started to hallucinate. "I noticed myself becoming almost schizophrenic from lack of sleep. My legs were a different person and my arms were a different person still. I was sort of going to pieces." He felt like he was losing his mind and decided that, too if no one had come to rescue him by the tenth day, he was going to strike out on his own and try to make for the coast.

During the long hours when he couldn't fall asleep, Clark had made himself useful by calling in airstrikes on the gun emplacements he saw around him. One airstrike, however, had come in unexpectedly close to his position. "I could hear that shell scream the whole way down," he said. The bomb slammed into the earth and sent debris flying; some of it tore away the vegetation that concealed him. The shrapnel barely missed him. Clark had to go scouting for more leaves and branches to cover himself.

Now one of the FACs circling above him got on the radio and relayed the escape plan. Golf had provided the code for Hambleton, but Clark was a much more difficult proposition. He wasn't a fanatic for the sport like his fellow survivor; he had no hobbies that involved distances and directions. Eventually, the planners had fallen back on geography.

As the FAC's first message proved, it wasn't as elegant a solution as golf. "When the moon goes over the mountain," the man told him, "become Esther Williams, get in the Snake, and go from Boise to Twin Falls." Clark didn't know what the hell the guy was talking about. He did understand that this was a code, and the Snake referred to the Snake River in his native Idaho, but the rest was as mysterious to him as Swahili. "Shit," he said, "I couldn't remember if Boise was east or west of Twin Falls." He told the FAC he had no idea what he'd just said.

The FAC consulted with base, then came back. "Go to Eglin," he said. Eglin was Eglin Air Force Base, which was in Florida. That was about as obvious as it got. Florida was east of Idaho, so he had to get in the river and head east. The danger, of course, was that if the North Vietnamese had a map of the United States, they could figure it out too.

After waiting for nightfall, Clark emerged from his hiding place and began making his way down to the river.

Hambleton picked up his survival vest and went through it, weeding out the things he wouldn't need on his journey. The heavy pen gun flares went first. Next went the oxygen mask. He debated over his flight helmet, then decided it was too bulky to carry with him.

What remained were his radios, .38 caliber revolver, survival knife, first-aid kit, boots, gloves, flares, and some Thai paper money. And the single remaining ear of corn. He stuffed that in one of the vest pockets.

Hambleton packed the items he was leaving behind into the flight helmet and placed it at the bottom of his hiding place. He covered it with dirt, uprooted a small plant, and stuck it in the loose soil to disguise the spot. He found a branch and backed out of the little covert, sweeping away his footprints as he went.

21

THE FIRST AT TUCSON NATIONAL

HAMBLETON COULD JUST MAKE OUT the moon, covered by drifts of cloud. It was dusk; he would be able to see only a few inches in front of his face. He brought out his radio and called for the FAC orbiting above.

The voice came on instantly. He asked if Hambleton understood the mission and the airman rogered back. Then, "very casually," the FAC said he understood that Hambleton was "quite a golfer."

Hambleton was bewildered. "Here I was," he thought, "about to step into a virtual minefield and he starts talking golf." He asked the man to repeat his last statement.

"Golf, Bat. Understand you play golf."

Hambleton confirmed he played golf and that he knew a lot of the major courses.

"I hope you remember them."

"I do."

"Outstanding!" the FAC replied. He said that they were going to play nine holes. The first would be the one Hambleton was most familiar with. "Play the first hole at Tucson National," the voice said. "When you're finished, call me."

Hambleton was disoriented and anxious and the conversation had him utterly turned around. *"Finished?"* he thought. He didn't even know what he was starting.

Naturally Hambleton remembered Tucson National. It was his home course; it lay to the northwest of the sprawling city, its green links laid out among the parched tans and purples of the Tucson Mountains. He and Gwen had played it countless times.

He closed his eyes and saw the first hole. It was a slight dogleg, 430 yards long, skirting a small pond on the right as you approached the green. There was nothing remarkable about the thing. If they wanted him to walk 430 yards, they could have chosen the seventh as well. They could have chosen half a dozen holes he kept in his memory.

Then it struck him. When you teed up the ball on number 1 and struck it, you were facing southeast. Southeast was the general direction of the river. The reason for the obscure sports code now came to him. His deliverance from Vietnam would hinge on his arcane knowledge of the sport of Hogan and Nicklaus.

Hambleton told the man he was beginning his journey and signed off.

Wearing the life preserver he'd ejected with, Mark Clark padded down the muddy bank toward the burbling water. He saw no one.

Clark pushed his way through the underbrush that choked the shore. The vegetation was thick, and his life preserver, though uninflated, was bulky. He shoved the branches aside and stepped through the tangle of vines. He was taking his first steps into the cold water when suddenly an inflation cord for one side of the life preserver snagged on an overhead branch. There was a loud whooshing noise. Clark looked down in horror as the life preserver started inflating with a hissing roar. "It scared the living hell out of me," he said. The preserver wasn't just making a horrendous racket; its growing shape looked in the darkness like a bright orange buoy, or a child's balloon, which was the last thing that Clark needed as he began his attempt to escape the North Vietnamese.

Once the thing started inflating, there was no way to stop it, so Clark stood there on the bank impatiently listening to the shriek of air. After the preserver had finished filling, the noise fell away. His heart beating fast, Clark paused, listening for the sound of feet rushing toward him. But all he could hear were insects and the plashing of water. He pushed into the river.

Hambleton looked around his hiding place, his home for the past eight days, and felt a pang of fear at the thought of leaving it. He stood upright and noticed "a touch of euphoria" along with the anxiety. He was no longer hunched over like a "stalked animal," and that simple change in physical posture seemed to boost his confidence. He took out his compass and found the heading: 135 degrees southeast. He stepped out of the foliage and ventured out onto the path, counting his steps as he went. Each stride was about a yard. He had to complete 430 of them before checking back with the FAC for his next heading.

His body felt stiff, his joints having soaked up the moisture from the mud and damp leaves. But his eyes gave him the most trouble. In the darkness, they'd lost any sense of depth perception. He couldn't tell if a dark shape ahead of him was a bush four feet away or a tree forty feet away. He was like a blind man staggering through the landscape. "I felt my way more than saw it."

It was dark now, with only the faintest glow in the southwest; Hambleton guessed that glow was a bridge burning after being struck by American bombs. He moved slowly. Walking the route in the dark was just barely doable because he'd been looking at this landscape for days and knew the terrain's basic layout. But what would happen when he headed into the unknown territory beyond the village? It was terrifying to think that he would be blundering around just when he needed to be at his stealthiest.

Nothing ran into him on the path, and he managed to navigate it without tumbling into the paddies on either side. After thirty minutes, the navigator found himself exhausted; even the slightest exertion caused his lungs to burn and his legs to go wobbly. He spotted a clump of undergrowth and pushed his way through the foliage, then grabbed the radio and whispered into it. "Estimate end of first hole," he said.

The FAC acknowledged. "Next is Number 5 at Davis-Monthan."

Hambleton thought back. He must have played Davis-Monthan a hundred times when he was the commander of the Titan II missile site. Number 5 was laid out due east, four hundred yards. He looked at his compass and turned toward a heading of ninety degrees. He took a few minutes to rest before standing up and starting out. He estimated he was in the midst of the gravel mines now, and he grimaced slightly every time he placed a foot on the path.

The rice paddies on either side of him were rectangular pools of blackness. The only noise was the ragged sound of his own breathing. As his eyes grew accustomed to the dark, his range of vision increased slightly; the path in front of him now had a distinct shape, as did the bushes three or four feet away. But his physical condition was beginning to worry him. As he made it to the end of number 5, he found that he was out of breath. He was more run-down than he'd realized.

When he'd finished, the FAC announced, "Number 5 at Shaw Air Force Base." Hambleton had to reach farther back in his memory. He thought back to his times playing the South Carolina course as a younger man, saw the hillocks and the flag bright yellow against the impossibly lush kelly green of the grass. Which way did it run? His thoughts were muddied with exhaustion. *Northeast,* he said to himself after a moment. When he studied his compass and looked out at the landscape around him, he realized that the FAC was taking him straight toward the village.

For the first time, doubt seeped into his mind. The FAC and the others directing his escape had a bird's-eye view of the terrain; they must be guiding him around dangers they saw from above. But the village not only had villagers — obviously. It also had NVA soldiers he'd seen as recently as two days before, and antiaircraft batteries manned by gunners. Why would he go through there?

He checked the compass again. The heading was correct. He kept off the radio and began walking. When he'd made it two hundred paces, he had to stop. He squatted down, his hands on his knees, breathing rapidly. As he crouched over, panting, he watched the ghostly outlines of the huts.

He started moving again, bent at the waist so as to minimize his profile for anyone looking out from the village. He spotted some foliage to his left and dropped to his hands and knees, crawling over the soft earth so as not to leave any footprints. When he reached the bushes, he listened. Nothing. He couldn't hear people stirring or chickens clucking or any sound of life. It was as if the villagers had vanished en masse in the middle of the night.

He got the FAC on the radio and announced the completion of the third hole.

His body felt wrung out; the exertion of his short walk, along with the constant anxiety about revealing himself to the enemy, had exhausted him.

The FAC's voice whispered on the radio. "Fourteenth at the Masters," he said.

The so-called "Chinese Fir." Par 4. Dogleg, 420 yards. East by northeast. Only hole without a bunker. Number 14 was famous and famously difficult. It was the spot where the big band singer Don Cherry had rolled in a beautiful putt for birdie during the qualifications for the 1957 Masters, eliminating Ben Hogan from the field.

Hambleton sighed. "That has many, many traps," he said.

"Roger," the FAC replied, "you are right."

Then Hambleton thought, *east by northeast?* That would take him straight through the village. He got back on the radio. "Birddog, confirm. Fourteenth hole at the Masters?"

A delay. Then FAC came on. "That is affirmative."

Hambleton couldn't understand what the planners were thinking, but he guessed they'd photographed the entire route and saw something they didn't like on either side of the village. The resolution on those photographs, even from thirty thousand feet, was fantastic. You could read a headline on a newspaper. "Surely they wouldn't let me go through if they thought it was extremely dangerous," Hambleton thought to himself.

The moon was covered by high clouds and the terrain in front of him was as black, he said, as "india ink." He waited fifteen minutes, studying the huts and listening for any sounds. Nothing. Perhaps everyone was asleep. He could see the first faint glow of the sun to his east. He was running out of time if he hoped to make the river by daybreak. He rose up and started walking.

Hambleton sidled up next to the first building and spotted a path that led through the village to the east. He guessed it was the main route from the rice paddies and decided to take it. At least he wouldn't blunder into any farm equipment or bicycles next to the houses, which might awaken the people inside the huts. After he took a few steps on the path, his foot struck something and he went sprawling to the ground. He looked back to see what he'd tripped over. A dead pig lay on the path.

It was a good sign. In villages as poor as this, a dead pig would have immediately been butchered for food if anyone was still around. Hambleton picked himself up and hustled over to a building just off the path. He listened. No sounds. He slipped ahead. He could see now that the town was just three blocks long. Hambleton had the feeling he was walking through a "deserted movie set of plaster and chicken wire."

At the end of the path, he found a shed filled with hay. He was completely spent. "Except for the last few feet, I certainly hadn't rushed, but my heart was pounding as though I had just climbed the top of Pike's Peak." He dropped to his knees and burrowed into the hay. He fell asleep to the sound of transports moving south on a nearby road.

Fifteen minutes later, Hambleton snapped awake. Something was out there. He listened. Soon he heard voices — young male voices. Was it a patrol, or were they pursuers coming for him? As he listened to the men talk, he realized that the voices were coming not from the road but from one of the nearby huts. It was probably a crew of one of the AAA guns that had been targeting American planes for the past few days.

As the minutes ticked by, the voices fell silent. Hambleton swept away the hay that lay on top of him and moved to the doorway. The night was dark, the fields black, and he saw no campfires or flashlights. The soldiers had to be asleep. But would one of them be left on guard, to watch for planes or monitor the radio?

Quiet. His throat was parched. He chewed on a piece of the dry grass to get some saliva working. He estimated he was halfway done with his journey; the river was about a mile away now.

He raised the FAC and whispered into the radio. "Number four at Abilene," the voice said.

Hambleton smiled. In one of his all-time glorious moments of golfing, he'd shot a hole in one at Abilene. On the fourth hole. Obviously, someone he'd been with that day — or one of the many pals he'd bragged to — had passed on the story to the USAF. It was almost like a wink from an old friend. The exact contours of the hole were imprinted on his mind with the freshness of a childhood memory.

It was east-facing, 195 yards, dead straight. When he looked at his compass and studied the landscape, he saw that the route went right through the village and out toward the open spaces beyond it. He felt pinpricks of fear. He had no idea how many NVA or VC were roaming out there. And he didn't know if the men whose voices he'd heard were really asleep.

The navigator edged out onto the main road, trying to make as little noise as possible. The dirt was hard-packed here, and once he was past the hut he thought the voices had come from, he moved swiftly.

He saw no one in the darkness. The soldiers he'd heard must be passed out. After counting a hundred strides, he spotted a burned-out hooch just off the road, its roof gone. He needed to rest. A hundred yards was about the maximum he could do in one go. He moved off the road and approached the darkened doorway.

As he stepped inside, something came rushing out of the shadows. Hambleton fell to his knees in shock, then realized it was just a chicken that had been rooting around in the hooch's interior. The navigator's heart was slamming in his chest. He hadn't been prepared.

Hambleton watched the chicken skitter out onto the road. Suddenly, he felt ravenously hungry. The bird would be his first real meal in many days. He had to catch it. He would eat it raw if he had to.

The chicken was perched near the ditch at the side of the road closer to him, pecking for bits of food in the gravel. As he got closer, Hambleton realized it wasn't a hen, as he'd first thought, but a rooster. A less appetizing meal. But he was determined to catch it and have it for dinner. He reached into his pocket and brought out his survival knife with his right hand.

Hambleton held his breath and watched the bird as it came closer to his right foot. He leapt at it in the semidarkness and fell to his knees as he attempted to grab it. Just then, out of the corner of his eye, he saw something else emerge from the hooch in the semidarkness. This time, a human figure.

22

DARK ENCOUNTER

Hours into his journey, Mark Clark was weak, cold, and exhausted. The river was leaching heat from his body, and progress was agonizingly slow. The current pulled him along, but he was having trouble staying upright. The river bottom would drop away suddenly and send him tumbling downward. The effort drained him. Every hour he would pull out his radio and call the FAC: "I'm still on my way down. Don't give up hope, I'm coming."

Clark was far younger than Hambleton, but he found the river, which was full of snags and submerged branches, to be unusually treacherous. At one point he was walking along when he felt his feet snarl in some branches below the surface of the water, dragging him toward the bottom. Clark went under, spluttering for air. As he thrashed beneath the surface, he managed to reach up and pull the handle on his life preserver, inflating the other side. The airbag bloomed out in the darkness, and Clark found himself being pulled back up. He cleared the surface and took a huge breath. "I just about drowned myself," he thought ruefully.

As he went, Clark spotted soldiers walking in patrols along the riverbank. There were tanks and transport trucks and troops, but no American faces. He kept on.

· · ·

Hambleton stood stunned. The man or woman — he couldn't in the confusion and darkness tell which it was — came flying at him, crashing into his left side. As the figure crossed the last few inches, Hambleton saw a flash of something bright and metallic raised in the air. Then he felt a sharp pain in his shoulder.

It had happened in a second or two. His heart was beating furiously. He'd been found at last, and now this person was trying to kill him. Hambleton shoved the figure away and scrambled to his feet. He still had the knife in his right hand. The figure came at him again and he saw the blade, held up high, catch the moonlight. Hambleton rushed at the figure and brought his knife forward, stabbing at the shadowy thing. He felt the blade chunk into the chest wall. The figure rushed close to him, and Hambleton could see its face. It was male, a Vietnamese peasant, the smell of fish oil on his breath. The man grunted in pain.

Hambleton jerked the knife back and the man seemed to deflate, slumping to the ground. Hambleton was breathing hard, staring at the figure in the blackness. The body didn't move. His assailant was clearly dead or dying. The rooster was clucking in the distance. All else was quiet.

Hambleton felt as if he was going to vomit. Then it occurred to him: *What if there are more?* He needed to get away. He turned and started running down the road.

Raw fear pushed him forward. His arms and legs shook with the exertion and his heart stabbed painfully in his chest. He felt like he was having a coronary. He was barely able to stay upright, and then he wasn't. He went tumbling to the road, rolling along the dirt before he lurched back up and careened forward.

He knew he was making too much noise and that he would attract anyone in the area. "Stop it!" he thought. "Stop it! You can't blow it now. You can't blow it now. *Calm down. Calm down.*"

His breath was coming in gasps. He collapsed to his knees, completely spent. His body gave way and he fell back, his arms flung out, his back smacking against the roadbed. He lay there, breathing hard, listening to the rasp of his breath. He couldn't go any farther.

The image of Gwen came to him, but it almost immediately slipped away. His vision was blurred; he tried to concentrate on the moon, but when he stared at it, there was a second one next to it, and then a third.

Hambleton turned his head and looked toward the roadside. He spotted a shape in the darkness. It was a wooden pig trough. It would offer him shelter, to get out of sight of any pursuers. He crawled over to it, so spent that he didn't smell anything, even though the place reeked of pig shit. He felt "slightly more alive than dead."

He had to see how badly he was injured. He jerked the zipper down past his sternum and got his left shoulder out of the flight suit. His fingers felt for the wound. He found it; the cut appeared to be shallow. The tough fabric of the flight suit had probably blunted the impact. He pulled out the first-aid kit from his survival vest and daubed some disinfectant on the wound, then fumbled for a dressing and put it on.

He sat in the mud and slop, trying not to dwell on what had just happened, but the thoughts came anyway. Who was the man and what was he doing in that hut? He hadn't been able to make out what the guy was wearing. Perhaps he was VC.

But he'd killed him, knifed him in the chest and left him to bleed out on the dirt road. The thought wouldn't leave him. It had been self-defense, but Hambleton felt no thrill at escaping death. "Actually killing a man face to face had been the most terrifying thing he had ever done in his life," wrote his biographer. His training hadn't prepared him for the reality of death, for the physical sensation of it.

And then he'd stumbled down the road making an enormous racket instead of crawling to the ditch and scanning the terrain for the dead man's comrades. Survival school had taught Hambleton that panicking was the worst possible thing he could do. But he'd done it anyway, "galloped off like a wild fool." Not only had he lost count of how many strides he'd taken, but also he'd expended a huge amount of energy. He'd always thought of himself as cool under pressure, but he'd come undone.

Hambleton could feel his mind slipping, losing focus. He had to concentrate. He called the FAC. The voice told him to play number 4 at Corona de Tucson.

· · ·

At about 10 p.m. on the night of April 10, as Clark was slowly pushing downstream, Tommy Norris and his team of Vietnamese sea commandos left the French bunker. Their faces were blackened and they each carried an AK-47 rifle, several grenades, and some spare ammunition, along with one canteen apiece. The commandos wore tiger-striped camo blouses with blue jeans; Norris had on his olive-green shirt and jeans, which made less noise than the standard-issue uniform. They knew Hambleton hadn't gotten to the Mieu Giang yet. Tonight they would focus on saving Clark.

The team made their way to the river, rippling under the moonlight, where Norris reached his hand in and tested the water. It was cold. The current was a knot and a half, difficult for all but the best swimmers. "I said, 'Uh-oh, I'm not going to put my guys in that.'" Norris and Lieutenant Tho decided the team would have to go overland.

The men moved away from the riverbank and headed west. The terrain was covered with small trees and underbrush — bamboo, nipa palm, elephant grass. As they pushed farther west, Norris kept a sharp eye out for rice paddies and fields; he didn't want the men to blunder out into the open. Along with exposure, noise was a constant worry. With the enemy thick around them, one clink of a canteen neck against a knife or a belt buckle could give them away.

When they'd walked just over a mile from the bunker, Norris heard the sound of machinery ahead. He stopped his men and peered through the semidarkness. Headlights a ways off. A line of NVA tanks and transport trucks was moving across the Cam Lo bridge. As Norris watched, the lead truck turned east off the bridge and headed directly toward him.

They'd barely left the bunker and already they were in danger of being spotted. For a second or two, Norris thought about calling in an airstrike. But the trucks were so close that the American bombs might hit his men, or even Clark, if he was near the bridge. He had to think of something else.

Norris pointed toward the river, and the Vietnamese commandos slipped into the bushes and pushed their way through the thin branches and waxy leaves. Hiding themselves in the underbrush, they watched as the procession of headlights continued toward them. Stealth was their primary tactical advantage. Norris briefly considered attacking the convoy but quickly rejected the idea. It would result in a clatter of gunfire, costing them their cover and, at best, ending the operation, at least for the night; at worst, they'd be captured or killed.

When the lead truck was five hundred yards out, its headlights swerved away. The convoy had turned onto a small road and was now heading south toward the mountains. Norris breathed a bit easier.

The men stood and began walking again, watching the river for any sign of Clark. The NVA was seemingly everywhere. A patrol moved by, the soldiers talking and laughing. Norris signaled for the men to take cover, and they slipped deeper into the underbrush and waited until the troops passed by. As they moved upriver, two more squads skirted their perimeter, and the men squatted in place, their fingers gripping their AK-47s. There were guard posts, both on the roads and on the river itself, soldiers in silhouette smoking and chatting as they gazed at the landscape in front of them, watching for intruders.

The farther upriver they got, the more Norris realized that the Mieu Giang wasn't just confined to a single body of water; at points, it divided into three different channels. Especially at night, it was easy to follow the wrong one and get completely turned around. If they didn't stick to the main channel, they could miss the American coming down. It was slow, painstaking work, and Norris felt each minute pass. "We'd burned up so much time. I was so afraid that Clark would pass us before I got to the water to intercept him."

They were 250 yards from the base, then 500. He kept glancing at the river, watching for a white face on its surface. More soldiers came on foot. Norris was aware of a truth of working behind enemy lines: every patrol you passed on the way in, you would have to pass again on the way back out. Even though they'd been lucky so far, each unit of NVA they evaded decreased their chances of getting back to the French bunker alive.

The radio chirped softly. Andersen was calling for a progress report. They were already past the five-hundred-meter limit that the Marine officer had set. Norris whispered a quick update, not mentioning his exact location, and went back to the search.

Finally, after hours of slinking through the shadows on the riverbank, the men came to a well-covered spot with a good view of the water. Midnight had passed; it was now the very early hours of April 11. They were about 1.2 miles from the base. Norris made a decision. There were too many NVA patrols along the banks; eventually their luck would run out, and one of the patrols would stumble on them. Norris told the Vietnamese commandos they would stay there and wait for Clark to come floating down the river.

Two of the commandos slipped down to the water to find out how fast the current was running and to look for any obstacles. Flares, called "illumination rounds," or "illum," launched by the NVA, lifted into the air and hung there, fizzing loudly and lighting up the river and its banks in stark white.

Norris got on the radio and, keeping his voice as low as possible, called in to the naval gunners for some illum of his own. He heard the crump of the guns, and more light poured down from the black sky, turning the upper section of the river fluorescent bright. He listened to Clark's progress on the radio while peering at the furrowed water. The airman would be coming down the south bank. The thing now was to wait and not miss him.

The men squatted in the bushes and studied the river, gurgling about ten feet away. Out of the darkness came a different noise: the tramping of feet. After a few minutes, Norris heard voices. He turned toward the sound. A patrol of NVA soldiers was approaching very close to the bushes his men were secreted in. He tensed. If they had to take on the patrollers, they could do it and probably kill them all, but the sound of the gunfire would be like an alarm bell for every soldier within a quarter mile.

What were these soldiers doing off the road and so close to the riverbank? The thought shot through Norris's mind that the squad had finished its patrol and the men were taking a shortcut back to their camps. Which would bring them right on top of his men.

If it was five or six, they could cut them down in short order with controlled bursts of their AKs. But the mission would be over. They would be running for their lives.

Just then, Norris heard the sound of loud breathing from the river. He turned to look and saw a white face on the dark water. "Oh, Jesus, why me?" he thought.

23

THE GROVE

In the command posts and chow halls and hooches of the American bases in Southeast Asia, among the mechanics and the pararescuemen, the drivers and the food servers, the story of Gene Hambleton had begun to leak out, despite the attempt by Norris et al. to make it "go dark." In fact, by the night of April 10, he was the talk of the American military in Southeast Asia. Door gunners and the men who drove the generals and the guys who fueled up the airplanes in Saigon and at Da Nang and Korat huddled together and passed along the latest scuttlebutt. In the ready rooms of the USS *Hancock,* anchored offshore, Navy pilots and their crews eagerly followed the unfolding drama. There was little operational detail — the mission was still top secret — but there was an awareness that Hambleton was out there and on the run.

It wasn't just the massive rescue mission that piqued the interest of the Air Force and Army guys, though that was intriguing; it was more the thought of this old dude out there in the jungle, seemingly outwitting the enemy at every turn. "He was a fifty-three-year-old man running around up there in the DMZ by himself," said Master Sergeant Daryl Tincher, who'd initiated the rescue effort at Joker, "beating the North Vietnamese and the Vietcong *by himself.* He was giving them all they wanted. With his decisions, with his intestinal fortitude. He became a household word, the first words out of people's mouth in the command post."

Is Hambleton still free, they'd ask one another as they fueled up an F-4.

Have the gomers got him yet? When the answer came back, the men would smile and whistle softly to themselves. *Hoo-wee, he must be one tough old bastard.* Hambleton's will to live, said one officer involved in the rescue, "was the most intense we had ever seen." Stuck in the middle of this gigantic invasion with just a .38 in one hand and his balls in the other, he was becoming an inspirational figure; you just had to root for the guy. It got so bad at Joker that Tincher had to order his men to leave their HQ and go to their hooches to get some rest. "I had five sets of controllers on that mission," said Tincher. "And you had to run them out of there. My radio operators, my hi-fi radio operators, my telephone people, my weathermen. Everyone wanted to be part of it."

By the spring of 1972, the conflict was at a standstill. Support back home was cratering. The proportion of Americans who believed that sending soldiers to Vietnam had been a mistake had risen to 60 percent, a number that had nearly doubled in the last four years. But this little war within a war, Hambleton's run to the river, held out the slim possibility of victory. The men loved it. The news and gossip about the downed airman spread all the way back to the Pentagon, where desk-bound majors and intel specialists followed the story as if it were Rod Carew's latest hitting streak, arriving in the office every morning and asking one another the question of the day: *Still running, is he? Well, I'll be damned.*

For many Americans back home, Vietnam was a war without the possibility of heroes. That wasn't true for the men actually in-country; they either knew men who'd done wondrous things under great pressure, or they'd heard the stories that were passed from hooch to hooch: medevac helicopter pilots going into shit-crazy LZs and carrying out wounded troops, or PJs who'd stayed beyond their allotted time on the ground, fighting off NVA regiments with an AK-47 and a few grenades. Word traveled quickly. The story of USMC Captain John Ripley, who'd singlehandedly blown up the bridge at Dong Ha, was already widely known and admired only days after the event. Hambleton was the latest, and the most unlikely, of these underground heroes.

What the military didn't realize was that the cheek-by-jowl relationship between the reporters covering the war and the troops on the ground meant that word was slowly, very slowly, seeping out to the regular world.

Hambleton finally collected himself and made his way down the main road out of the village. He'd lost count of his steps, but he staggered forward, trying to estimate the distance he'd covered. He found his body was behaving strangely. As he walked, he was tilting backward slowly, like one of those toy birds that sipped water then leaned back at a crazy angle. Except that his body never came back forward. After a few minutes of this, he would end up sprawling backward and collapsing on the road. This happened again and again. He was completely unable to control himself.

Hambleton had no idea if the problem was muscle exhaustion or something neurological, or if he was suffering some kind of psychological aftereffect from killing a man. But he had to find a way to counteract the tilt. Finally, he began walking with his head pitched forward, "like the crazy-looking Road Runner bird." This corrected the backward incline and allowed him to stay upright while better avoiding the bumps and divots in the road. But the increasing signs of deterioration were worrying.

He cut a bizarre figure. His body seemed unwilling to obey his demands to walk straight. His arms felt ahead into the darkness to keep him from running into anything—"I felt like I was wrapped in a great black cape"—and his legs were shaky. He shuffled like a man in leg chains, in short, halting steps. When his feet tapped against a bump or divot in the ground, he would totter and try to regain his balance. Sometimes he didn't make it and fell off the path entirely. It occurred to him that anyone watching his progress would think he was blind drunk.

He found a pair of coconut trees and collapsed next to them. His throat was parched. He hadn't had water since his journey began. He massaged his face with his hands, trying to stay awake. Dawn was now only a couple of hours away; he was determined to make the river by then.

As he sat there, Hambleton was overcome with a new feeling. *I'm going in the wrong direction,* he thought. Once the idea entered his mind, he found it impossible to shake. *I must have turned west back there somewhere. I'm headed deeper into enemy territory. I've made a terrible mistake.*

He took out his compass and checked it. It told him he was headed east. But it didn't matter. "I had that sinking feeling I was doing something wrong and I wasn't facing east at all. For the first time I felt as though I was going to panic."

The land around him looked suspiciously familiar. He thought he recognized a couple of features of the terrain from the beginning of his journey. Was he actually walking in circles? His hand shaking, he picked up the radio and called the FAC.

"I'm out here in the same stuff I've been in all along tonight," he told the man. "There are no landmarks except lights in the sky north of me and more southeast of me. This is the right direction, isn't it?"

"Roger. This is the right direction."

"I was getting concerned," Hambleton admitted. The FAC told him he was doing fine and that the next hole was ready. He gave him the name and Hambleton started to get up.

He took a couple of steps before his foot caught on a root and he went crashing to the ground. He found himself in a puddle, his face and body splashed with mud. He staggered up and went on.

He began talking to himself. "Don't give up now. Keep going. The biggest part of the battle is over." He imagined arriving at the river and finding his rescuers already there. It was possible. They knew where he was going, so why wouldn't they have sent in a team to gather him up as quickly as possible?

He came to a fork in the path. One trail led away to his left, to where he couldn't tell. Straight ahead another trail—not the main path—led to terrain that looked very much like the place where he'd hid for the past six days.

Hambleton stood there, debating. If he went left, he would be veering away from Quang Tri and the river. Maybe the path doubled back and led to the water, but he couldn't be sure. If he went ahead along the less trodden path, he would be going in the right direction. But why would the path turn like that?

He was too exhausted to think of taking extra steps. He decided to push ahead into the foliage. He took a few steps and the path beneath his feet disappeared. He was now on rougher ground and it immediately taxed his strength. After a few minutes he realized he was in the middle of a banana grove. Its crude furrows caught his feet and he dropped to his knees, unable to go any farther. Paranoia needled his brain. He felt his spirits drop; he was, he said, "exhausted and disgusted with myself because I couldn't control my body." If he couldn't walk, he would never make it to the river.

He got back up. He was lurching ahead when he ran into something sharp. He reached up and felt a barbed wire fence. Shocked, he jumped back. He was on someone's property; perhaps he'd blundered into another village, whose people would soon be waking up.

With a heavy heart, Hambleton decided he would have to turn around and retrace his steps. He couldn't take the risk, in his physical condition, of coming upon any Vietnamese villagers. He wouldn't be able to run away, and they would easily kill or capture him.

But he had no energy left. His body felt like it was made out of cold clay, without any human spark inside. He found a banana tree and leaned his back against it, then slumped to the ground, spent.

A thought sprang into his mind. The Negritos in the survival school in the Philippines had mentioned during his training that banana and bamboo trees contain fresh water in abundance. They store it in their trunks and, during the night, the water flows down to the roots. In the morning, it burbles back up the trunk. He turned and put his ear to the trunk. Immediately he heard the sound of moving water.

Hambleton felt for his survival knife and pulled it out. He reached back as far as he could, then thrust the knife forward, stabbing the banana tree mid-trunk. When he wrestled the blade out, a stream of water poured from the gash. He turned and brought his lips under it and took gulp after gulp. The water tasted clean. Slowly, he felt some of his strength return.

After he'd drunk all he could, Hambleton stood up and began his walk back out of the banana grove. Once he got clear of the broad-leafed branches, he found the fork in the path and his original route. The trail led due south. But as he pushed ahead, it began to curve back eastward. Clearly the path skirted the edge of the banana grove. He was relieved.

The energy the water had given him ebbed quickly. After only a few minutes of walking, he still hadn't cleared the edge of the grove. He had to turn off the path and rest against the trunk of a banana tree. As he lay with his back propped against the tree, he looked at his watch: 2:30 a.m. He realized he couldn't continue and closed his eyes.

Thirty minutes later, he awoke. He got back up on the path and headed east. The nap had cost him time. It was doubtful he would reach the river by daylight. He began to scout the edges of the path for a place to hide.

He made his way toward a patch of trees and pushed through the foliage. Just then, he heard voices. He froze. What would anyone be doing out at 3:45 in the morning unless they were chasing him? He dropped quietly to the ground and put his back to a tree, facing the way he'd come. Now he listened. The thicket he found himself in was heavy with foliage; any pursuers would have trouble finding him. He turned and looked around the tree trunk. Beyond the edge of the brush, he spotted something else. It was something tan set among the dark greens and browns of the terrain. It looked for all the world like a sandbar.

He cursed himself. What the hell would a sandbar be doing in the middle of the Vietnamese countryside? Hambleton moved to the edge of the thicket and stared at the tan shape. He removed his glasses and cleaned them. He was having trouble focusing his eyes, so he lay down on his stomach and rested them for a moment. When he opened his eyes again, the cloud cover above him had swept past and the moonlight shone down on the landscape. He pushed himself up and knelt, looking around the tree again. He stared at the light area for four or five minutes. Finally, his eyes adjusted long enough for him to see it clearly. He wasn't looking at a sandbar. It was the Mieu Giang.

Hambleton stood up, staring at the rolling water. "I was so damn excited, I thought, Jesus I've made it." He began to stumble forward. His self-control evaporated. Were his rescuers already there, impatiently waiting for him to show? Or had he already missed them?

The navigator thrashed through the foliage, blundering on, shoving the thick leaves aside with his arms. Suddenly, the ground dropped away from under him and he was falling down the steep embankment, his body turning somersaults. After a few seconds, he slammed into a tree trunk. He couldn't move; he thought he would pass out.

The American lay there, breathing shallowly, trying to regain enough strength to make it to the water. He could hear it burbling and rippling along. He began to stretch his legs and arms, feeling for breaks in the bones. But there was no sudden pain, only the throb of bruised muscle. He managed after great effort to topple over on his stomach. He raised his head and looked ahead. There was the river, a broad roiling shape, only yards away.

Hambleton began to crawl on his belly. When he finally reached the river's edge, he put his hands into the water and splashed some back and forth. The navigator was exultant. *He'd done it!* He'd nearly cracked his skull in the last hundred yards, but he was at the river. The rescue team would be here any minute. Would they come before dawn or would they need daylight to navigate to where he waited? He didn't know. All he could think of was that he was close to home, to Gwen, to freedom.

Painfully, he reversed course, his flight suit filthy with the riverbank mud, and pushed himself back toward the tree that he'd collided with. It would give him some cover while he waited. Once there, he heard the buzzing of a plane overhead. The FAC had found him.

He pulled out his radio, worried that it might have been broken in his fall, but to his relief it powered up immediately. He called in and after a moment, the FAC responded. It was a different voice from the one that had guided him to the river.

The voice asked him if he was "feet wet." The term usually referred to airmen who'd ditched in the sea, but Hambleton knew what the man was asking. He confirmed he was at the river.

"That is fine. That is great." The FAC told him he could relax now, that the "plan would be working out shortly."

The FAC buzzed overhead, settling into an orbit. His questions seemed to revolve around one thing: Hambleton's physical condition. Whether from bravado or from worry — would they think he was too weak to complete the mission? — the navigator hid the fact that he'd been having trouble staying upright on the path. Something was wrong with him, but he didn't want to jinx his chances. He said nothing.

Unbeknownst to Hambleton, the FAC was already deeply concerned by what he was hearing. Some of what the navigator was saying was sheer gibberish. He would stop speaking for long periods or utter something nonsensical. Andersen, listening in, was alarmed as well, and kept checking in. "They seemed to want to keep verifying that I was still there and alive," Hambleton said. He thought he sounded better than he did.

The FAC needed his exact location. Hambleton couldn't name any landmarks around him, because the NVA was presumably monitoring the transmissions, so they worked out a plan. Hambleton could hear the plane coming up the river. When it passed directly overhead, he clicked the transmit button on his radio. They repeated the process several times, with the O-2 vectoring in from different angles, until the FAC was satisfied.

The voice told him to hide in place. He was to relax for the rest of the day.

Clearly, the rescue team hadn't yet arrived.

24

CLARK

Tommy norris listened closely. Someone upriver was exhaling and inhaling loudly in the darkness, "a-huffing and a-puffing." It sounded, on that quiet night, like an exhausted marathoner sucking wind at the end of a race. It had to be Clark. Who else would be swimming in the Mieu Giang in the middle of the night?

The North Vietnamese patrol was inching closer. Norris turned to the sea commandos, who had brought their rifles up in case he ordered an attack. "All I could see were blackened faces and wide eyes." Norris switched his gaze back to the inky darkness above the surface of the water. Whoever was out there was making far too much noise, especially with the patrol so close.

Norris was in a bind. If he ordered his men to fire on the enemy soldiers, the NVA would swarm down on the riverbank and he might have to leave Clark behind, not to mention Hambleton. But if Clark kept making that infernal racket, Norris was sure the NVA soldiers would hear him. And then they'd kill or capture the airman.

He shot a glance upriver. He could see a head bobbing out of the water, a pale face. Clark, unquestionably. But he couldn't call out a warning. He had to let the airman pass. Only if the patrol opened up on the American would he and his men return fire.

The breathing sound went drifting by. Norris listened to the footsteps of the men in the patrol. They didn't hesitate or stop. Apparently, the noise of pushing through the underbrush had masked the sounds Clark's breathing was making. Norris was astonished. Once again, his team had gotten lucky.

He waited sixty seconds until the patrol had completely gone, then quickly slipped into the water. He was shocked by how cold it was. He switched the radio back on and told Andersen he needed illum. A minute or two later, flares sparkled high above, big shock-white orbs of light drifting down toward earth on their parachutes. Norris cut through the water with quick strokes, making excellent time; the current was with him now. He wanted to get ahead of the American and then grab him as he went past.

Finally, when he'd reached a point where he was sure he'd overtaken Clark, he angled toward the riverbank. Now he would wait for the airman.

But Clark had vanished. The man had been wearing an orange life preserver that was designed to be spotted in situations just like this one, and yet Norris couldn't see him anywhere. His eyes swept back and forth from one bank to the other, but there was no hint of bright color. *Maybe I let him pass by in my excitement,* Norris thought. He swam along the bank, pulling back the foliage and checking the undergrowth. Nothing. "I've really done it now," he thought. "I saw him, I had him. Where is he?"

Worried and growing increasingly cold, Norris started back upstream. After exhausting himself against the current, he reached the spot where he'd entered the water. He glimpsed Kiet and the other Vietnamese sea commandos. They were sitting on the bank, looking "tired, cold and frustrated"; clearly, chasing after some phantom American while dozens of NVA soldiers walked past their position was beginning to wear on them. Norris ordered the men to begin searching the banks. They spread out and started quietly inspecting the overhanging shrubbery and bushes for any sign of the American.

Time was passing. The work was painfully slow; the river turned and twisted on itself, and each square foot of shore had to be checked.

The SEAL got on the radio and called Andersen. "He got past me," he told Andersen. "The next contact he has with the FAC, tell him to hole up on the south side of the river. We'll find him."

Andersen began to reel off a long list of questions: *Where are you? How'd Clark get by you?* At that point, Andersen's voice cut out. Norris would attribute this to "some radio trouble," but that wasn't actually true. "I'm sitting out there in the middle of no-man's-land," Norris admitted later, "with a whole bunch of bad guys around and I didn't want to talk to him so it was kind of like [making static noises] radio's off!" He'd simply switched off the power. It was a Tommy Norris solution.

Norris entered the water again, along with Lieutenant Tho, to look for Clark, while the others prowled the shoreline. Norris called in more illum. The river downstream was lit up as bright as Georgia Avenue in Silver Spring on a sunny summer afternoon. But no Clark.

Norris was terrified that he'd blown the mission. He'd disobeyed Andersen's direct order and gone upstream on his own initiative, and now the target had gotten by him. There was a whole river to the east of him and Clark could be anywhere on it.

He checked his watch. Almost 4 a.m. They had only had about an hour and a half before they had to be back at the bunker. They couldn't be out in daylight; that would be suicide. Every additional minute they spent looking for Clark decreased the time they'd have to make it back to friendly lines.

Clark went on, chilled to the bone. The FAC began calling him on the radio. Clark took a breath and rogered. The voice came back, instructing the airman to head to the south bank and stay there. Clark confirmed. He turned and made his way toward the ghostly line of the shore.

Once he reached it, Clark found an old sampan bobbing on the current, one of the broad, low boats used by Vietnamese fishermen. He slipped in behind it, then pulled out his camouflage net and drew it over his head. He waited, watching the river. Another artillery flare arced into the sky, and the white light lit up the water from bank to bank.

Norris swam slowly downstream, eyeing the shore. Petty Officer Kiet was shadowing him on the riverbank, checking for footprints in the mud. As the commando came around a bend in the river, he saw a quick movement. It was a man, covered in a camo net, wearing a bright orange life preserver, watching Kiet from behind an old busted-up sampan. Kiet knew it had to be Clark.

There was something else glinting in the moonlight. It was the barrel of a .38 revolver held just over the water's surface and pointed directly at Kiet's face. Clark had him sighted down. The two men stared at each other. "For a second," Kiet said, "neither of us moved."

The sea commando slowly turned the barrel of his rifle away from the airman. Then he took the gun and slung it behind him on its strap. He didn't want to escalate the situation; clearly, Clark thought he was NVA.

He knelt down and began waving to Norris in the water.

Norris saw the commando's signal and then spotted Clark. He and Tho began to swim toward the boat. Norris carefully slung his AK-47 behind his back, out of sight. If it was Clark and he saw it, he might think Norris was NVA and freak out on him.

He began to speak softly. "Mark, I'm an American. My name is Tom Norris."

Clark didn't trust his own ears. In his deteriorating mental state, he thought the NVA had tracked him. "Oh good Lord," he said to himself, "how did they find out my name? What have I done now?" The airman pushed himself away from the bank and began edging along the back of the sampan.

He heard his name called again. This time something registered. *It's an American*, he thought.

Norris swam closer, talking all the while. He said that he knew Clark had spent time in Idaho and that the code word for the river they were in was the Snake, which was also a river in Idaho. Then he said, "I'm here to take you home."

Norris was by now within a few yards of Clark. The airman's eyes swiveled to stare at him. Norris took off his hat so the American could see his white skin and round eyes. He swam up to Clark, talking softly. When he finally got close enough, he could see the relief in the man's face. Clark's lips broke into a smile.

Just then, one of the Vietnamese SEALs came sliding down the bank out of the brush. Clark's eyes went wide and he snapped his head toward the man. "No, no, no, he's with me," Norris said quickly. Clark visibly relaxed. Norris came around the sampan and began explaining what the plan was, talking in an even voice.

They weren't safe yet. There were enemy patrols and outposts from here to the bunker. Norris told Clark to follow behind him in the river and do exactly what he did: "If I drop, you drop; if I turn, you turn." Norris was impressed by the airman. Despite being exhausted and chilled to the bone, Clark was composed.

Norris got on the radio and alerted Andersen that he had the first survivor and that he was headed toward the bunker. He didn't want the South Vietnamese rangers to mistake them for enemy and shoot at them when they emerged from the water.

The men began swimming downriver. Norris could hear the NVA moving on either bank, but minute after minute passed and they slipped by in the dark water. Clark swam adequately and they made good time.

The pale gray of the French bunker appeared on the south bank. The South Vietnamese commandos called out quietly to the rangers hidden in the brush. When the rangers responded, Norris headed toward the bunker. He pulled himself up on the bank and saw the sea commandos helping Clark out of the water. Together, the exhausted men trudged up the hill and into the bunker. There they found Andersen waiting.

The Marine took charge, checking Clark for wounds and getting some chow into him. Knowing they would soon go after Hambleton, Norris and the commandos stretched out and tried to get some sleep. Andersen had called for an armored personnel carrier to take Clark to the rear, and soon it came clanking up the road.

Andersen escorted Clark to the APC. The Marine officer never recorded his feelings at that moment, but he must have been thrilled. After so many disappointments, the Division had accomplished — at least once — what they'd set out to do six years before.

The vehicle moved off and Andersen found Norris. He asked him what had happened out there. *How far did you go upriver? How did you end up missing Clark?* "Knowing his position on our working area," Norris said, "I did not tell him how far we went that night or about the enemy patrols we encountered." Essentially, he lied so that he'd have a chance at Hambleton.

Resting on the stretcher, Clark was grateful to be alive. He realized now that Norris and the South Vietnamese commandos had come upriver in the darkness, into terrain crowded with the enemy, to save his life. He found this remarkable. "*I* wouldn't have gone in there after me," he thought to himself.

25

PLACES LIKE THE MOON

THAT MORNING, miles to the north of the downed airmen, Bill Henderson was marching toward Hanoi. He would cover ten miles on the trails, and then the guards would lock him up at night with shackles on his feet as he sweltered in the 100 percent humidity.

His captors had turned out to be a bunch of teenagers who'd treated him fairly well, even offering him a Vietnamese cigarette after confiscating the pack of Winstons they found in his pocket. "It was good for me," said Henderson, "because they weren't some ideological assholes." The young soldiers had treated his chest wound with sulfa powder and put a dressing over it. The cuts on his face were beginning to heal.

A day after his shootdown, he'd been brought in front of a rather plump NVA major, more menacing than the teens who'd captured him. "I'm going to ask you some questions," the major said, "and you're going to answer them." The man asked Henderson his name, rank, and serial number. "I gave him that. They published this shit in *Stars and Stripes.*"

The major continued. "What plane were you flying."

"I'm not going to tell you that," Henderson said.

"If you don't tell me, I'm going to kill you."

Henderson didn't have to think about it. "I'm not going to tell you that," he said again.

The major studied Henderson for a minute, then walked away. His guards grabbed the American and led him off.

As the pilot walked north, he was astonished by evidence of a massive invasion force. "There were millions of NVA out there. There were SAM missile launchers being dragged down southward. The B-52s would come in and blow the shit out of them." The hospitals he passed, if you could call them hospitals — they were really just forward aid stations with the most basic supplies — were packed with badly wounded men lying in a stupor. But the tidal rush of olive-clad humanity continued unabated.

Henderson was now seeing up-close the people, the houses, and the fields he'd bombed for months without much of a second thought. The countryside was ripped up with bomb craters. One NVA officer, Nguyen Quy Hai, was commanding a battalion in the sector. "There were lots of bombs," Hai recalled. "After they fell, I could see human thighs hanging in the trees. There were bodies that had been hit and had exploded." Hai didn't feel hatred toward the American soldiers; he didn't feel anything toward them. That emotion was a self-indulgence. "We were running out of food, bullets, clothes, everything," he said. "I had no time or energy to think about the Americans."

The North Vietnamese photographer Doan Cong Tinh was shooting pictures of the invasion and the airstrikes. "After the bombs fell, some soldiers died, some were injured," Doan said. "The towns became places like the moon. The houses were gone." Another NVA soldier witnessed the attacks and what came after; it was hard not to. "When we walked," he said, "our feet would be covered in blood." It was for this reason that people in the North had a saying about their soldiers' fate: "Go south," it went, "and die."

Nguyen Thi Uong, a twenty-five-year-old local, could hear the American bombers and fighters flying over her village nightly. "There were many bombs," she remembered. "After the planes left, the inhabitants of the villages would come out and bury the dead. And then we would visit with the dead ones' families." If the bodies weren't buried quickly, the dogs would eat them. Hunger roamed the countryside, afflicting every living thing. "We had no food to eat," Uong recalled. The villagers had strong feelings toward the pilots who flew the planes. "If we fought them, why would we not hate them?" she said. "Yes, we hated them. If we couldn't capture the downed airmen, we killed them."

Now among the enemy, Henderson didn't have an *oh-my-God-what-have-we-done* moment. He reacted like a soldier. He didn't hate the Vietnamese, but he didn't apologize for what was happening either. "It was the price of war," he said. "You lock into survival mode. I'd been trained to deal with this." Weren't the NVA shooting at American planes? Wasn't that battle?

After about four days — he'd lost track of the exact time — his guards loaded him into a transport and he continued his journey toward Hanoi. One afternoon, the driver pulled up at an Army barracks. Henderson was taken out of the back and marched into the building. He found himself in an officers' mess, where his guard pushed him into a seat. He waited. Eventually an older NVA colonel came in and sat across from him. Henderson realized that they were waiting for the man's underlings to serve them tea.

Henderson was expecting another interrogation: What were you flying? What were your orders? Stuff he'd already refused to answer. But the colonel wasn't interested in those things.

Once the tea had been served, the colonel looked at the pilot. Then he asked a single question: "Why are you here?"

Henderson stared at the man. He found himself at a loss for words. The Vietnamese colonel had grown up with war, first with the French, now with the Americans, and he was apparently seeking the reason why this had been his fate. *Why are you here?*

It occurred to Henderson that he didn't have a good answer. "I had no fucking clue," he said. "I was there because I was told to go there because I signed up because I needed a job." But how do you tell this to an enemy colonel who has probably watched hundreds of his men die from American bombs? How do you convey that your presence in Vietnam didn't spring from some personal crusade against communism or the deep belief that East Asia must remain free from Soviet influence but was a result of the lack of jobs for Dartmouth music majors in 1968? That is, that there was no personal reason worth speaking of?

Henderson sought for the words that would convey this truth to the Vietnamese officer. "My government said I should be here to do these things," he said finally. "I don't know why."

The colonel regarded Henderson for a moment. Then he dropped his eyes and shook his head slowly. He got up and left the room.

José Astorga, the door gunner from the Blueghost 39 chopper, was also on his way north. He'd been handed over to the North Vietnamese and was transported by truck and then by canoe, a bamboo splint on his broken leg. His clothes were filthy and he was weak, having lost a lot of blood in the crash. He had a high fever and was vomiting frequently. Soldiers would come up to him and slap him around, just venting their anger. At one point, the VC turned him over to regular soldiers. "They took me to a village and decided to execute me."

"OK, go ahead," he told them. But this wasn't defiance, as it had been with Henderson.

The soldier brought up his rifle and pointed it at the American's chest, but just then an officer spotted what was happening. He quickly walked over to the soldier and told him to stop. The soldier lowered his rifle and the officer took Astorga to a hut in the village. He left him outside while all the soldiers went in to decide his fate. When they came out, the officer said, "We decided to let you live." Most likely, the North Vietnamese were simply playing with his mind.

Something inside Astorga had broken. The unrelenting pain and the certainty of his own death had unnerved him. José Astorga was ready to die. "Go ahead and shoot me," he told the man. The officer must have been startled by this; there were very few American prisoners who asked to be killed. He ignored Astorga's request, and his escorts grabbed their prisoner and ordered him to resume marching.

Later on, somewhere in North Vietnam, Astorga and his keepers were on the road. After hours of marching, they arrived at some kind of junction and Astorga saw a thin white man standing up in a bamboo cage. It was Bill Henderson. The Vietnamese told Astorga not to talk to the captured pilot, but the two exchanged names and spoke briefly.

He made it to a camp near Hanoi, where a doctor put a cast on his leg. He was kept in solitary for a month. Astorga had survived, but he'd been changed.

26

ZEROED IN

Hambleton spent the morning of April 11 studying his surroundings. The sun was beginning to light up the eastern sky and he could make out the basic features of the landscape around him. The river flowed past steep embankments on either side. West, the way he'd just come, there were trees and bushes lining the top of the slope. To the north there was thick foliage.

There was no way in hell he was making it back up that embankment, so he headed toward the foliage. When he'd found a good spot, he began to dig a hole. Once it was completed, he gathered some leaves around him and pulled them over his body. He was hungry, but the bananas he'd passed coming in were green and inedible. And why was he thinking of bananas when in a matter of hours he'd be feasting on sirloin and French fries?

A sense of well-being came over him. He'd made it through. Snug as a bug. He'd had to kill a human being to make it here, and the memory of it horrified him, but he'd survived. He didn't think to himself at that moment that he'd proved his father wrong and achieved something so unlikely and bitterly won that it would make his brother Gil's wartime heroics seem almost routine. Instead, Hambleton was flooded with a sense of gratitude—specifically, toward Jesus, or "the Boy," as Hambleton called him. "I found myself thanking the Boy for all of His help.

I was . . . thoroughly convinced it was because of [Him] that I wasn't lying in one of those rice paddies on the other side of the village, bleeding to death."

He couldn't keep his eyes open and fell into a light sleep. On and off that afternoon, he would drop off, then come awake with a startled jerk of the head. On waking up the second or third time, he heard voices. He turned his head and tried to locate the source, but it could have been coming from either embankment.

When Tommy Norris awoke on the morning of the eleventh, he stepped outside the bunker. Daylight shone down on the top of the bluff and he could see the South Vietnamese rangers relaxing. They were playing cards and cooking some food. The sound of laughter and meat sizzling on the campfires floated over the forward base toward the river.

Andersen was on the radio, prepping the rescue of Hambleton. He called in airstrikes along the river, hoping to clear out any guns that might spot the navigator coming down. As he spoke to the FACs, the Marine officer learned that a convoy of Soviet tanks was approaching the Cam Lo bridge; he ordered it taken out. Fast movers came sweeping in and dove on the column, destroying three tanks and leaving a number of transport vehicles with smoke billowing from their burning frames. The fewer assets the North Vietnamese had on the river, the better it would be.

Norris heard a sound in the distance: the cough of an artillery gun. He froze. The shell came in long, arcing over the bluff and hitting harmlessly about a hundred yards to the west. After it had exploded, Norris looked around, a feeling of anxiety growing inside him. The rangers had barely looked up. They were goofing around, snacking on their freshly cooked treats, and generally having a good time. Nobody was scurrying for cover or even glancing up at the sky. The men were acting like they were on R&R in Thailand or something, not sitting across the front line from a large contingent of enemy.

Norris caught the eye of the South Vietnamese lieutenant, Tho. "We've got big trouble," he said. He began running around, trying to corral the South Vietnamese soldiers into the bunker and under their tanks. "You're going to get hit hard!" Norris screamed at the men. Andersen came out of the bunker to help. Then, the whistle of more rounds in the air, followed by B-40 rockets and mortars.

Shells hit yards away from the bunker. Norris saw bright flashes and men twisting in midair. He raced to them, now lying prone, some dead, some grievously wounded. Body parts were scattered on the ground; blood mixed in with the mud and grass. The unhurt rangers were panicking; Andersen thought they were going to break and run. Amidst the whistling of the shells, the Marine called out in Vietnamese that he would shoot anyone who deserted the outpost.

Norris grabbed survivors by their shirts and shoved them under the tanks and inside the bunker. He screamed at the gunners to get in their tanks and open up on the enemy positions across the river. As more rounds thudded into the hill, he ran from body to body, leaving the dead and pulling the wounded to the bunker. Once they were all inside, he began doing triage. Some of the men had been hit by shrapnel and were bleeding badly.

The NVA were zeroed in. The rounds slammed into the earth, shell after shell, sending sprays of mud and shrapnel spinning through the base. Norris emerged from the bunker holding the radio, trying to call in airstrikes. The South Vietnamese lieutenant was standing next to him. Norris was talking to the Air Force when he felt something, a slight displacement of air, a sixth sense that told him a round was about to fall. Before he could move, the shell hit yards away and the man next to him immediately cried out and dropped to the ground. Norris put down the radio and bent over him. "A big piece of shrapnel went through his right arm and tore it to pieces," he said. The American grabbed the lieutenant, dragging him into the bunker. Once inside, as the concussions rocked the concrete structure, Norris filled a needle with morphine and injected it into the man. He started bandaging up the wound as best he could.

Another Vietnamese soldier appeared at Norris's side. "Lieutenant Colonel Andersen has been hit," he said. The American had been outside trying to coordinate artillery and call in a medevac when a round came in close. Norris ran outside and found the Marine on the ground, unconscious and bleeding from the head. A fragment of steel had penetrated his skull just above the right eye. Norris picked up Andersen and carried him into the bunker. He inspected the officer's wound as more rounds shook the ground in the bunker, but he couldn't remove the shrapnel.

He called for two armored ARVN personnel carriers that were about half a mile away to come in and retrieve the wounded. But the South Vietnamese refused. They wouldn't start out until the bombing stopped. Finally, after ninety minutes, the enemy guns went quiet. Men were moaning and the bunker reeked of blood. Norris got the first APC to the base and the men loaded Andersen and the other injured soldiers in.

His leader was down. Half of the rangers were dead or badly wounded, along with Lieutenant Tho. A frisson of panic jumped from soldier to soldier. Even the normally poised Norris was shaken. "I'm like, 'Oh, man, I am just going to lose it. This is not a good thing.'"

Andersen was taken to another outpost deeper in the rear; from there, he was flown out on a helicopter. Eventually he would arrive at a Saigon hospital, hours away from the forward operating base. But he'd become so obsessed with completing the mission and bringing in Hambleton that he would end up climbing out a hospital window and making his way to Major General Marshall's office, eye patch and all, where he persuaded the commander to lend him his Sabreliner jet to fly him to Da Nang. From there, he planned to hitch a ride back to the French bunker. Someone with higher rank got wind of Andersen's plan and quickly vetoed it. Andersen was out of the battle.

Tho was evacuated out as well, accompanied by his senior enlisted sailor. Around sixteen men—Norris, Kiet, two sea commandos, and "about a dozen very scared Vietnamese rangers"—were all that remained of the rescue team. Those numbers could drop quickly; if the outpost was attacked again, Norris believed the commandos would abandon the mission. On the afternoon of April 11, the odds of getting Hambleton were growing longer.

Meanwhile, the FAC was calling on the radio. When Norris finally picked up, the officer gave him a report on Hambleton. The navigator had missed several of his hourly check-ins. And when he did make his calls, he literally couldn't talk. There was only silence on the other end, alternating with slurred gibberish. "He's not going to make it," the man told Norris. They couldn't wait for Hambleton to swim downriver like Clark.

In the steamy afternoon heat, Norris posted guards to watch for any enemy approach. The tank crews kept near the hulking forms of their vehicles and tried to get some sleep, and the three remaining sea commandos caught a quick nap. Norris was fully tasked with trying to set up the Hambleton rescue. The FAC gave him the airman's estimated location, about two miles upriver. It was much farther away than Clark had been. But they were going to have to go get him.

27

ESTHER WILLIAMS

As NIGHTFALL APPROACHED, Hambleton heard a surge in the sound of a plane's engine. He called in on the radio.

The FAC asked him if he was OK. Hambleton, lying, said yes. "Good, because you gotta make like Esther Williams."

Hambleton's mind was drifting. He repeated the name robotically. *Esther Williams, Esther Williams.* Where had he heard that before?

The FAC repeated the instruction. A long pause. "Not reading you," Hambleton replied. It took more playing around with words and a mention of the Swanee before he thought, *Oh, Esther Williams the swimmer.* The FAC wanted him to get into the river and cross it.

He looked at the river. It was wide, he couldn't tell how wide, maybe two hundred feet across. He felt a surge of gloom. His body was growing colder and weaker. "Oh God, I thought. I'll never be able to make that." He was barely able to walk; how did the Air Force expect him to swim across it? "Then I thought, if I don't, I'm dead."

Other fears surfaced: wildlife, for instance. He knew that Vietnamese rivers were badly polluted, but what kinds of creatures hid under its surface? Bloodsucking fish? Bacteria that would slip into his bloodstream and attack his organs? There was a range of waterborne diseases in-country: hepatitis A, typhoid fever. Some of the mosquitoes carried the pathogens for godawful things: yellow fever, malaria, dengue fever, and Japanese encephalitis, which dropped you into a coma and had a death rate of 30 percent. And then there would be the leeches.

But he had to get across. In the end, he decided he could bear anything except snakes. "I think I despise snakes," he said, "more than anything in the world."

There was still light in the west. He wanted to wait until seven before heading out; the descending darkness would conceal his trip across the river from anyone peering down from the banks.

He heard sounds from above, what sounded like voices "very far away." He crawled out of his hiding place and down to the riverbank, listening. Yes, there were voices, but no sounds of anyone coming through the bushes. He felt a pall of dread settle over him.

The navigator quickly began to go through his survival vest, tossing aside anything he couldn't use. He'd have to get lighter to have a chance at crossing. The first-aid kit chunked to the ground, followed by the Smith & Wesson .38 — too heavy — and other items. He took the radios, which were water-resistant and should be able to survive a trip across the river, flares, the thin mosquito net, which he packed into his pocket, and his survival knife. If the NVA got to him before his rescuers, he knew what to do with it.

Hambleton couldn't leave the items lying on the riverbank; they would be a tip-off to his pursuers that he'd crossed there. He looked up the face of the embankment. Among the rocks he saw the opening of a hole or cave. He crawled up the slope on his hands and knees and pushed the extra gear inside. He covered the items with dirt, then hurried back down.

More noises from above, growing closer. They were coming from both directions now, north and south. Hambleton couldn't wait any longer. He hurried down to the river's edge and waded in. The current was gentle, meandering. That wouldn't be the problem. It was the temperature: the cold seemed to knife through him. After a few steps, the frigid water poured in over the tops of his jungle boots and soaked his socks. He cursed, thinking the boots would weigh him down, and hurried back to the shore, dropped to the ground, and struggled to get the boots off. He left them on the riverbank and, barefoot now, made his way back to the river in the semidarkness.

The water was shallow and he hurried forward. Suddenly, the bottom dropped away and Hambleton plunged into the depths, his head sinking under the surface. He kicked furiously, trying to lift himself higher in the black water. Darkness enveloped him as he thrashed. When his head cleared the surface, he spit out a spray of water and sucked in a breath of air. He'd dropped into some kind of hole carved out of the river bottom. He began swimming.

After progressing only twenty feet, Hambleton realized he could go no farther. Muscle fatigue was cramping his legs and arms. He stopped kicking and found to his surprise that the river had gone shallow again. He was able to stand on the rock-strewn bottom, the water gurgling at armpit level. He started to walk forward, hoping he wouldn't tumble into another hole.

Pain shot up his legs. The rocks he was walking on were uneven and as sharp as blades. They were cutting the soles of his feet. He gasped. There was no way; he couldn't make it across. It had been a mistake to leave his boots. Now he'd have to go back and retrieve them, losing more time and allowing his pursuers to get closer. "You really are a jerk," he said to himself.

Gritting his teeth, Hambleton turned back and began paddling through the water. As he got closer to the shore, he glanced upward at the embankment. There were no unfamiliar shapes against the starlit sky. Wincing with pain, he staggered out of the river, water streaming off his hair, through his beard, and down his flight suit. Where the hell had he left his boots? The darkness was near-total now, and he couldn't pick out any details on the ground near him.

He felt around with his hands and almost immediately touched the toe of a boot. Dumb luck. But there was only one. His hands searched for the other but came up empty. The socks were right next to the pair and he pulled them on, then the single jungle boot. He yanked the zipper up the front. Where was the other one?

He remembered that he'd taken it off near a toppled tree. He turned and spotted a jagged shape in the near distance. He crawled on his hands and knees until he found the exposed roots. Again he began to feel along the ground with his hands. His fingertips touched leather. He pulled the other boot on and zipped it up.

Hambleton hurried to the river's edge and waded in. This time he anticipated the deep hole he'd fallen into and started swimming. Once he was past it, he dropped his feet to the bottom and pushed forward, the water chest-high. He proceeded cautiously, anxious not to fall into another depression in the riverbed.

Time seemed to slow. He couldn't see the far bank and he found no other holes in his way, but still his strength was quickly ebbing in the frigid water. After pushing through the current for what seemed like an hour, he felt the ground rise up under his feet. He was near the shore. He crawled out and lay flat on the muddy bank. He found that he was as limp as a "little girl's rag doll."

The navigator lay there gasping for a few moments until he'd gathered the strength to go on. He crawled toward the bushes he'd spotted from the other side and pushed through. He pulled out his radio and called the FAC. "I just made like Esther Williams," he said. "Now I'll rest for half an hour before turning left." The FAC radioed his approval.

As Hambleton was crossing the river, Norris, Kiet, and the two other sea commandos left the protection of the bunker and headed upstream, with the American walking point, moving ahead fifty yards through the darkened foliage, then stopping to listen. The enemy activity was as heavy as the night before. Not long after leaving the bunker, Norris and the other men heard an NVA unit approaching and slipped into the undergrowth. They spotted the same guard posts on the river that they'd seen on the way to rescue Clark. Moving in short bursts, Norris and the others managed to evade the patrol and made their way slowly upriver. The SEAL wondered about their incredible good fortune in avoiding contact: he theorized that the idea of an American or South Vietnamese squad penetrating this far into such thickly populated terrain was so unlikely that the patrollers weren't looking for them. But he wondered how many times they could traverse the same ground without running into the NVA.

The commandos were thinking the same thing. Norris heard the other two whispering to Kiet. He couldn't tell what they were saying, but their voices were growing more urgent. Norris had a bad feeling. "They wanted to go back," he realized. Finally, one of the commandos spoke up: "I'm not going to follow an American just to rescue another American."

Norris couldn't fault the commandos. It wasn't their brother who was stranded out there; it was his. Even for him, the night journey was eerie. But the young SEAL couldn't tolerate a mutiny in the middle of his mission. He told the commandos that they were all going upriver; it would be safer if they stayed together. The men relented, but Norris knew their patience was nearly gone.

After hours of slipping through the dark countryside, Norris and his squad reached the predetermined spot, half a mile downriver from the Cam Lo bridge. In the pitch black, he could hear trucks moving over the structure. He called the FAC and told him to have Hambleton get into the water so the team could see him. The clouds above had parted; a crescent moon shone down. It was good news. Norris would be able to spot a human figure in the water.

They waited. They could hear North Vietnamese soldiers coughing and moving around on the paths and open areas. Peering at the river, Norris could see only the fretted surface of the water. *Is he too weak to come this far?* Norris wondered. *Or maybe he just stood up where he was and is still obscured by the overhang.* Either way, there was no American visible in the river. He and the team began to scout up and down the northern bank, peering across for telltale signs of the airman.

Hambleton gathered some leaves and covered himself in them. Then he lay on his back. "It seemed all the muscles in my body had been stretched farther than they were meant to be and just couldn't snap back." Everything hurt. He couldn't raise his head without wincing. He couldn't stay awake. He sank into a heavy sleep.

Forty minutes later, he awoke. The FAC told him he still had farther to go. Hambleton warned him he could do only thirty minutes of walking with thirty minutes of rest.

He was in a kind of irritable stupor, the state that old-time Arctic explorers got into in the later stages of malnutrition. "Everything I did became a chore." His body was sluggish, his thoughts disjointed.

He was drifting off to sleep again when he heard more voices. Wincing, he sat up. The voices were coming from the west, and he saw when he looked back upriver figures outlined in the glow of their flashlights. Hambleton stared. "A sickening feeling came over me and I tried not to face the fact that it was just a matter of time before they, too, crossed the river and would find me." If he moved into the water, one of the searchers might spot him, so Hambleton simply looked on as the figures slashed at the undergrowth with their gun butts and wooden sticks. They seemed to be focused on a certain area of the riverbank. Had someone reported seeing a man there? The search went on for twenty minutes before the figures dispersed.

Hambleton pulled himself to his feet and started downriver. The depth of the water was constantly changing, going from knee-deep to over his head in a single step. He was spent and just wanted to lie down. There were trees lining the riverbank, and he stayed under them, grabbing onto the branches and the low-hanging vines to pull himself forward. It was pitch black under the shrubbery. His feet splashed the water as he staggered on, his progress excruciatingly slow. After walking for a few minutes, he took a step and tumbled into a hole in the river bottom. His head sank below the surface as he gasped for breath. Now completely submerged, he thrashed his arms and legs, trying to push himself upward. A few terrifying seconds passed before he finally made it back to the surface.

After thirty minutes of walking, he crawled out of the river and collapsed in a field of grass that came down to the water. He wanted nothing more than to lie there and sleep. But within a minute or two, the sound of voices came floating down to him again; they were coming from the other side of the river now and they were moving closer. Panic fluttered in his chest, but he was too weak and cold to stand up; even crawling was beyond him. How could he make it to the river? Hambleton decided he would have to roll down to the water. He took a breath, gathered his strength, then pushed his left shoulder into the air and toppled over.

His chest smacked into the mud. Hambleton took another breath, then pushed his right shoulder up and repeated the movement. He was rolling in slow motion toward the river.

The FAC came up on the radio, whispering. "You gotta move, you gotta move. It's hot on that side." Hambleton was nauseated with fear. The soldiers seemed to be following him. He stopped moving and his gaze probed the dark bank for his pursuers.

He could hear their sticks striking the branches of the foliage, the leaves crashing together as the unseen men pushed their way through. Hambleton stared at the beams of their flashlights, praying they would stay up on the banks and not dart toward the river.

It went on for fifteen minutes, maybe twenty, as he lay there watching. Then the flashlights moved away. The sound of thrashing slowly faded, then stopped.

He moved toward the water. Just as he was about to wade in, there was a splash. Instinctively, Hambleton reached for his survival knife and peered through the foliage. His heart bumped fast; had his pursuers decided to cross the river after him? As he stared at the inky river, he saw a large hump slowly emerging out of the water. It was round and broad and moving toward him. Hambleton stared at it, then realized it was the shell of a big mud turtle. He let his breath out with a gasp. Adrenaline sped through his veins, causing his body to shake.

Hambleton scurried into the water on his hands and knees, wanting to get away before the searchers returned. In his hurry, his elbow smacked into something solid. His face twisted in pain and his arm went numb. He ducked his head, trying not to cry out. Once the feeling in his arm returned, he felt along the riverbed to see what he'd hit. It was a long, thick rectangular piece of wood. As he felt along its surface, Hambleton could sense that it had been cut from a log. It was about nine feet long. It could be only one thing: a railroad tie.

Here's the answer to my exhaustion, thought Hambleton. If he could dig it out of the riverbed and float it, he could hang on and move faster down the river. He began to shove the tie, pulling it this way and that, trying to dislodge it from the mud. After a minute or two of agonizing effort, one end lifted up from the riverbed with a sucking sound and popped above the surface. Hambleton was holding on to the other end. He draped his arm over the wood and pushed into the water. The tie took much of the burden off his body. "Joyous relief came over me."

Norris was frustrated. An hour went by. Nothing. He listened to the FAC talking to Hambleton on the radio, asking for his location. Hambleton's answers were bewildering; Norris couldn't make heads or tails of them. Was he even speaking English? An hour passed without a trace of the airman, then another. The team was moving through the foliage, pulling back the vines on the shoreline, looking for signs of him. As they searched, they spotted several encampments of enemy companies and heard vehicles coming and going over the bridge.

He could tell from the commandos' body language that they were growing more anxious. Dawn was getting closer and they were far from their base. Finally, Norris signaled Kiet that they would head back. He was bitterly disappointed not to have found Hambleton. How many times could they come into the NVA's sector and not get hit? What would they do if Hambleton couldn't move?

The team began its slow journey back to the bunker.

Hambleton's progress was pitiful. He was still holding to the thirty minutes of travel and thirty minutes of rest, but he could stagger only a few feet at a time. The darkness made progress more difficult. He would occasionally trip on an underwater vine, and branches kept smacking him in the face as he stumbled blindly forward. But the log took the pressure off his legs, and he was able to last longer in the water than he would have without it. When he gripped the wood, his hands came away covered in sooty ash. Something had burned one end of the tie. He wondered if it was part of a railroad bridge that had been hit by an American bomb, sending the burning wood into the river.

The first streaks of daylight appeared; it was now the morning of the twelfth. He had been on the run for ten days, with little rest and barely anything to eat or drink. Hambleton began searching the shoreline for a place to hide. There. A thickly wooded patch of foliage a short distance from the river. He dropped his feet to the rocks and pulled the tie out of the water, slowly hauling it up onshore so it would appear to anyone passing by that it had washed up on its own. He crawled into the brush. Once inside, he searched for fruit or nuts, anything to sustain him, but found nothing. Farther on past the bushes, however, he saw a hill and at the top of it the leaves of several banana trees. He thought that once he regained a little strength, he would climb up and see if any of the bananas were edible.

He pulled out his radio and called in. The FAC asked him to pinpoint his location. They would try the same triangulation process they'd used the day before. The FAC warned Hambleton that there were enemy in the area and to stay concealed.

Once the FAC had his approximate location, Hambleton went to sleep inside the thicket. Around ninety minutes later, he woke. He could hear the sound of the FAC's plane above. He checked in on the radio. There was a message for him: a plane was going to attempt to drop him another survival package. "Someone will be by shortly."

The navigator had hoped that his rescuers were close, but he needed food, and so he waited impatiently for the Madden package. He could hear birds chirping in the trees above, but no sounds of voices or dogs or chickens, no sign of a village nearby. At around 4 p.m., he heard the drone of an approaching aircraft engine, deeper than the buzzing of the FAC. It sounded to him like an A-1. He watched the blue patch of sky through the branches and spotted the plane as it zoomed past, a package under one wing.

The pilot called him on the radio, asking if he was on line with his position. Hambleton confirmed. "OK. We will back off and do it again. Keep your eyes peeled."

The plane disappeared, the sound dying off, and then fifteen minutes later it was back. Hambleton watched its approach and saw the package drop away from the wing. It was falling straight for his hiding place, and for a few seconds Hambleton thought it might actually crash right into him, but it sailed overhead and *pock*ed into one of the banana trees on the embankment above. He would wait until darkness fell, then go hunting for it.

He took stock of his physical state. "My hair was matted, my beard was long, the reading glasses — smudged and water-spotted — covered very tired eyes and a very dirty, soggy flying suit hung loosely over my thin body." His shoulder was still throbbing with pain. His smell was funky and powerful. He felt a twinge from his lower leg. He pulled up the leg zipper on the suit. There on his calf was a blood-colored leech. He could feel its tiny, razor-sharp teeth embedding themselves in his flesh.

Hambleton gripped the slimy thing between his fingers and slowly pulled it off, then threw its body into the bushes. His first-aid kit was back at the place where he'd entered the river, so he squeezed the wound, letting fresh blood wash through the teeth marks. Then he dried it with his handkerchief and zipped the flight suit back up.

His belly was racked with diarrhea. He unzipped and urinated into the bushes, but the cramping pains soon returned. It had to be the river water he'd drunk; the bacteria were beginning to work on him. He was going to lose water more quickly, along with any nutrients he managed to consume.

As the minutes ticked by, Hambleton drifted in and out of consciousness. He thought obsessively of the food and fresh radio batteries waiting for him a short walk away. After thirty minutes, he'd convinced himself that the heavily wooded embankment would hide him from the eyes of his pursuers. He decided to try to climb it.

In a daze, Hambleton pushed himself upright and staggered over to the foot of the embankment. But as soon as the incline increased, he found he was weaker than he thought. The ground sloped at a forty-five-degree angle. Hambleton snatched at vines and roots and tried to pull himself along, but his thigh muscles were in agony and he fell back. He tried again and made it almost halfway up the slope before his legs went numb. He lost his footing and rolled back down to the bottom in a spray of dirt.

Hambleton sat on the ground and thought. "My fifty-three-year-old legs just wouldn't get me up the damn hill." He was clearly too weak to force his way up the incline in a straight line. But what if he attempted to cut angles into the hillside, as if he were climbing the side of a pyramid? He got up and began walking sideways to the hillside, crabbing up at a gentle angle before reversing course and doing the same thing on the way back. His legs were able to stand the strain, and after an hour he collapsed at the top of the hill, thoroughly spent.

The navigator lay on the ground for a few minutes before gaining the strength to lift his head and look around. He expected to see the box sitting in the middle of neat rows of banana trees, but to his dismay the terrain looked very different. The ground was strewn with broken bits of machinery, what looked like pieces of airplanes and dented fuel tanks. Clearly, some plane had come angling down and crashed here, spraying parts across the hilltop. For a moment he thought he was looking at the wreckage of Bat 21. Could it be that the bodies of Bolte and his other crewmates were close by, lying among the engines and the twisted aluminum?

His mind was fixated on the care package. He had to find it. He crisscrossed the area again and again, searching for the shape of the box in the fading light. Even when darkness fell, he staggered across the hilltop, hoping that by some godforsaken chance he would topple right over the thing. But eventually his spirits flagged and he admitted to himself the obvious: the package had overshot the hilltop and was lying somewhere in the distance. He would not find it that night.

Disappointed and freshly exhausted, he stumbled down the hill to his hiding spot. When he reached the shrubbery, he dropped to the ground. "I settled into my hole and felt in despair over all that energy, all those hours, and nothing."

He called in to the FAC to report his failure. "No luck," he remembered telling the man. "I couldn't find it. Should I stay tonight and try tomorrow?"

The FAC immediately vetoed that idea. "No, keep moving. Above all, don't go back. We want you back on the Swanee tonight." Hambleton couldn't understand his insistence but was too tired to argue. He would switch to his spare radio. He would get back in the water tonight.

The FAC's memories of that night conflict sharply with Hambleton's. The pilot later reported that Hambleton had been much too weak to move very far on the afternoon of the twelfth and that he'd never gone to look for the Madden pack. The evidence supports the FAC's version of things; he was tracking Hambleton's movements carefully that night, and he wasn't delusional from lack of sleep, food, and water.

Hambleton remembered each part of the climb vividly: the zigzagging up the slope, the small bushes he grabbed to pull himself up, the "debris of mashed metal . . . and damaged fuel tanks" that cluttered the top of the embankment. But how could he believe that he'd actually climbed an embankment with a forty-five-degree slope when much of the time he was unable simply to walk along the riverbank without collapsing? Most likely, the whole episode was an elaborate apparition that unfolded behind his closed eyes while he lay half-conscious on the bank, the wreckage of the plane something his nutrient-starved brain had created out of his memories of the shootdown and his dread of what had happened to his fellow airmen. You could go further: perhaps a bout of repressed survivor's guilt impelled Hambleton to visualize the EB-66C's crash site, which doubled as a tomb for Major Bolte and the others, and he remembered it as an actual discovery.

Certainly his hallucinations were becoming more frequent and more true to life. Without the navigator realizing it, he'd slipped into a new phase, one in which reality and various phantom realities exchanged places seamlessly.

28

"SOME KIND OF RESCUE"

THAT MORNING, back at the bunker, Norris sensed a change in the two sea commandos' moods. They were brooding. He guessed, just by their body language, that their doubts about chasing after an American had only strengthened overnight. Norris was already thinking that he might have to go out alone.

As they ate, the crump of mortars sounded again from over the river. The men scurried into the bunker and dove under the tanks; they watched the geysers of mud as the shells struck. No one was hit, but the attack further unnerved the commandos. Another round of mortars followed. Norris got on the radio and, minutes later, American fast movers swept in and smoke bloomed up from the opposite bank.

It was hot and muggy. Norris was walking around half-naked with just a shirt and his boots on. His jeans were hanging on a branch, drying. He called the FAC and they talked about Hambleton's condition, which was worsening, if that was even possible. What if they found him and the guy was unable to walk out? Marching two miles through enemy terrain with an incapacitated, wildly delusional airman was not an appealing thought.

In their two forays upriver, Norris had come to trust the commando with the wrathful expression, Nguyen Van Kiet. Now the two of them brainstormed about what to do with Hambleton. The night before, Norris had spotted a number of sampans, moored along the river banks. What if they grabbed one and used it to smuggle the American out? It would be easier than carrying the navigator on their backs.

The two men agreed the idea had potential. If they went with a sampan, Norris would need oars. He got on the radio, called Da Nang, and ordered a set of XRV12 paddles, which are usually used for Army rubber boats. "You want *what*?" the officer on the other end said. Norris repeated the request, and finally the man understood. He promised to get them to Norris posthaste.

That afternoon, the FAC continued to loop around Hambleton's position. Every so often he would turn the plane and look down, studying the terrain for any sign of NVA troops. He saw none, leveled off, and continued his circuit. A moment later, he turned back and angled the wing down again, glancing at the ground below.

He spotted something down there, a human figure. The startled pilot turned the plane for a better look and realized with a jolt that it was Gene Hambleton, standing in the middle of a sandbar and waving at the plane with a white handkerchief.

The FAC was horrified. Hambleton had exposed himself in broad daylight to any enemy who happened to be in the vicinity. What the fuck was he doing?

He thumbed the radio transmit button. "Bat 21 Bravo!"

The FAC could see the figure bring the radio up to his mouth. "Roger," the voice said.

"You goddamn dummy," the FAC shouted. "Get back in the wilderness!"

The figure below paused, then turned and lurched toward the bushes. Within ten seconds, the navigator was no longer visible to the naked eye.

The FAC was now beyond concerned. Had Hambleton even been aware that he'd done it? (The navigator wouldn't mention the incident in his memoirs.) Did Hambleton have any mental reserves left, or was he going to start wandering across the countryside like some escaped mental patient? His psychological state was obviously deteriorating at a rapid clip. What if he started looking for his pursuers, blundering into North Vietnamese villages and calling out for help?

The FAC raised Norris on the radio. He explained what he'd seen, then added, "This guy is losing it." Norris absorbed the news. It was increasingly clear that Hambleton wasn't going to last much longer on his own.

Norris spent the afternoon getting ready for that night's mission, seeing that the commandos had something to eat and that they cleaned their guns before nightfall. The hours passed quickly. As he organized the men, the armored personnel carrier arrived, bringing the paddles he'd requested, along with some medical supplies for Hambleton. Norris didn't pay much attention as the hulking vehicle pulled up and the metal door swung open. But soon afterward he heard voices shouting behind him. The SEAL turned and saw a white man striding toward him past a group of startled rangers. This in and of itself wouldn't have been that unusual — the guy could have been some back-office prick from Da Nang or something — but the man was carrying in his hand not an AK-47 or an M16 but a microphone with a fuzzy knob-headed top to it. And behind the microphone guy, an assistant was setting up a large television camera on a tripod in the mud next to one of the tanks. It looked like the two of them were getting ready to cover the local commissioners' meeting back in Silver Spring, or do the seven-day forecast.

Norris was struck dumb for a moment. After he'd recovered, he called out to the approaching man, "What are you doing here?" The man stopped. He said that he was an American reporter and he'd heard there was "some kind of rescue going on" and he was here to cover it.

Norris's mind reeled. *Cover* his rescue? What did that mean? The SEAL had no inkling that news about Hambleton and the beleaguered mission to save him had spread like wildfire through the camps and bases of Southeast Asia, or that Hambleton had become a kind of folk hero to thousands of American airmen. Now it was about to become world news. What Norris *did* realize was that if a major television network broadcast any kind of a report, the situation could quickly get out of hand. The North Vietnamese, who were surprisingly media savvy, would be eager to deny the Americans a heroic victory. They could train their guns on this lonely hilltop and wipe out his little band of commandos. They could send units to the river to capture or kill Hambleton. They could do any number of other things that Norris didn't even wish to think about at the moment.

Not only that, the broadcast would reveal Norris's plan. It would reveal his *location*. It would, in fact, be an utter shitstorm that would beggar all description.

The SEAL found his voice. "The heck you are," he shouted to the man. (Norris later swore that he didn't resort to using a vulgarity even in this situation.) "I want you back in that APC and I want you out of here *now*."

The reporter didn't budge. He was clearly no newcomer to Vietnam and had probably faced down his share of spit-flecking military types. "We have clearance to be here," he said. Meanwhile, his assistant kept working on the camera, looking through the viewfinder and slowly adjusting the focus. Norris felt an explosive mix of rage and disbelief rise up from his inner core. This was a secret, classified operation with the lives of many Americans and South Vietnamese on the line. Did the press not know the meaning of "secret" or "classified"? What bizarro, upside-down world had he stepped into that morning that some journalist thought he could just saunter up to a hot front line and interview a Navy SEAL about a rescue *that hadn't even happened yet*?

Norris walked over to where his AK-47 was propped against the bunker and grabbed the stock. He whipped the rifle up and jacked a shell into the chamber, then turned and pointed the muzzle at the reporter. He was so blind angry by that point that he later forgot what exact words came out of his mouth, but the man listened, looked at the gun in the hands of the rage-filled, half-naked SEAL, quickly turned around, gestured to his assistant, ran for the APC, and, after his partner was aboard with the camera and the tripod, closed the door. The APC moved off up the hill and Norris put down his rifle.

As dusk fell, Norris was getting his gear ready for the journey when he saw Kiet approaching. The commando squatted next to him. The other two Vietnamese commandos were refusing to go out that night, he told Norris. "They said it was too dangerous and that it was not worth risking their lives again to save one American," Kiet said. "They have lost their fighting spirit."

Norris could hardly blame them. "Each time you go," he said, "it's harder and harder to do it again." The larger irony didn't register with him particularly. During the early days of the red fiery summer, the Americans had pulled their planes and artillery away from the South Vietnamese in order to save Hambleton; now the South Vietnamese commandos were pulling themselves off the Hambleton mission in order to save themselves. There was a bitter symmetry to it.

Norris accepted the mutiny as a fait accompli. He told Kiet he would be heading out alone that night. Kiet was to stay at the base with the other commandos and keep watch on the river, ready to help him when he returned the next morning, he hoped, with Hambleton.

Kiet shook his head. "No, *Dai Uy,* I'm going with you."

Norris was struck by the offer, but he thought the Vietnamese sailor was underestimating the odds of disaster. "Look, Kiet," he said, "this might be a one-way trip. We might not be coming back."

Kiet said, "If you go, *Dai Uy,* I go."

Hambleton had been asleep for hours. It was noon before he came awake. All he could hear was the low burble of the flowing water. The sun was up and the day was growing hotter, but his body wasn't absorbing the heat. "I was weak and exhausted," he said. "I looked at my skin and I was beginning to look like a wrinkled prune. My feet were cold as ice and I had no feeling in them." His weight was down to 125 pounds; with his six-foot-two frame, he looked emaciated.

He wanted to move. He called the orbiting FAC and said he was going into the river.

"Stay there until dark," the voice told him. But Hambleton couldn't quell the rising panic he felt. Except for the man he'd killed, he'd run into no Vietnamese for the last ten days. He'd been extraordinarily lucky, and he had the feeling that luck was going to run out today. He felt shaky and kept checking in with the FAC, just to hear a human voice.

At around 6:30 that night, Hambleton decided he was getting into the water. Walking was out of the question; he lacked the energy even to get to his feet. He couldn't manage to crawl, so again he thought he would roll down the bank to the water. The incline gave him a bit of momentum and he pushed himself over and starting tumbling, his shoulders smacking into the earth. After five or six turns, he made it to the bank. He found the railroad tie and got behind it, grunting as he shoved it ahead.

His body felt feeble and shaky. He could no longer walk unaided; for every step he took, he had to reach out and grab a vine or a root and pull himself forward. He couldn't make the same time. And he was beginning to realize now just how disjointed and bizarre his thoughts were becoming. A few feet ahead of him, at the other end of the railroad tie, Gwen appeared, perched daintily as though she were sitting on a park bench. He was grateful to see her and started talking, just saying whatever nonsense came into his head. The substance of the conversation drifted away from him; he couldn't hold it in his mind. But he enjoyed the conversation immensely. It was as if they were sitting together on the couch in Tucson talking about a dinner they were planning for some friends. It was so good to see her.

An instant later, he was staring at the blackened end of the wooden tie. He shook his head. He had to stay focused. But his thoughts slipped out of his grasp again and went scurrying into the darkness. He would make a decision — to turn the tie closer to the bank or to move his arm higher on the wood — and five or ten minutes later would realize that he was walking along, having completely forgotten to follow through with the idea. He told himself he would break off walking after thirty minutes, but an hour later found that he was still marching through the water like an automaton.

He had to get some rest. He paddled toward the shoreline and pushed the tie onto the bank. He found a patch of vegetation to collapse under. Before he dropped away into sleep, he called the FAC.

The man's voice was excited. "Your buddy is now in the clubhouse," he said.

Hambleton, his mind foggy, couldn't understand what he was talking about. What buddy? What clubhouse? Then it came to him. Clark. He had landed near the river; he had been the first to be rescued. The clubhouse must be a base hospital or somewhere secure.

Hambleton mumbled a reply. He thought to himself, *I'm next.*

He slept for a bit, then waded back out into the river, holding on to the railroad tie. In the moonlight, he passed under a bridge that had been blown apart by a bomb. He watched the banks in case he spotted an American face.

In the cockpit of the O-2 orbiting above, the FAC called, "Bat 21 Bravo, Bat 21 Bravo, come in." There was no answer. When Hambleton did key down the transmit button, what swam into the FAC's earphones were groans and nonsense words. The FAC asked him repeatedly about landmarks he'd seen, trying to get an exact fix on his position. But again and again, either Hambleton was silent or there would be a string of sentences that had nothing to do with the question. Only rarely was he coherent.

The navigator was fading in and out of consciousness. The rescuers began to worry that Hambleton might pass out for good along the riverbank. If he was well hidden and they didn't get to him soon, he could slip into unconsciousness and die of exposure or dehydration.

29

THE SAMPAN

AFTER A FEW HOURS of agonizingly slow progress, Hambleton could hardly pull himself along. His arms were old ropes. He stumbled on, feeling drunk with tiredness. An image of the Mieu Giang did register faintly in his brain; it was lovely in the fading light, "like a smooth but cloudy mirror."

The navigator saw something slipping over the surface of the water toward him. *Jesus Christ, a snake.* His heart pounded painfully in his chest as he watched the thing slither toward him, leaving a dark trail in the water. In his panic, it looked to be fifty or sixty feet long. It was the biggest one he'd ever seen.

He couldn't draw attention to himself. Maybe it would just move on past him. Hambleton watched the snake fearfully, "wondering what I would do when we were eyeball to eyeball." Finally, he couldn't stand it any longer. He slapped his hand on the surface of the water. The snake immediately veered away. As he watched it go, Hambleton spotted a second one coming at him from behind. He hit the water again and the thing darted away.

Had they been apparitions, creatures from deep in his subconscious? He couldn't be sure, but he was shaken. Had he entered some kind of breeding ground for the goddamn things? Was he going to have to fight snakes all the way to his rescue team? He couldn't bear to think of it.

In his rare moments of lucidity, Hambleton was increasingly anxious. "A fear came over me that maybe they didn't know where I was . . . Maybe they had misunderstood some of my directions." He obsessed over the idea that they were looking in a completely different section of the river from where he actually was. "Frantically," he called the FAC and asked if he was absolutely positive the rescue team knew where he was.

"Everything is fine," the voice told him.

Hambleton asked how he would be able to identify his rescuers.

The FAC told him to call out with his rank—lieutenant colonel—and his favorite color. If the individuals responded with a different color, it was his rescue team.

He couldn't feel anything below his knees. He had to stop. Hambleton pushed to the shore and found a place underneath the tree cover. He looked down. The skin on his hands was pushed into pale ridges from being in the water; they were the color of a fish belly. But his feet were in worse shape, completely without sensation. He took off his boots and socks and tried to massage some life into them, but he had little strength left. Exhaustion was lapping at his mind like a tide. He sprawled back on the ground and fell asleep instantly.

Thick clouds covered the moon that night as Norris and Kiet, disguised as local villagers in long dark shirts, slipped down to the riverbank. They began walking upriver, following the wandering course of the Mieu Giang to an abandoned village they'd spotted the night before. When they reached the outskirts, they squatted down and studied the huts. Everything was dark; there were no fires burning, no flashlights, no movement at all.

Convinced the huts were empty, the two men waded into the water and felt under the surface until they found a bunch of sampans that had been intentionally sunk in the river. (The villagers did this so the canoes' reeds wouldn't dry out.) After pulling up several of the boats, they finally found one that looked to be in good shape. They hauled it out of the river and dumped the water out. Then they got in one by one with their paddles and laid in the radio, medical supplies, canteens, compass, and AK-47s, along with extra ammo cartridges.

The men sat cross-legged on the bottom of the boat and began paddling toward a thatch of thick vines hanging over the riverbank. They swept under the foliage, then pushed ahead, their paddles making small splashing noises. As the pair pulled the oars through the water, they were looking ahead for the next section of brush; they crossed the river several times to take advantage of the overhang.

Enemy soldiers were walking along both banks, scanning the shore and the nearby fields. Norris saw others talking, cooking, and relaxing. No one stopped the boat or called for it to stop; at a glance, they would look like villagers returning home after a long day of fishing.

The problem of the split river reappeared. There were channels cut into the Mieu Giang, separated by sandbars, and it was difficult to tell in the darkness which one was the main tributary. At one point, the two men struck out on a broad stretch of river but soon found they'd chosen badly. It brought them only to a leafy shore; there was no way forward. Hidden underneath a bunch of the foliage, Norris pulled out his map and studied it by penlight, the circle of white shining on the rubber. Then he got on the radio and asked the FAC to find them and tell them where to go. When he was confident he knew where they were headed, the two men moved out again.

An hour into the journey, Norris and Kiet found themselves enveloped in mist. A fog bank had come sliding down the river. The mist hid them from the patrolling soldiers along both banks, but it confused Norris's sense of his location even further. Again, the pair moved up a branch of the Mieu Giang, only to find themselves stranded. They paddled back and tried another stream and finally hit on the main tributary.

The fog swirled around Norris and Kiet, opening to reveal sudden glimpses of the landscape. At one point the mist parted and Kiet spotted several NVA soldiers in a bunker on the north side of the river. They were asleep. Sounds drifted by. Men talking in Vietnamese, the tramp of marching soldiers, the snap of wood fires. All at once, Norris heard tank engines revving loudly in the mist. "It was like pulling into a bus station," he said. What on earth was out there? He peered ahead, but the fog was too opaque to make out anything. Finally, after a few minutes, the mist thinned and Norris saw a row of tanks lined up to be refueled. He and Kiet quietly paddled toward the other side of the river and kept going.

Hours passed as the two men ducked and hauled their way up the river. Finally, they reached the spot on the map where Norris believed Hambleton was hiding. The sampan moved slowly along the south shore. It was difficult to pick out details on the bank: in the fog, trees and rocks looked like men crouched over or lying on the ground.

As Norris and Kiet watched the water, the fog parted and then swept downstream. The sampan was suddenly in the clear. Norris looked up and spotted the Cam Lo bridge just a few yards away. NVA soldiers marched across, their eyes pointed forward. Norris and Kiet eased away from the crowded bridge, turned, and headed downstream. In the fog, they'd passed the unconscious Hambleton.

Hambleton was back in the water, barely moving. Something loomed up ahead. It looked like a hill emerging out of the water's surface. The navigator stared at the mound with growing dismay. How was he going to climb that hill in the middle of the river? He was far too weak; climbing anything was out of the question. He would have to get out of the river and call the FAC and tell the voice that he was done, that he could go no farther and they would have to look by the hill and come get him.

But wait a minute. Could hills grow out of rivers? The water didn't curve around the dark shape he was seeing. Instead, it seemed to flow right up its slope to the top and then topple over the summit. But that was impossible, wasn't it? Hambleton felt his tenuous grip on reality slipping further.

He thought he heard someone speaking. "There can't be a hill there." It was his own voice. "Get back on track," it said.

He took a few more steps, but the hill stubbornly remained. He decided he would leave the river and rest for a while. Perhaps the hill would go away. He clambered out of the water and lay on the bank, closing his eyes. He was almost afraid to open them again. If he looked downstream and the large mound of earth or whatever it was still stood in front of him, what would he do? He couldn't arrive at a plan of action.

Finally, he opened his eyes and pushed himself up on one elbow. He turned and glanced nervously downstream. The hill had disappeared. It had been a hallucination. He was almost giddy with relief.

His flight suit reeked. It was covered with mud, and more of the foul-smelling stuff stuck to him as he crawled back to the water. He lurched forward, holding on to the railroad tie. But after thirty minutes, he had to stop. If he went any farther, he was afraid he wouldn't have the power to get out of the water.

He pulled himself out and lay on the bank. He brought the radio up to his mouth. The FAC asked him how he was feeling. "Very weak," he said. The FAC told him he was doing beautifully, that he was on hole 16. If he could just manage two more, he would be close to home.

"I'll try," he said. "But can they be short ones?"

He thought: *Two more and I'm done. Just two.* He got back in the water and staggered on. After an hour, he spotted a little sandy beach that sloped up gently from the river. He got to it and rolled out of the water. Then he crawled on his hands and knees toward some foliage.

The FAC promised him that he was doing well. Just one more hole.

It was about 3:30 a.m. He told the voice that he would do his best, but he doubted he could go any farther. He picked himself up and walked toward the wooden tie. But his foot caught a rock and he tumbled to the ground.

Could he keep on going? He had an image in his mind of himself wading through the current and falling in the river and sinking unconscious into the water, then drowning there. He didn't want to die like that, not after coming all this way.

He turned and crawled back to the bushes. "I just don't know if I can play another hole," he told the FAC. The voice told him to hold on, he would get right back to him.

For forty minutes, Hambleton lay under the foliage. Finally, he heard the voice of the FAC calling him. He picked up the heavy radio and listened. The voice told him that he had to go on. The next part was very short. His "playing partner" would join him soon. Couldn't he just get back in the water and wait?

Hambleton asked how long before this playing partner showed up. "Not long now." A few minutes.

The navigator took a few breaths, trying to animate his muscles with just enough energy to get him into position. Then he began to crawl. He could see the sky starting to lighten. Day was coming.

He got to the river and sat by the bank. He wouldn't move; he would just wait here as instructed. The minutes rolled by and his mind blinked on and off. The color of the sky changed from blue-black to pewter. He listened for the sound of his rescuers but heard nothing.

There was a bend in the river just ahead of him and he watched it closely. It was about 5 a.m. Dawn was approaching. He peered through his mud-smeared glasses.

He thought he spotted something moving. He took off his glasses and looked. There was something poking out from beneath the overhanging branches. It was a sampan, occupied by two figures. Hambleton was about to yell, but the thought crossed his mind: What if it's just some Vietnamese fishermen? What if he gave himself away at the very end of his long journey?

His throat had gone dry, whether from excitement or mere thirst he couldn't tell. He wanted to get a look at the men in the sampan. He peered at the front of the boat as it emerged a little more from the foliage but he was immediately disappointed. It was a Vietnamese face, probably just a villager trawling the river. "My spirits sank to a new low."

At almost the same time Kiet saw Hambleton. "Tom," he said quietly and pointed. Norris quickly spied the survivor up ahead. Hambleton continued to watch the craft from about forty feet away. The sampan was behaving strangely, paralleling the shore at ten feet or so, barely advancing in the current. It drifted closer toward him and he caught a glimpse of the second man. Hambleton was astonished. The man's skin was white. How was that possible? Hambleton wanted to "jump up and down and holler and yell," but he still wasn't sure these were his deliverers. His body was shaking with excitement, his heart beating wildly.

The sampan came closer. Fifteen feet, ten. Hambleton stared intently at the second man. His skin was pale white and he had round eyes. The navigator felt relief flood through him. The sight was "the most beautiful thing he had ever seen."

Finally, Hambleton decided he had to signal the men. He moistened his lips and called out, his voice hoarse, "Lieutenant colonel. Red."

"White," the second man said immediately. The two men put their paddles in the water and the boat stopped moving.

The sampan pulled closer and Tommy Norris said quietly, "Colonel Hambleton, get your ass in here."

30

JOURNEY'S END

THE NAVIGATOR WAS TOO WEAK to climb into the boat. The two men reached over, gripped his flight suit, pulled him across the sampan's edge, and lowered him onto the bottom. Hambleton was shaking from the cold. Norris told him his name and Kiet smiled at him. "Colonel," he said. The sea commando, like Norris, was overjoyed to have found the navigator. "It was like diving to the bottom of the sea and finding gold."

Norris crouched over Hambleton's body, checking him for wounds. He looked at the infected finger. The puffed-up flesh was oozing pus and Norris thought it might be gangrenous. Hambleton was little help. He was delirious, mumbling to people and things that weren't there. They had gotten to him as the man was spending his last reserves.

Daylight was approaching. Norris brought out a survival vest and pulled Hambleton's arms through it. In case they capsized, at least he wouldn't drown. Norris debated what to do next. Should they try to out-run the daylight and make it past the patrols and outposts, or should they hole up and wait for darkness? The foliage was thick. If they decided to hide, they would probably be safe for twelve or fourteen hours. But he gave it only a few seconds' thought. Hambleton couldn't wait for medical attention. He might die right there in the sampan.

Norris signaled to Kiet that they would take the chance and head downriver. The Vietnamese commando brought out his knife and sliced fronds from the foliage hanging over the water, then draped them across

Hambleton's body. As he did this, Norris called the FAC on the radio and, using their prearranged code, told the man that they had Hambleton and would try for the base that morning. "I also told them that we were going to need some air cover, as there was no way we were going to make it past all those NVA troops and bivouacs without some help."

Kiet finished covering the navigator with the fronds and said quietly, "We go now." The two men pushed off the bank with their paddles. As they took their first strokes in the water, the FAC came back on the radio with an update. There was no air support available.

Norris was gobsmacked. The Air Force had diverted a massive amount of assets to save Gene Hambleton, and here he had him in his sampan *and there were no planes available*? Norris grabbed the handset. What about fast movers, Air Force or Navy? The FAC came back: Nothing. The problem was twofold: The airfield at Da Nang, where a large proportion of the Air Force's planes were stationed, was under a major rocket attack. Nothing could get in or out. And the US Navy aircraft carriers in the Gulf of Tonkin had not yet begun launching aircraft for the day's missions.

Norris couldn't believe his luck. He'd have to proceed downriver naked to the NVA guns. All he could rely on was Navy artillery.

The sampan hugged the riverbank; Norris and Kiet proceeded slowly, as if they were out for a leisurely paddle. As the two men bent over their oars — Hambleton, in his delirium, could hear the sound of rushing water through the skin of the sampan — the light was getting stronger. Norris and Kiet scanned the shore for NVA. It was one thing to steal through enemy territory under the cover of night; it was another to do so in clear daylight.

Hambleton was now perhaps a mile from safety, but he'd actually entered the most dangerous part of his journey. On the surface of the Mieu Giang, he was exposed as he'd never been before. And with his extra weight, the freeboard on the sampan was down to three or four inches. Any sudden movement could tip them into the river.

The current pulled them along. They slipped underneath the hanging vines, moving as quietly as possible. Kiet's and Norris's eyes swept the riverbank continuously. Norris spotted figures in his peripheral vision, but no one called out. They must have resembled two villagers fishing for the day's first meal. The extra speed of the current helped; by the time the NVA soldiers had a chance to register the sampan with the two strange men, they were almost past them.

For fifteen minutes, the boat moved in silence. Then, a hoarse shout from the riverbank. *"Eh, lai day!"* (Hey, come here). Kiet shot a glance toward the men who had called out. Three armed North Vietnamese soldiers, at least one of them high-ranking—Kiet spotted a white star on one man's belt buckle, signifying elevated rank—were gesturing and yelling at the two of them to stop. Two soldiers were carrying rifles and the third a K-54 pistol. All three were staring intently at the figures in the sampan. "It sent chills up my spine," Kiet later recalled.

The commando turned back and looked at Norris, who made a sign with his finger. Get ready to shoot, it meant. Kiet nodded. Then without speaking, he and Norris began to turn the boat slowly away from the men, pretending not to hear them. They bent over and dug their paddles deeper into the water, putting their backs into the stroke.

Clearly suspicious, the men began chasing the boat, shouting at the two to stop. How much longer would it be before the bullets came? The sampan was ripping downstream now, crashing through vines and foliage extending out from the bank. Norris waited for the water around him to erupt with rifle fire. He spotted a bend ahead of him. If they could reach it, they might lose their pursuers. The veins on his neck popped as he and Kiet whipped the paddles into the water and pulled with every ounce of strength they had.

Twenty yards. The men were running alongside, bellowing "Stop! Stop!" in Vietnamese. Ten yards. Silence. Five. And the boat went shooting around the bend.

The sun was coming up. Full light now. The sampan was visible to anyone on either bank. They passed NVA outposts carved into the shoreline, and Norris spotted mortar tubes and rocket sites sticking up from the ground but saw no soldiers milling around. They were probably sleeping. He knew the spot where he'd heard the tanks refueling had to be coming up, and he worried that there would be more vehicles there filling up on gas. But when the sampan approached the depot, he could see that the tanks had disappeared. He did spot a large field truck sitting next to a ramshackle building, and then soldiers, the crews from the fuel tankers. But they were busy covering their vehicles with camouflage to protect them from the day's airstrikes.

The sampan glided by the outpost. Once they were past, Norris—unable to resist—picked up the radio and called in the coordinates so that fighters could drop their bombs on the tankers.

At one point Kiet whispered that they had to get under cover. Once they slipped behind the brush, Norris watched the commando in the front of the boat. Norris had no idea why they'd stopped. For ten minutes, Kiet said nothing. Hambleton, passing in and out of consciousness, absorbed one fleeting impression: the Vietnamese commando had "the greatest pair of eyes of anyone I know." He could see things on the riverbank the two Americans had no inkling were there.

Finally, after ten minutes, Kiet said, "We go now," and the two put their paddles in the water.

The forward base was getting closer. Norris heard someone talking. It was Hambleton, who was "starting to moan and babble." It sounded like he was having some kind of an anxiety nightmare beneath the fronds. In his weakened state, the stress of the past eleven days was working on the navigator.

Norris whispered for him to shut up. If he could keep it together for just a little while longer, they would be home free. But Hambleton's voice only grew louder. Norris reached forward and shook Hambleton. "Quiet," he whispered. Finally the airman's rantings faded away and he dropped into unconsciousness.

They were close now. Perhaps just one more bend in the river and the bunker would be in sight. Norris and Kiet steered the sampan toward the south bank, where the bunker would appear. The sun was hot on their necks.

The sampan came around the bend and suddenly the water in front of it began to boil and churn, and an enormous noise shattered the quiet. Branches and vines splintered off the slim trees. The surface of the river erupted in violent little bursts of water. Someone on the northern bank was shooting at them with a heavy machine gun.

Norris and Kiet turned the boat quickly and raced toward the shore-line. The sampan slid in under an overhang of vines, the clattering roar of the machine gun echoing in their ears. Norris jumped out of the boat to check the banks for NVA. If they were pinned down by the machine gun and bracketed by troops on the other side running to find out what the shooting was about, they'd be dead within minutes.

The SEAL knew he'd been lucky. The gunner who'd spotted them coming down the river had been watching from a village perched on the bank. He'd seen the prow of the boat as it came around the bend and opened up on them. But he'd been too quick. Had he waited a few seconds longer, he would have been able to fire broadside into the sampan at almost point-blank range, killing the three men with ease. His eagerness had got the better of him.

Bullets sheared through the foliage, and now mortar rounds joined the one-sided battle. Norris could hear the gasp of the shells exiting the mortar tube, and rounds ripped through the brush farther up the slope. He peered upward through the branches, studying the riverbank nearest him but couldn't see any soldiers coming to investigate the gunfire. He breathed easier. But there was no way they could get past the machine-gun nest. If they tried it, the gunner would carve them up. Their AKs were no match for a tripod-mounted machine gun. He needed an airstrike, and he needed it now.

Norris scrambled back to the sampan. Hambleton was moaning again underneath the fronds. Kiet held the boat pinned to the bank with his paddle. Norris grabbed the handset and raised the FAC. "We really need some air support," he said.

He waited.

Da Nang was still under rocket attack; no fighters could get out. But the aircraft carrier USS *Hancock* was sitting in the South China Sea, its decks and holds filled with fast movers. When the FAC put out an urgent call for help, the pilot of one of the *Hancock*'s A-4 Skyhawks — their wings loaded with five-hundred-pound bombs — answered. He was leading a flight of five fighters and they were only five minutes away; the FAC asked the pilot to proceed toward the Mieu Giang immediately.

The Skyhawks instantly turned toward the river. The FAC radioed the

SEAL and informed him that he had some fast movers approaching. Norris sheltered along the south bank. The FAC dropped a smoke rocket, which thumped into the brush near the machine gun, still spurting fire. Now they waited on the fighters.

Norris and Kiet could hear the Skyhawks streaking overhead, their engines sucking in an acre or two of air and tearing it to pieces. A concussion wave bloomed across the water as the bombs struck, and dirt and flame shot into the air. Two A-1s that had finally managed to lift off from Da Nang joined the fight, strafing the area along the north bank with smoke bombs, which provided perfect cover for the three men in the sampan.

The gunfire stopped. The air above the river was still again.

Norris and Kiet speared their oars into the water and pushed the sampan toward home.

When they emerged from the smoke, Norris saw they were only five hundred yards from the bunker. He wanted the cover of foliage, so they swerved the boat toward the shore. They quickly covered the distance to the outpost. When the bow of the sampan slid onto the packed mud of the bank, Norris jumped out.

The sampan stopped. "Where are we?" Hambleton asked from beneath the fronds. "End of the line," Norris said. The navigator, temporarily alert, felt relief flood through him.

He stood up and tried to step out of the boat. but his strength failed him and he tumbled to the ground. Kiet helped Hambleton stand. Norris bent over and picked him up and hoisted him over one shoulder. Kiet had gone ahead and alerted the rangers, and he came back now with several men. In his half delirium, Hambleton could see people running toward him, what looked like Vietnamese soldiers. He wondered if, after all he'd been through, he'd somehow blundered into a trap.

Gunfire erupted from the opposite shore, and the men ducked and hurried back toward the bunker. Bullets pitted the slope, and little geysers of dirt erupted around them. Finally they made the top of the hill and ran into the blockhouse. The men laid Hambleton on a stretcher and covered him with a blanket. Hands reached for his boots and unlaced them. He could feel someone massaging his feet. "They felt like two chunks of ice," he said. He looked at their faces, their uniforms, still bewildered.

One young soldier next to him was wearing an NVA uniform. Hambleton goggled as his eyes swept past him to the next man. This one had patches on his camouflage identifying him as a Cambodian. Hambleton's gaze switched over to the other side. Here, a man looking at him was wearing a hat that read "LAOS."

He called out. Norris's face appeared at his side.

"What the hell have you gotten me into?" Hambleton said excitedly.

Norris looked confused. "What are you talking about?"

Hambleton gestured toward the uniforms.

"Don't worry about it," Norris said. "You're going to be all right."

The Vietnamese soldiers sensed his unease. One of them came closer to him. "Smoke, Colonel?" he asked in English.

The instant, junkie-like craving for tobacco momentarily blotted out any fear the American felt. He nodded. The soldier reached into his pocket and pulled out a red box. Marlboros. Hambleton sighed with pleasure.

The soldier selected a cigarette, put it between Hambleton's lips, and lit it.

The others cleaned Hambleton's wounds and brought him food, which he devoured. Another ranger found a small bottle of wine and poured some for the airman.

"I was overcome with a flood of emotions," Hambleton said. "I was so relieved and happy." He called Norris over and promised, if he lived to be a thousand, he would do anything he could for him.

Suddenly Hambleton heard a high whistle, and a mortar round hit the outside of the bunker. Three of the soldiers leaned over Hambleton to protect him. He was moved. "Kindness needs no words in a time like that." He could hear the rangers outside returning fire and more shells thudding into the base and striking the three-foot-thick concrete walls. Despite the bombardment, Hambleton no longer had to worry about evading the enemy. "I savored the thought that it was all over." He began to think about returning home. And Gwen.

Norris got on the radio and called for an APC. The South Vietnamese officer on the other end said they wouldn't come down to the bunker until the rockets stopped. The SEAL called the FAC and told him to send some fast movers at the NVA outposts that were dropping the mortars on them. The skies filled with American aircraft, all hitting the emplacement across the river. The rockets stopped.

As the APC approached, the sound of its metal tracks outside the bunker reminded Hambleton of the enemy tanks he'd heard moving along the roads when he was hiding in the stand of trees. The vehicle pulled up in front of the bunker and the men carried Hambleton out on the stretcher. Norris helped load him in, then he, Kiet, and the other two sea commandos boarded as well. A hatch above Hambleton's head was pulled open and he could see the rangers riding on top of the APC, turning their heads this way and that, looking for the enemy. Occasionally he heard the report of an M16.

The APC bounced along the road for thirty minutes, reaching the city of Dong Ha, which was still under NVA attack, late that afternoon. It stopped, and the doors were pulled open. Men, Americans, came in and lifted Hambleton out on his stretcher. He saw the drooping rotor blades of a US Army medevac helicopter. He was overjoyed.

"LAY THAT MAN DOWN"

The navigator heard a whirring sound; he turned his head to look. There were eight or nine television cameras and a cluster of men carrying microphones. The journalists walked with the stretcher as Hambleton was hurried toward the chopper. One asked about the men who'd died in the rescue operation. "It was a hell of a price to pay for one life," Hambleton said. "I'm very sorry."

The attendants loaded him onto the chopper and pulled the door shut. The engines whined, and Hambleton could hear the sound of small-arms fire. The pilot pulled back on his stick and the medevac helicopter lifted into the air. Hambleton saw concerned faces above him. A paramedic, then another. They pulled off his shirt and went to work on him, inserting a needle into his arm and another into his emaciated torso. They began to clean his wounds with disinfectant. Another face—a doctor?—lifted his hand and turned it, studying the pus-filled finger. Hambleton got a glimpse of the dark, swollen thing. The doctor shook his head. Hambleton wondered if he was going to amputate it. The doctor moved on to his left arm, which he discovered had been fractured from his fall down the hill when he'd first spotted the river.

The chopper landed next to a field hospital, and the airman was rushed into the emergency room. As the stretcher-bearers brought him in, Hambleton could see doctors and nurses gowned and scrubbed up and waiting for him. "Fifteen or 20 in all swarmed over me like a bunch of mechanics at the Indianapolis Speedway during a pit stop." Hands removed the old dressings on his wounds and replaced them with fresh ones. Special creams were applied to his still-freezing feet to help with blood flow. Empty IV bottles were replaced with full ones. His blood pressure was taken and his wounds were reexamined.

After he'd been checked and rechecked, Hambleton's stretcher was taken from the examining table and hoisted onto a cart. He was wheeled to another helicopter, this time an Air Force Jolly Green, waiting outside, the doctors and nurses walking alongside the cart, still working on him. Inside were more doctors and paramedics. The chopper flew him to another, better-equipped hospital at Da Nang.

Days before, Hambleton had worried that the military had forgotten him, but now he was in danger of being smothered with attention. "I was again given the royal treatment and wheeled into a ward," he remembered. The airman was placed in the hallway while his accommodations were prepared. He looked around. There were seven or eight injured airmen in hospital beds, all craning their necks to see who the celebrity patient was. He smiled. He was delighted to be back among people again. He'd missed making small talk with the guys, and besides, he had the best goddamned rescue story in the history of the United States Air Force.

As he looked around, Hambleton noticed something. There were no empty beds in the hospital ward; he wondered where the doctors would put him. Finally he spotted some activity at the end of the ward; workers were pulling mops, buckets, and other janitorial supplies out of a small room. He watched as a cot appeared and was wheeled in. Then the attendants came and got Hambleton, carrying his stretcher into the room—which was really a broom closet, with no windows and bare cement walls—and laying it on the cart. They turned and left.

More nurses and doctors arrived. One of them handed Hambleton a mirror and he stared into it. "I saw a face I hardly recognized—sunken eyes and a . . . beard!" Emaciated and exhausted, he looked years older than he was.

After two hours of tests, Hambleton asked for some food. A nurse called an attendant and he brought two white paper cups. One contained chicken broth and the other "the most god-awful gelatin I ever tried to eat." But he finished off both cups with gusto and washed the meal down with a Coca-Cola and a pitcher of water.

Finally, the last nurse left, closing the door behind her. But after days and nights on his own, Hambleton found the silence to be almost unbearable. When an attendant opened the door, he saw a handwritten sign taped to the other side: KEEP OUT. NO ADMITTANCE.

Obviously, Hambleton was being kept in isolation. But why? He asked the man what was going on. The attendant said some colonel had phoned the hospital and insisted that only medical personnel were to be allowed to see the navigator. That's all he knew.

Hambleton was too exhausted to argue. He was alive. He was safe. He would soon see Gwen. After days of sleeping on the ground, he found the mattress and the feather pillow were too soft. He actually missed the hard ground of his hiding place in the copse of trees. But eventually he nodded off.

Word filtered out by radio and through base scuttlebutt that Hambleton had been rescued. The men at Korat and Joker and others on bases across Southeast Asia who had nothing to do with the mission were elated. The fifty-three-year-old airman had overcome long odds. He was free.

Andy Andersen was still recovering from his shrapnel wound when he heard the news. Soon after, his second-in-command, Major Gerald Bauknight, showed up at the hospital and told him about the talk he'd had with Colonel Frank Zerbe, and about Zerbe's threats to leave them dangling in the wind if the mission failed. "Andersen said, 'Well, I'm going over to Zerbe's apartment right now.'" The Marine climbed in the jeep and the two men drove over to where Zerbe was staying. When they arrived, "Andersen went in there and chewed out the colonel, told him where to get off." The fact that Clark and Hambleton were both safe — and that Andersen had been wounded in the operation — most likely saved the Marine from serious consequences from the military command.

With Zerbe dealt with to his satisfaction, Andersen searched out his fellow operatives who'd been risking their lives for months on end to rescue a living American. He gathered them up and brought them to an Officers' Club to toast the mission's success. "The whole group got together and got totally drunk," Bauknight said. "They had a great old time celebrating."

In Tucson, Gwen Hambleton was asleep. There had been a small incident earlier in the night. She'd woken and sat straight up in bed; something prompted her to speak out into the darkness. "Hang in there, Gene," Gwen said. "They're coming." Her dog Pierre stirred at the side of the bed. But all else was quiet. Gwen checked the clock. It was 11:30 p.m. She went back to sleep. At that moment, her husband was on the river, delirious and fearful, waiting for Norris.

Now, four hours later, something woke her again. She turned in the bed and realized it was the phone. She sat there, allowing the ringing to fill the room.

She had been preparing for this moment for days. The Air Force would call — especially in the middle of the night — only with significant news, either good or bad. The nightlight threw the wrinkles of the duvet into relief. She took a few seconds to compose herself, then found the base of the lamp on the night table next to her. She twisted the switch and light flooded the room. Then she reached for the phone.

"Gwen Hambleton speaking."

The man on the other end introduced himself. He was a sergeant at the Casualty Affairs Office at the Air Force Military Personnel Center. He apologized for calling in the middle of the night. Gwen said nothing. "We've just received a message from the 388th Tactical Fighter Wing," the sergeant said. "We have your husband."

Gwen felt lightheaded. "Oh, dear God," she said.

The sergeant asked if she was all right. She told him that yes, she was. He offered to have a doctor sent over from the base hospital at Davis-Monthan. "Thank you, no, Sergeant," she said.

The man told her that Hambleton was now at Da Nang Air Base and that he was suffering from exhaustion and was badly dehydrated. He didn't mention any other injuries. He gave her an address to send mail to and told her the details would be in a telegram that would reach her within the hour. Gwen thanked him and hung up.

Gwen began to weep, crouched over on the bed. Her dog Pierre watched her, fully awake now. She sobbed for several minutes.

After she'd composed herself, Gwen stood up and went to the bathroom, where she washed her face and combed her hair. Feeling refreshed, she went to her closet, found the brand-new dressing gown that she'd purchased for her trip to Bangkok, and put it on. Then she walked through the house, turning on all the lights. It was the middle of the night in Tucson, but the windows of the Hambleton house blazed as if a gala party were in progress.

Gwen ended up in the living room, where she went to the stereo and turned it on. Music filled the room. She walked to the couch, turned, and sat down.

After Hambleton had breakfast the next day, a visitor was announced. He was an official from the Department of Defense, and he asked questions for thirty or forty minutes. A larger team from military intelligence followed soon after to conduct a standard debrief of his escape and evasion experience. They talked for three hours. Later, a typed memorandum of the meeting was delivered to his room for Hambleton to read over and approve. The navigator never revealed what he and the intelligence officers spoke about, but he did say he believed that his background had played a part in the intensity of the rescue mission. "I've had some pretty sensitive jobs," he said. "I had access to plans that not too many people had access to," and with his memory for detail, he'd "never forgotten them."

After the intel guys had said their good-byes, six men—lieutenants and captains—walked into the room. Hambleton didn't recognize any of them; they certainly weren't from his squadron. One by one, the men gave their names, but he still had no idea who they were. Finally, one of them spoke up. "We're the O-2s and the FAC boys, sir." These were the men who'd watched over him for eleven days.

"No!" Hambleton said. "Really?"

One of the men reached into his back pocket and handed Hambleton a water bottle. Hambleton unscrewed the cap and tasted the contents. It was a Manhattan. He sipped the cocktail, laughing and talking with the other officers. He recognized some of the voices.

Hambleton found it hard to express his feelings adequately to the men who'd guided him out of danger to the safety of this room. "I had always bragged I wasn't the emotional type," he said. But in front of the half-dozen men who had worked so diligently to save him, he was overcome with gratitude. He reached out and shook each man's hand, wishing he could convey to them the deep thankfulness he felt.

The next night, the base came under attack. A shower of NVA rockets detonated, shaking the hospital. The explosions were close and loud. Hambleton lay tensed in his bed, terrified that having survived his long ordeal behind enemy lines, he was now going to be taken out by an ordinary bomb. But the mortars soon ebbed away.

The following day, an ambulance took him to the flight line and he boarded a plane for Clark Air Base in the Philippines. One of the first things he asked to do there was to call Gwen. The administrators agreed and the navigator dialed her number. But he ended up with an earful of static; the call wouldn't go through. After a few failed attempts, Hambleton asked a Red Cross official in the hospital for help. The official spent a frustrating hour trying to reach Tucson, but in the end all he could promise was that a telegram would be sent.

Once he arrived at Clark, Hambleton was eager to keep going all the way back to the United States, but the doctors at the base were concerned that the eighteen pounds he'd put on since his return was mostly water weight. They worried that the water might get into his lungs on a long flight, so they decided to hold him a few extra days. Hambleton, lonely and still weak, agreed.

That night, at 3 a.m., the navigator was lying in his bed when the walls around him began to shake. He snapped awake: the medicine bottles in the cabinets were chattering like castanets, the glass clinking louder and louder. An earthquake measuring 7.5 on the Richter scale was rolling through Manila. The dresser and the other furniture in the room began swaying, and outside he could hear a low, powerful rumble. Hambleton thought to himself that he was surely cursed; everywhere he went, disaster followed.

Hambleton was gaining his weight back, and each day he felt a little stronger. His finger and shoulder wound had fully healed. Finally, he was able to call Gwen. She told him what she'd been going through, the terror of seeing the Air Force officials pulling into her driveway, the wait to hear if he'd survived that first day on the ground. "Thank God he's alive" was all she could think when the Air Force told her they'd maintained voice contact with him. She'd been praying every day for his rescue.

Gwen recounted the friends calling her and wishing her strength. And she told him that she'd willed herself not to cry during the entire ordeal, perhaps believing it would be a sign of weakness. It wasn't until she learned that he'd been rescued that she hung up the phone and, sitting in her bed alone, began to weep. "But for joy," she told Hambleton.

Gwen told him that one day toward the end of his days behind enemy lines, a feeling had come over her. She'd said to herself, *Gene has what it takes to survive.* Hambleton thought back later on that part of the conversation. "I'm no believer in ESP," he said, but he synced up her conviction that he was going to make it and found it had occurred at the exact time he decided to go with the Air Force plan for him to walk toward the river.

While Hambleton was still in the hospital, he got a call from his wing commander in Thailand, who asked him if he could stop back at Korat before he returned home to the States. The Bat 21 event was already changing how rescue missions were conducted. "This episode absolutely stunned the rescue community," says military historian Darrel Whitcomb. "The message was: There are places helicopters can't go." Search and rescues had to be approached as combat events, and other options besides the Jolly Greens had to be contemplated. The commander wanted Hambleton to speak to his airmen and talk about his evasion techniques so that they might survive when the rescue choppers weren't able to come for them. Hambleton badly wanted to get to Tucson, but he agreed. "I am an Air Force man," he said. He was carried out of the hospital on a stretcher and loaded aboard a plane headed for Thailand.

As the plane came in for its landing at Korat, Hambleton propped himself on his elbows and looked out the small window. "I couldn't believe my eyes. Every fellow in my squadron who wasn't flying was there. Along with them were the F-4 and F-105 boys." Hambleton was moved, and "mighty happy." He was glad to be alive, but it was just beginning to register on him that his ordeal meant something to thousands of ordinary airmen still fighting the war.

Two corpsmen came aboard and took either end of his stretcher as a nurse stood by him. Hambleton saw two figures climbing up the ramp: his wing and squadron commanders. The first man saw the two soldiers gripping the handles of the stretcher and said, "Lay that man down. He ain't going to be *carried* off this airplane."

The men laid the stretcher down and Hambleton slowly got to his feet. He was wearing hospital pajamas, and he felt awkward at the thought of facing his friends and crewmates in such clothing. The wing commander had anticipated this: he'd brought with him a pair of jungle boots, a squadron hat, and a new flight suit complete with patches. He gave them to Hambleton, saying, "You're going to walk off." Hambleton nodded and pulled on the flight suit. His legs were shaking; he hadn't yet built up the muscle he'd lost while on the run. But once he was dressed, his boots on, his cap firmly affixed, he took a few steps down the ramp, flanked by the two commanders.

As he made his way toward the tarmac, Hambleton was startled by a roar. The men standing below him erupted in a burst of applause and shouting. "It was the greatest ovation of my life," he said. Hambleton waved to the men. As he did, he felt a pang of remorse. "I thought quickly . . . that I shouldn't be getting all the cheers. They belonged to all those boys who did all the work to pull me out of that trouble."

When the squadron dudes quieted down, Hambleton spoke. He thanked the men for the welcome but added that it was the pilots and corpsmen and the pararescuemen who'd gone after him that they should be applauding. Then he was whisked into the wing commander's vehicle and driven to the Officers' Club. It was time for some de rigueur Air Force partying.

As Hambleton walked in, he saw signs on the walls welcoming him home. The tables and chairs had been pushed back, and the men began to surge in behind him, the pitch of conversation rising steadily as more airmen poured in. Officers came over and shook his hand and congratulated him and laughed and asked him questions about the eleven days. He spent the next hour with a circle of constantly changing airmen grouped around him, listening intently to his stories. For them, he was the embodiment of a great and unspoken thing they were all part of: the intense devotion of one American fighting man to his brothers.

After an hour, he could feel his strength fading. The squadron's flight surgeon had been watching him closely and offered him the use of his old hooch as a place to rest. Hambleton gratefully accepted and said goodbye to his fellow airmen. It had been a wonderful party.

Hambleton spent ten days at Korat, giving talks to hundreds and hundreds of airmen as they returned from their missions. (Several of the airmen he spoke to would later that year face their own "escape and evade" ordeals as the air offensive continued.) Then he boarded a C-9 plane back to Clark and then on to Travis Air Force Base near Fairfield, California. The next morning he flew the final leg of his journey to Davis-Monthan. When he emerged from the airplane, he saw throngs of people waving, and a volley of cheering washed over him. Newspaper photographers and television cameramen rushed toward the Jetway. A convertible waited to take him on a motorcade through the city.

He smiled broadly, searching the crowd for Gwen. He'd been longing to see her for many weeks. He'd imagined whole conversations with her when he was fading in and out of consciousness on the river, and now he wanted to hold her, talk to her. He spotted his wife running toward him. She was wearing a dark blue dress with white and red piping, a white bag hanging off her right arm. Gwen had clearly thought about her outfit; she meant to be seen wearing the colors of the American flag.

He felt his throat tighten. "Those hallucinations couldn't possibly equal the real thing." Gwen came running up to him and the two embraced, Gene pulling her close. A photographer for the local paper snapped a series of pictures of the two, Gene thin in his flight suit and dark blue Air Force cap, a white hospital band around his right wrist. In the first, he's embracing Gwen — her back is to the photographer — and is whispering something in her ear. Her arms gently encircle his waist, and she seems partially collapsed into his taller frame. In the second, they've begun to walk away from the plane, and he has his right arm wrapped around her shoulder and is pulling her tight to him, his face partly turned away from the camera. She is quite clearly crying. It's only in the third shot, when they are walking, he with his left hand in his pocket, that her lips show the beginning of a smile. But her eyes are closed and she has the expression of a child who is trying to appear happy although she is still feeling some kind of sorrow or pain. "She suffered worse than I did," Gene would later say. The photographs attest to this.

32

BEYOND A NORMAL CALL OF DUTY

At FIFTY-THREE, Gene Hambleton was a certified war hero. Correspondents for CBS News and other networks were waiting in Tucson to talk to him and marvel at his survival; the interviews appeared on the national news that night. Newspapers across the country and as far away as Bangkok and São Paulo ran stories about the airman, with headlines such as "RESCUED U.S. NAVIGATOR BARELY ESCAPED N. VIETS" and "11 DAYS BEHIND ENEMY LINES." A piece even ran in the *Bloomington Pantagraph,* one of the newspapers read in Hambleton's hometown of Wenona, Illinois, which must have pleased him no end, and another in Piper City, Illinois, where Gwen was from. The rescue "brought jubilation to headquarters officers who have had little to cheer about," wrote one reporter, while another said that Hambleton "was a symbol to the men of his unit and the whole service of one American fighting unbelievable odds." Weeks later, the navigator told reporters that he'd been unable to pay for a meal, a cocktail, or a pack of cigarettes since he got back. "It's kind of embarrassing, actually," he said. "I've only spent $6.13 in over a month."

There were welcome-home banners strung in Tucson and a large family party in Illinois. At a ceremony attended by the top Air Force officers, he was awarded a sparkling array of medals: the Silver Star, the Distinguished Flying Cross, the Air Medal, the Meritorious Service Medal, and a Purple Heart, all at once. Journalists drove out to his father's place to interview the old man. For once, Iceal Sr. had warm words for his son, telling an Illinois journalist "how great it was" to know that Hambleton was safe. "He thought enough of this country to fight for it," he said approvingly. Hambleton clipped and saved both stories. "For some reason," wrote one columnist, "certain individuals are called to give beyond a normal 'call of duty.'" The navigator had become one of the elect.

Gwen invited reporters into her living room and told them the mission had been "fantastic . . . miraculous." She thanked the Air Force, the Marines, and the other services involved: "They have accomplished something that must have seemed impossible." Reporters found Hambleton upbeat, exhilarated to be alive. "I never lost hope," he told the *Arizona Daily Star.* "I knew I would come out of there."

Everywhere the navigator went, people stopped him and asked about the eleven days and the run to the river. "He wasn't a bragger," said his close friend Dennis Armstrong, "but if someone brought it up, he would talk about it." Old Air Force buddies wrote him from all over the world. "I was really shocked to see your name in the paper," wrote one USAF officer from São Paulo, including with the letter some news clips about the rescue from the *Brazil Herald.* "SOME PEOPLE WILL DO ANYTHING TO GET THEIR NAME IN THE HEADLINES," read a telegram from his pals at Davis-Monthan Air Force Base. "WE DID NOTICE THAT YOU FAILED TO SHAVE AND THAT YOUR UNIFORM WAS REALLY TERRIBLE."

The navigator's saga represented a victory in a war that had produced so few. The feeling that American airmen had when he was on the run —*that man is giving the North Vietnamese pure hell*—now radiated out into the general American public. People wanted to sit with him, touch him, hear him speak. And Hambleton didn't disappoint. He recounted the events of his journey to the river with suitable drama and encouraged his listeners to draw the same lesson he had from it. "You never know how strong you are," he told them. "You never know how long you could hold out."

Hambleton did revel in the attention. He even filled out the paperwork and ordered a vanity license plate from the state of Arizona that read "Bat 21." People in Tucson would spot the plate and wave to him, and he would pull over and they'd talk for a while. He traveled all around the country for speaking engagements—recounting his ordeal to military men and their wives, to high schools, Air Force cadets, ROTC programs. He appeared at grammar schools and children wrote him to ask how he was doing now and to thank him for his courage. As far as old-fashioned American glory went, it was everything he could have asked for.

One part of his return didn't go as smoothly as the rest. He and Gwen occasionally made it up to New Hampshire to see his brother Gil and his family, and though his nieces and nephews still reveled in the visits, there were new tensions in the house. Gene liked to talk about the shootdown and the rescue with Gil and his kids; he couldn't help himself. He'd been the overlooked Hambleton for so many years, living in the shadow of his brother's World War II exploits, and now it was his turn to shine a little. "I always thought it was Gene's way of saying, 'I'm an important person and just as successful as my brother," Gil's daughter Sharon says. "But my father always felt Gene overplayed the whole thing." Gil was quiet and serious and had never talked much about the flights over Germany, the darkness lit up by AAA, the dead squadron mates. And so he listened to Gene talk about the Vietnamese patrols — "There were times I could reach out and touch them"— and the F-4s and all of it in complete silence. Sharon could feel his disapproval. "He always felt that Gene should have been a little more humble about it."

Hambleton was not going to be humble. He was rightfully proud of how he'd handled himself on the ground. Even Tommy Norris himself had praised him for his tenacity. "I certainly admire the man," Norris said. "He deserves a lot of credit." Hambleton felt he'd proven something that had long been in doubt: he had what it took. He'd nearly gotten killed a few different ways in Vietnam, and he wasn't going to hide his light under a bushel for anyone.

After a year, Hambleton retired from the Air Force. An author, William Anderson, approached him to write his life story. The two worked steadily on the project, then sold the hardcover rights to Prentice-Hall, and *BAT-21* appeared in the fall of 1980. The first 25,000 copies sold out almost immediately, and foreign editions were printed in half a dozen countries, including France and Japan. The book was selected for a number of book clubs and became a selection of the Literary Guild of America. *Reader's Digest* published a condensed version. "The world is hungry for heroes," said Anderson.

Despite Hambleton's cooperation, the book was partly fictionalized; Anderson created composite characters, dreamed up events, and invented pages of dialogue. In the story, Hambleton remains clearheaded and in control until the end, something that amused Tommy Norris no end. ("He wouldn't have gotten out of there," the SEAL said, "if someone didn't come get him.") Anderson also created a fictional African American FAC named Captain Bartholomew, who guides Hambleton throughout the entire eleven-day operation. In the final pages, Hambleton meets Bartholomew for the first time and exclaims, "Well, I'm a son of a ... *you're black*!" Bartholomew replies, "Well, waddaya know. So I am."

A Hollywood producer snapped up the rights. Charlton Heston, Dean Martin, and *The Rockford Files'* James Garner all expressed interest in playing Hambleton, but the project eventually stalled. It wasn't the right time. "In the eyes of 'Tinseltown,'" said Anderson, "Vietnam was a dirty word." The television actor Jack Webb, of *Dragnet* fame, picked up the option when it expired but died before he was able to do much with it. The rights were then sold to the country and western singer Jerry Reed, co-star of *Smokey and the Bandit* and famous for his hit "She Got the Goldmine (I Got the Shaft)." Reed was hardly the high-powered producer the movie needed. It seemed like the project was sinking into a dim B-list purgatory.

But Reed came through. By 1987 he'd arranged financing, signed a hot director named Peter Markle, decided on Malaysia as a shooting location, and announced that Gene Hackman had agreed to play the downed navigator. The pairing of the actor and the character seemed preordained; not only did the two men share the same first name and last initial, but Hackman had been raised in Danville, Illinois, not far from where the navigator had been born and lived before his family moved to the nearby town of Wenona. The two Genes were both midwestern boys who'd worked their way up in the world.

Hambleton was over the moon. After all, how many Americans had

Gene Hackman play them in a Hollywood movie? The navigator flew out to the location as a technical adviser and relived his ordeal as it was painstakingly re-created in the Malaysian countryside. He bridled at some changes to the story: the filmmakers, for example, wanted to insert a knock-down argument between him and Gwen just before he shipped out to Korat, to make their reunion that much sweeter. "Gene would have no part of that," says his sister-in-law. The scene never made it into the film.

When it came time for the premiere, Gene and Gwen flew out to Los Angeles. The film was almost as fiction-heavy as the book, but after the screening, he gave it his full endorsement. And Hackman? "He was a better me than me," Hambleton said. He went out on the road to promote the movie and proved to be a good soldier, even if the truth about what had happened in Vietnam inevitably suffered onscreen. In one radio interview, the host asked Hambleton about the African American FAC (played by Danny Glover) who guides him home in the film:

> "Are you still in touch with Captain Bartholomew?"
>
> "Yes, sir. Yes, *sir,*" Hambleton answered. "I'm never going to let him get away. My guardian angel? No way."
>
> "What's he doing now, is he still in the Air Force?"
>
> "He lives in Rochester, New York."
>
> "Really?"
>
> "Yep. What he's doing up there I don't know but he lives in Rochester now."
>
> "Did you go to the premiere together?"
>
> "He didn't make it."
>
> "What did he think of the movie?"
>
> "I've had a couple of letters from him and he thought it was just absolutely great."

If Hambleton had simply been being droll, it would have been a strong performance. The tossed-off "he didn't make it" was especially good. Captain Bartholomew didn't make the premiere because, of course, he didn't exist. But Hambleton's remarks weren't a bit ironic. He thought the film was wonderful. He thought Gene Hackman was wonderful. He must have seen such white lies as the price of his own Hollywood moment, the dream he'd had since Wenona of making it out and doing something truly big.

As he settled back into life in Tucson, Hambleton always denied that he suffered any lingering effects from his eleven days on the ground. "I think I'm pretty much the person I was before it started," he told one interviewer. "It's changed my mind about a few things, about first of all the horrors of war and it's shown me anybody can do what they had to do when they have to do it." But others noticed things. Four years after he returned, Gwen's niece Vicky and her husband visited the couple in Tucson. Gene and Gwen welcomed them to their house, brought them into the living room, and sat down to talk. Soon Gene excused himself. Minutes later, the niece and her husband heard him in the bathroom, throwing up. They asked Gwen if he was sick. Gwen reminded them it was April second, four years to the day since Gene had been shot down.

There were other reminders. Sometimes, standing in the shower, he would hear a little *plink* sound and look down and see a piece of flak shrapnel that had worked its way out of his skin lying on the floor. But the anniversary was the toughest. The memories returned every year, along with the nausea.

For the families of the men who hadn't returned, the news had come most often in the evening. Jim Alley's parents were sitting in their home in Plantation, Florida, around 10:30 one spring night when the doorbell rang. It was an hour when the Alleys weren't used to receiving visitors, and both thought immediately of their son. Mr. Alley stood up and walked toward the front entrance, but before he could reach it, he paused, then stopped. Despite his wife's entreaties, he couldn't make himself walk the last few feet to the door and turn the knob.

Mrs. Alley had to get up and answer the bell. When she opened the door, there were Air Force men standing on her doorstep. The men spoke a few words and handed her a telegram. Years later, Mrs. Alley retained a clear memory that the officers had behaved cruelly in the way they delivered the news of Jim's disappearance, though she never said how. Perhaps they didn't linger to talk about Jim, which was, above all, what she wanted. "This was our only son," she wrote in a letter afterward. "He was a wonderful boy . . . We do not say this 'cause he was our son, but you had to know him to really know what I'm trying to tell you. He never got in any trouble . . . He made student of the year in the 12th grade. You don't find many boys like our son was . . . He thought as much of us as we did him. He called me at least once a week, when he left for the service."

The Air Force men didn't ask about any of this, didn't ask who the young man was whose death notice they were delivering. They handed over their message, turned, and left.

The news reached Centerburg, Ohio, around the same time. Hayden Chapman's sister Beth was returning home about 11 p.m.; she'd been out with the girls from her job. As she pulled into the driveway, she saw her husband standing in the doorway of their home, the light behind him framing the outline of his darkened body. She ran up the steps and he told her what had happened to Jolly Green 67. "I just collapsed on the floor," she said.

Chapman's nephew Brad, who'd hero-worshipped Hayden and would eventually become an Air Force pilot himself as a tribute to his uncle, recalled the moment when he heard. "My sister Julie answered the phone and said it was Grandpa. My mom got on the phone and listened and then she put her head down on the table. I remember what clothes I was wearing that day. I remember where I was in the house. Our life and our world basically ended."

Hayden's sister Carol was listening to the radio when the announcer read a report of a Jolly Green being shot down in Vietnam. "It scared me." She called her husband, who'd already received word of the crash. "You *have* to tell me," she said to him. "Is it true?" When he said yes, Carol began to scream. "It scared my husband to death. He didn't know what to do for me." In her mind, she was seeing Hayden not as a grown man but as the child she and her sisters had doted on and fought with, their games of 1-2-3 played in the backyard in Centerburg until it got dark. "I thought, 'That beautiful, beautiful boy.'" Many nights afterward, she would wake up and hear "blood-curdling screams" echoing in her bedroom and only after a few seconds realize it was her own voice making the sounds.

As the years passed, letters arrived for Hambleton from the families of the men who hadn't returned. He conscientiously answered (and saved) the letters that the grieving wives and sons wrote him. His responses to their questions — *What happened that day? Could my son still be alive?* — were full and gracious. "Please keep in touch if there is ever anything that I can help you with," he wrote Barbara Serex, daughter of Henry Serex, his Bat 21 crewmate. "Please don't hesitate to call on me. I wish you much good luck and nothing but happiness to you and your family."

In the 1980s and 1990s, Hambleton was invited to speak at Air Force survival and evasion schools across the country. He mixed easily with the younger airmen, who listened closely to his account of the Bat 21 ordeal. Often when he gave a speech, Hambleton would talk about the men who came to save him. He named them — Kulland, Alley, Chapman, and the rest — and gave quick bios of each one. He wanted the audiences to know a little about the airmen so that they wouldn't just be names hurrying by in a narrative. When he got on the phone and spoke to a reporter about Chapman, who'd piloted Jolly Green 67, he was effusive. "I have been all over the country, and every place I go they use the word 'hero.' Well I am not. The heroes were Captain Chapman and his crew, Lt. Tom Norris of a SEAL team that picked me up . . . I can't say enough about what Chapman was doing. I owe my life to him and all the other people involved."

Then, beginning in 1994, something odd occurred. US military teams had returned to Southeast Asia to recover the remains of those who'd died in battle and whose bodies were never retrieved. On that list were the men involved in the Hambleton mission. In April 1994, the families of the men aboard Blueghost 39 were notified that remains of their loved ones had been found and would soon be brought back to the United States. And three years later, the bodies of the men from Jolly Green 67 were discovered and repatriated.

The news had a peculiar effect on Hambleton. Now in his speeches he talked about the eleven men's sacrifice, but he stopped mentioning them by name. Before, he would give a little description of each of them, their hometowns, perhaps their rank. Small reminders of their individual lives. But now that their remains — bone fragments, in most cases — were being returned, he no longer did this. Perhaps the physical reminder of what had been lost was too much for him to bear. Perhaps it was the expectation that he would go to the airmen's funerals and face their families and their children that distressed him.

When the organizers of the ceremonies contacted Hambleton and invited him to Arlington to welcome the men of Jolly Green 67 home, the ex-navigator told them he couldn't make it. His excuses ranged from the barely adequate to the ludicrous-sounding: he had a previous speaking engagement, or he was miffed because the organizers wouldn't send him a plane ticket.

Many of his fellow soldiers going to the ceremony were incensed. How could Hambleton stay away? These men had died trying to save him, and now he was too busy to welcome them home? No one could fathom it. One of the airmen who helped organize the Arlington ceremony, Darrel Whitcomb, personally called Hambleton and invited him to attend, but the retired officer declined. Hambleton never gave what his fellow airmen considered a good explanation for his absence.

It seemed, after all that had been done to keep him alive, like a slap in the face.

Why did Hambleton refuse? We can only surmise what was running through his mind; he never gave a reason that seemed convincing. Perhaps a clue can be found in the many letters from the mission members' families, which he kept for decades at his home in Tucson. In late October 1974, Hambleton received a handwritten note from Jim Alley's mother. In it, Mrs. Alley expressed her deep gratitude for an earlier letter from Hambleton and talked about the couple's continuing bewilderment over Jim's fate. Things had not gotten better in the years since Jim disappeared.

> We cannot accept the fact that our son is dead. Only you know and we would like for you to tell us what really happened to the Jolly Green trying to rescue you! Would you help us locate the crash site? I'm planning on going over there . . . I pray every day that my son will be

home soon. It's been three years April 6th that he went down. I know on the news that we have boys still in prison over there, I pray our son is one of them. I would give my life for my son! . . . I always get a dozen roses and place them out by his flag pole, and we fly the flag. You know, sir, losing him and never getting anything of him is just about more than I can stand.

How could Hambleton face these men and women and tell them their loved one was surely already dead even before they got the telegram? That there was no hope of rest or peace for them? Meeting these people would be to confront what his moment in the sun had cost. It would be to consider the question "Am I really worth eleven lives?"

What could his answer possibly have been? Many of the men who'd died had children; he was childless. Many of them were just beginning their lives and careers; he was closer to the end of both. What did he have to show these families that could atone for the loss they woke to every day?

In private moments, the ex-navigator was tormented. "He was always very much embarrassed and concerned about the number of guys killed trying to get him out," said his closest friend, Dennis Armstrong. "He wasn't worth that and nobody was worth that. It shouldn't have happened." Hambleton was anguished that some of the men never had the chance to have families and the others never returned to see their children. "He was *very* sorry it happened. He had survivor's guilt, absolutely. He broke down. He would cry."

Armstrong recalled watching Hambleton talking to audiences about Bat 21. The airman was good at public speaking, personable and warm. His version of the events hit all the main points: the SAM exploding, the days in his hiding place, the long walk to the river. But when he reached the point in the story where his rescuers were killed, he would sometimes stop and turn away from the audience. Only after composing himself with some difficulty would he turn back and go on.

33

THE RETURNS

THE INVASION OF SOUTH VIETNAM, the red fiery summer, raged for six more months, killing 25,000 civilians and turning a million Vietnamese villagers and townspeople into refugees. The North saw 100,000 of their soldiers killed or wounded; casualties in the South were double that. Supported by an aggressive air campaign pushed by President Nixon, who ordered the renewed bombing of Hanoi and the mining of Haiphong harbor and other shipping ports, the ARVN often fought bravely and well. The South Vietnamese generals launched a fierce counterattack in June and July, reclaiming much of the territory they'd lost in the spring. By October, the offensive was over.

Nixon's aggressive strategy had risked a Soviet withdrawal from the spring summit planned for Moscow. But at the end of May, the meeting went ahead. Nixon and Kissinger flew to the Russian capital on Air Force One as the world watched and the television networks broadcast live coverage. On the first day of negotiations, after a boat ride on the Moscow River, the Americans met with Brezhnev and Nikolai Podgorny, chairman of the Presidium of the Supreme Soviet. Almost as soon as they sat down, the Soviet leaders launched into an extraordinarily bitter attack on their policies in Vietnam. "You are murderers!" Podgorny shouted. "There is blood of old people, women, and children on your hands. When will you finally end this senseless war?" It went on and on, at high volume, with each leader expressing his outrage in the most passionate terms. But Kissinger, listening closely, sensed all was not as it seemed. "For all the bombast and rudeness," he later wrote, "we were participants in a charade. While the tone was bellicose and the manner extremely rough, none of the Soviet statements had any operational content . . . The Soviet leaders were not pressing us except with words. They were speaking for the record, and when they said enough to have a transcript to send to Hanoi, they would stop."

He was correct. After Brezhnev and Podgorny ranted for several minutes, the shouting ceased and negotiations resumed in a much calmer tone. There was even a "joyous" dinner that night in which Russian vodka flowed freely and Nixon became so intoxicated that he only just managed to get out of the room without passing out. On May 26, 1972, the two countries agreed to an international arms control treaty known as SALT I, which, among other provisions, froze the number of ICBMs in each nation's arsenal. The agreement was widely seen as a breakthrough and was praised even by the president's enemies. "A FIRST STEP, BUT A MAJOR STRIDE" read the headline in the *New York Times* the next morning.

Nixon's punishing counteroffensive, along with the signs of a détente between the United States and the two major communist powers, also pressed the leaders in Hanoi toward the negotiating table. On January 15, 1973, the White House announced that, in light of progress in the peace talks, the president was suspending military operations in Vietnam and the final withdrawal of American troops would commence. Twelve days later, the United States and the government of North Vietnam signed the Paris Peace Accords; by the end of March, the last American combat troops left the country, after 58,220 of their fellow soldiers, and millions of Vietnamese combatants and civilians, had been killed. The war, for the Americans, had ended.

Nixon had gotten what he wanted, an "honorable" exit from the war. But the consequences for the South Vietnamese were dire, as the Americans knew. The South had barely been able to fight off the Easter Offensive with the full backing of the USAF. How could it survive once the planes and the pilots left? When he read the details of the agreement, Prime Minister Thieu of South Vietnam flew into a rage. Feeling betrayed by Nixon, he refused to sign. Nixon, who'd won a landslide victory in the

1972 election, attempted to sway Thieu with promises of military supplies and millions of dollars in aid. The Vietnamese leader knew that he had few good options; if he refused to sign the peace deal, the Americans could walk away without giving his regime anything at all. Eventually, he conceded.

In the next two years, the North Vietnamese, in violation of the peace accords, secretly built up their forces with the aid of both China and the USSR. The NVA swept south, taking provincial capitals on their way to Saigon. Rumors of beheadings and mass executions filtered through the city. South Vietnamese soldiers stripped off their uniforms and flung them onto the streets, and civilians threw rocks at Marines in their trucks as they sped by, furious that the Americans were leaving.

The final attack on Saigon began on April 29, 1975. People offered American soldiers gold and jewels to let them inside the US embassy compound, while diplomatic officials fed CIA documents into the furnace, along with millions of dollars in cash. The airport was being strafed by NVA rockets and the runways became unusable. The next day, helicopters ferried the American ambassador, Graham Martin, and the last of the Vietnamese refugees to the ships of the Seventh Fleet, anchored offshore.

The last contingent of Marines guarding the embassy grounds ran up the building's stairs, snapping locks shut on each floor before moving higher. Then, unsure whether they'd been forgotten, the soldiers sat on the roof passing around a bottle of whiskey before finally hearing the chop of rotors descending from above. Their commander, Master Sergeant Juan Valdez, was the last man aboard the helicopter as it rose into the sky. As they flew toward the sea, the Marines watched the capital burning below them.

As part of the agreement, American POWs returned home in 1973. One of them was José Astorga, the door gunner on Blueghost 39 who'd been wounded in the effort to save Hambleton. Astorga had spent a difficult year in a prison near Hanoi, a year he wished to forget. Before being captured, he'd learned the skills of a mechanic, which he hoped would lead to a job and an ordinary life back in the States. But that didn't happen.

"I was depressed, I was hallucinating," he said. Classic PTSD symptoms emerged: Astorga would dream about the helicopter crash and the NVA soldiers pointing their guns at him in the hole as the chopper burned, and he would die in his dreams and his crew would burn up all over again.

Astorga managed to get a civil service job, but after three months he walked into his boss's office and resigned. "People didn't understand," he said. "I wasn't able to adjust to society. Mentally, I couldn't do it. Something's wrong and I didn't know what." He felt guilty about his crewmates: Paschall, Frink, Kulland. He called their families and spoke about their loved ones, but in the back of his mind he always wondered if he could have saved the men. His mind dwelled, for large parts of the day, in Vietnam.

Astorga now lives in San Diego with his family. He's never held another job in the more than forty years he's been back. The ordeal destroyed romantic relationships in his twenties and thirties; he was far too erratic, too haunted to sustain one.

His path had changed so drastically on that spring day in 1972 that it could almost be said that one life ended and another, darker one began in the air over the Mieu Giang River. But he never regretted going after Hambleton. "It was worth it," he said. "We got him out."

After marching for days, Bill Henderson, the downed OV-10 pilot, ended up in a tiny room in a North Vietnamese prison. His face began to heal and his eyebrows and mustache, which had been burned off by the explosion, grew back.

There had been random moments of terror on the way north. In one village, some guys in shiny suits — obviously intelligence operatives — put a gun to the pilot's head. "You will answer our questions," one of them said. "I've answered all the questions I can," Henderson replied. The man dropped the gun. The American was taken to a plantation outside Hanoi and put in a nine-foot-by-nine-foot room.

The small cell was covered with ceramic tiles, which radiated the heat even after the sun went down. He lost weight rapidly. Boils appeared all over his torso and limbs, even on the inside of his eyelids. His body lost the ability to sweat; in the summer afternoons when the heat reached 120 degrees, his temperature shot up until he thought he would pass out.

The American was eating mostly pumpkin and what he suspected was rat meat. He was tortured, but he found the abuse to be "superficial and hilarious." The guards would come in and slap him around and stuff him into small boxes, where he'd have to crouch over to fit, but it was nothing that survival training hadn't prepared him for.

His room was covered with Vietnamese jumping spiders, and at night he could hear rats scurry across the floor, sometimes crawling over his leg or arm. But the heat was worse; he felt he was literally putrefying during the long afternoons. "I said to myself, 'Am I going to stay here and rot until the rats eat me?'" About two months into his captivity, depression washed over him. There seemed no way out of that room and back to America.

The weeks and months passed slowly. Shut away from the world, Henderson had time to think about his path in life, hours and hours in which he spent considering his career as a military aviator. "It reset me," he said. Perhaps it was the emergence of a long-buried desire, or the suffering he experienced or the suffering he witnessed, but in that tiny room Henderson decided he no longer wished to be a shit-hot pilot delivering the smash from thirty thousand feet. After a year in the prison, he was released and returned home a slightly different man. "Before I was shot down, I would have stayed in the Air Force. Flying, really flying, there's nothing better." But it no longer seemed like quite enough. "I said, 'That's great, but so what? I thought about what I wanted to do. How can I help people?'"

Henderson went back to school and became an organizational psychologist. He reunited with his wife, and they had three children. He suffered no symptoms of PTSD or regrets about his part in the war, but he did carry with him a card containing a prayer to one of the angels he believed had spoken to him in the plane after the missile struck. It didn't make him any more religious, but it did give him a feeling of being watched over.

He felt no bitterness toward Hambleton. Nothing needed to be said. "If you're going to hang your ass out there," he concluded more than four decades after the ordeal, "you expect your *compadres* to come after you."

34

"AS COMRADES"

GENE HAMBLETON SPENT his time golfing, churchgoing, and being with Gwen. He had a regular group of buddies who met at the local barber shop to shoot the bull and tell Air Force stories. But his ordeal in Vietnam had made him less sociable; he stayed home more often. "It changed him," Gwen told a friend. The couple's devotion to and dependence on each other only grew.

In the spring of 2002, Gwen was diagnosed with lung cancer and began chemotherapy. The prognosis was grim; both Gwen and Gene were lifelong smokers. As Gwen grew sicker, the two became distraught at the thought of leaving each other. "She fought for every day," said her sister Mary Ann Anderson. "She struggled to live because she knew that he needed her." Gene stopped doing much of anything except caring for his wife; as she grew thinner, he fed her, bathed her, and spent long hours by her bedside.

In the fall of 2003, Gene received the same diagnosis. After speaking with his doctor, Gene refused treatment. "He told me he had a spot on his lung but he wasn't going to do anything about it," said his niece Pam. He felt the chemo would take the physical strength he needed to look after his wife. "It didn't surprise me," Pam said. "They'd been through everything together."

One of the last things he wrote to Gwen was a card for her birthday. "Honey, I do love you and always have. Thank you so much for a very wonderful 61 years we have had together." One Sunday, he slipped away to attend church. While he was there, ushering, Gwen's sister came in and told him that his wife was failing. He ran to see Gwen, but she was dead by the time he reached her bedside.

Gene was sick at heart. "I knew when she died, he wouldn't make it a year," said his friend Dennis Armstrong. Nine months after his wife's death, Gene came down with pneumonia. He was brought to Tucson Medical Center, where he passed away on September 19, 2004. His ashes were interred next to his wife's at the Abraham Lincoln National Cemetery in Elwood, Illinois which had been built on the site of the old Joliet Arsenal, where the two had met years before. His congregation, the Spanish Trail Lutheran Church, put a note on their message board that sat on the church's front lawn. "BAT 21 HAS BEEN RESCUED," it read.

One of the last to return home was Jim Alley. In the spring of 2010, forensic teams searching the field where Jolly Green 67 had crashed found a number of bone fragments. They notified the Alleys and the families of other crew members that the remains would be returned to them and asked for a family member to be sent to Hawaii to receive them.

Alley's father—who'd kept his son's yellow '67 Camaro in his garage for decades—had passed away two years earlier. "My dad had the perfect family, and then Jim died," said Jim's brother, Tim. "Everything just went downhill. In pictures, you see that he never smiled again." Alley's mother was in a nursing home suffering from the final stages of Alzheimer's. His sister wanted nothing to do with the ceremony; that part of her life was over. So Tim was left to fly to Hawaii, where JPAC, the Joint POW/MIA Accounting Command, is headquartered.

After Jim was reported missing, the family had followed his wishes and adopted a baby boy. Tim had been born to a cousin of the family, a single mom who felt she was too young to care for him; the Alleys took him in as their own when he was six weeks old. Tim grew up knowing that he was a replacement of sorts, a living reminder of the boy who hadn't returned. "He was this hero I could never live up to," he said. The Alleys were strict with their young son. Tim's childhood was conditioned by the unspoken demand that he not die. When he finished high school, he took the Marine Corps exam, passed it, and announced to his family that he was going to join up. "I wanted to be like Jim," he said. "But my father told me they'd already lost one son and weren't going to lose another." Tim became a fireman instead.

When the day arrived, he boarded a Delta flight in Fort Myers. He was happy to be on his way, eager even. "I'd looked up to my big brother my entire life," he said. When he arrived in Honolulu after the seventeen-hour flight, he was met by the Air Force mortuary personnel and brought to his hotel. The next morning, he went to JPAC's facility. He took a tour of the lab, met the commander, shook the hands of the service members. After the tour was over, the director asked him, "Would you like to meet your brother?"

The remains were waiting in a funeral chapel on the base. Tim entered and stood nervously as two soldiers approached him carrying a green wool military blanket. When the soldiers got closer, he could see that four or five bone fragments had been placed on the blanket, including a piece of a human femur. The soldiers showed the remains to Tim, turned, and put the blanket in an open silver casket that stood on a trolley. Tim approached and saw that inside was a blue Air Force uniform, laid out on the white silk lining as if it covered the body of an airman. The medals Jim had earned were pinned to the chest. "I broke down there a couple of times," Tim said. He reached into the casket and touched the bones. "I put my hand on Jim and told him good-bye and said I was glad to bring him home."

The casket was loaded onto the Delta flight. The plane landed at Fort Myers and Tim was allowed off first; Jim's casket was put in a hearse right there on the tarmac. The hearse left the airport with Tim riding behind in another vehicle, a sheriff's car leading the small procession as it headed north. Each county they passed through along the route sent an official vehicle to accompany the hearse. When the cars came to the Charlotte County line, Tim felt a light pressure on his eardrums, the chop of helicopter rotors agitating the air. He glanced out the window and saw a Vietnam-era Huey hovering at the front of the procession.

Exhausted, wrung out, Tim looked at the big chopper and the flashing blue lights of the police car ahead passing through towns whose streets

Jim and his friends had ridden down in their Pontiac Tempests and Ford GT40 Mark IIIs in the months before Vietnam. He knew that even this small motorcade wouldn't have happened in the early seventies, when Jim had died. The bitterness of those years had largely faded, allowing his brother to become not a symbol of an ill-starred war but simply a soldier returning to his old haunts. "It was more like a homecoming that should have happened back then," Tim said. The sound of the Huey thrummed in the air until the hearse reached the county line, then the chopper flared its rotors and turned back, and fire trucks from Tim's department took over and escorted his brother to the funeral home in the small city of Arcadia. There the rest of the family, those still alive after these many years, were waiting to wake Jim Alley.

A lot of people had come to the funeral home, some of whom hadn't even known Jim but wanted to pay their respects regardless. For hours, the men and women talked and sat and milled about. Finally, toward late afternoon, the last mourner spoke to Mrs. Alley and walked out into the parking lot, and Tim and his mother were left alone. Tim asked the funeral director to open the casket; his mother took a red rose and placed it inside. Tim had found a photograph of his father, mother, sister, and himself; now he put it down on the blue wool of the uniform, so the Alleys would be together, at least this once, the snapshot plus the remains forming a wholly intact family that never existed in space and time. Then Tim placed a plastic model car next to the photograph, the same toy-sized yellow '67 Camaro that Jim had kept in his room, a reminder of his dream car and of a time before his draft notice arrived in the mail, before the reports of a shootdown near the Mieu Giang, before everything.

Tommy Norris stayed in Vietnam and, six months later, set out on an intelligence mission behind enemy lines with three South Vietnamese sea commandos and another young SEAL, Petty Officer Michael Thornton. After landing their rubber boat on the seashore, the soldiers came under fire from a large contingent of NVA and were forced to fight their way back to the beach. The men became separated; Norris was firing at the NVA alongside one of the commandos when a bullet struck him behind the left ear, shattering his left eye socket and blowing off most of his forehead. He fell to the ground.

The South Vietnamese soldier who'd been left with Norris saw his grievous injury and, assuming the American had been killed, ran off, leaving him alone and unconscious in the path of the approaching enemy. When the soldier told Thornton what had happened, the American raced four hundred yards back to where Norris lay and found his fellow SEAL. "The whole side of his head was completely gone," Thornton said. "I thought Tommy was dead." Thornton shot two NVA soldiers charging toward the position, threw his fellow SEAL over his shoulder, and ran back across open beach to the sea, firing his gun as he went. There he and another wounded American fought off about 150 enemy soldiers, waded into the water, and swam for hours before being picked up by the American cruiser *Newport News*.

After he was pulled aboard, Thornton carried the unconscious SEAL down through the ship to the surgery and laid him on the operating table. The doctor on call looked at Norris and came over to Thornton. "Mike, there's no way he's gonna make it," he said. But the salt water had cleaned the SEAL's wounds and the sun and the warmth of Thornton's body had prevented him from going into shock. Norris survived, to the astonishment of his caregivers. Later, a doctor would seek him out to tell him his stubbornness was almost an affront to medicine. "We didn't think we were gonna save you," he said. "But you just wouldn't give up." A year later, Thornton was awarded the Medal of Honor for his bravery.

Norris returned stateside and spent years in hospitals trying to recover from his wounds. He'd lost his left eye and even some brain matter in the skirmish at the beach, and now began a series of grueling reconstructive surgeries to repair the damage. He wanted badly to stay in the Navy, but the service determined that his injuries were too severe and retired him. Norris entered a kind of limbo. His doctors told him his wounds prevented him from working, and he experienced severe headaches that would completely immobilize him. Four years after the Hambleton mission, the thirty-two-year-old Norris was living with his parents, unable to move on from the war, his face still bearing the scars of his ordeal. Still,

Norris was humble. "My injury," he said, "when you see the death and destruction to other people that you see in a war — I mean, what I have is nothing. So I lost an eye and part of my brain and had some other bodily injuries, but what is that? I have another eye. You just go on."

As he slowly recovered, the stories about his rescue of Hambleton and Clark continued to circulate in ready rooms and American base camps around the world. Finally, the Navy asked Norris to write up his memories of the rescue so he could be recommended for the Medal of Honor. He refused. He didn't feel that the act of saving Clark and Hambleton qualified him for the medal. The two parties went back and forth. The Navy was frankly exasperated with Tommy Norris. *Who refuses the highest honor his country has to bestow?* Finally, they told the ex-SEAL they were going to put him in for the medal whether he submitted his memories of the rescue or not. Norris relented.

The ceremony took place on March 6, 1976, at the White House. President Gerald Ford read out the citation, which praised Norris's "conspicuous gallantry and intrepidity in action," before hanging the gold medal with its five-pointed star around Norris's neck on its pale blue ribbon. Norris, characteristically, never thought he was worthy of the honor. "I don't feel that I was anybody special," he said. "It was a time and a place and a mission that needed to be accomplished, and I was fortunate to be the one that was successful in that."

Norris was a legend but also basically an invalid. He couldn't get a job. Finally, in the late 1970s, he went in for an interview with the FBI; his college major had been criminal justice, and he'd always dreamt of becoming an agent. It seemed hopeless; he was past the maximum age for applicants, and he couldn't even meet the basic physical requirements. The agency had only ever employed one other one-eyed agent in its entire history, and it wasn't looking for a second.

Norris wouldn't take the FBI's gentle "no" for an answer. He wrote the director of the FBI, William Webster, and asked for a chance. "Surprisingly, he wrote back and said, if you can pass the same tests as anybody else applying to this organization, I'll waive your disability." Norris passed the exam, aced the physical protocol, went through his interview, and was placed in the queue of eligible agents. Finally, he was selected for the 1979 class at Quantico.

In the early 1980s, Norris joined the Hostage Rescue Team, considered the elite of the elite, as one of its founding members. Later he became a "shooter" on the Salt Lake City SWAT team. "You heard stories about him," says James Gagliano, a former FBI agent. "I was a young New York City SWAT member training at Quantico. We were dangling on ropes out of a Huey and the Salt Lake team was training at the same time. This one guy comes down a rope and he's just so strong and wiry. I said to one of my friends, 'Who's that guy?' And he's like, 'That's Tommy fucking Norris. If you two ever cross paths, you better bow *and* genuflect.'" With that, says Gagliano, "I had to meet him. I went up to him that night at the bar and introduced myself. He could not have been more gracious."

Early in 1985, Sikh terrorists began plotting to assassinate the Indian prime minister, Rajiv Gandhi, during his visit to the United States that summer. They went looking for an American who could not only kill the young leader but also provide them with training, machine guns, grenade launchers, fake passports, and C-4 plastic explosives for a "military expedition" back to India. The men wanted to start a revolution. The stakes were quite high: Gandhi's mother, Indira, had been murdered by Sikh terrorists the year before, and her murder had set off violent riots that claimed the lives of three thousand people. Another assassination of a Gandhi could lead to massive unrest.

The conspirators finally found their assassin, an Alabama man referred to in court documents only as "A." This individual was introduced to the Indian men as an expert in guerrilla warfare and "someone with experience in the use of explosives and automatic weapons," which all happened to be true. The would-be killer met with the men in a New York hotel room, where the extremists made it abundantly clear how serious they were: not only did they want the American to shoot Gandhi, but they also wanted training in how to bomb bridges and hotels in India, attack government buildings, and blow up a nuclear power plant. When A inquired exactly how much C-4 plastic explosive they'd need, the men told him enough to bring down something the size of the Brooklyn Bridge and a thirty-six-story building. The men even asked if A could get them chemical weapons.

A, of course, turned out to be Tommy Norris, who was working deep undercover. (Perhaps his quite noticeable facial scars helped convince the Sikhs that he was, in fact, a real-life killer from the Alabama hinterlands.) FBI agents were listening in as the men talked and, after two more meetings, swooped in to arrest the terrorists. Gandhi completed his visit to the United States without incident, and the "assassin" slipped back into the shadow world. The FBI refused to confirm or deny that A was the legendary ex-SEAL who'd saved Gene Hambleton.

Through it all, he remained unimpressed by the myths that had grown up around him. Once, when he was working out of the Coeur d'Alene office of the bureau, he flew to Washington for a dinner for Medal of Honor recipients but forgot the medal itself. Norris called the office and asked another agent if he would go to his house, pick up the five-pointed star, and FedEx it to him. The agent climbed up to Norris's attic and found the medal where Norris said it would be — sitting in an old shoebox. Many recipients display the award prominently in their homes. Not Tommy Norris. "The medal does not belong to me," he said once. "It belongs to all the soldiers over there that fought and lost their lives."

Now retired from the FBI, Tommy Norris lives in Idaho.

Nguyen Van Kiet stayed with his commando unit when the Americans left. As the North Vietnamese closed in on Saigon and the regime of Nguyen Van Thieu fell, he narrowly escaped a bombardment at Cat Lai, just outside Saigon, and boarded a ship crowded with sailors and soldiers. The sudden collapse of the South Vietnamese defenses allowed Kiet no time to find his family — he had a young wife and child — and he was forced to leave them behind. Even if he'd been able to reach them, his status as a South Vietnamese special operations sailor would most likely have doomed his loved ones to years of shame and physical suffering. "I did not want anyone to know they were related to me," he said.

Kiet and other South Vietnamese Navy men steered their ship out into the Saigon River and headed toward the Philippines, nearly a thousand miles away across the South China Sea. They joined up with other large and small boats to form a flotilla of refugees moving east. "We were sad," he said. "It was really hard for us to leave our families." At one point, as the boats made their way toward Subic Bay, an American naval officer boarded the ship and asked the evacuees to lower the South Vietnamese flag. The men and women gathered around and saluted as the yellow flag with its three horizontal red stripes — signifying the nation's three geographical regions — was brought down. "We knew then that we had no country."

Kiet eventually ended up in a refugee camp in Guam, joining thousands of other Vietnamese men, women, and children who were awaiting resettlement in America as part of Operation New Life. After three months, Kiet was flown to Camp Pendleton in California and then moved north to Washington, where he found a job in a sawmill.

The sea commando was every inch the hero that Norris was, but as a foreign national, he couldn't receive the Medal of Honor. Instead, the US military awarded him the Navy Cross, the highest honor possible for a non-American service member. The diminutive sailor attended a ceremony at a naval base near Seattle, where a high-ranking officer read out the citation: "Due to Petty Officer Kiet's coolness under extremely dangerous conditions and his outstanding courage and professionalism, an American aviator was recovered after an eleven-day ordeal behind enemy lines. His self-discipline, personal courage, and dynamic fighting spirit were an inspiration to all; thereby reflecting great credit upon himself and the Naval Service."

Worried about his family in Vietnam, Kiet kept news of the award private. If the communist authorities there learned what he'd done for an American soldier, they might have punished his family severely. There were only three men in the room that day: Kiet, the Navy officer, and Tom Norris, who stood next to his friend as he accepted the Navy Cross. It was Norris who'd recommended Kiet for the honor.

Kiet learned some English and became an American citizen about seven years after arriving in the country. But for more than a decade, he was afraid to write or call his wife and children, who were living in the town of Di An, about twenty miles north of Saigon, now known as Ho Chi Minh City. "I believed if I didn't make any contact, they would be OK."

The reports that filtered out were grim. "They lived very poor and very hard with the communist regime. They tried selling pieces of furniture, one by one, to get food."

After eleven years at the sawmill, Kiet came down with a severe cough caused by the dust from cutting wood planks. Following an operation, he moved to Seattle and went to work for Boeing as a mechanic. In 2005, Norris, Darrel Whitcomb, and the FAC Harold Icke, who'd taken part in the Hambleton mission, returned to Vietnam to film a documentary on the rescue. Kiet was also invited. But contacts in the Vietnamese community told him that if he returned to the country, he wouldn't be allowed to leave again. Kiet asked Norris and the others to see what they could do to help his daughter. The veterans visited the US embassy in Ho Chi Minh City and met with a diplomat there. The man listened to the story and immediately went to work. Shortly after, Kiet's daughter flew to the United States and was reunited with her father.

In November 2000, Kiet attended a gathering of Southeast Asia rescue veterans at Nellis Air Force Base, just north of Las Vegas. Gene Hambleton was there, and he recounted the story of the eleven-day ordeal to the rapt audience. At the end of his talk, Hambleton spotted Kiet standing on the far side of the stage and walked over to embrace him. "Thank you for rescuing me," he said.

Kiet lives in Seattle with his second wife, Thuy, and their extended family.

The Air Force has taught the rescue of Gene Hambleton to its recruits as an example of the maxim that, even in a technological age, courageous men are still necessary. The operation is also used to train soldiers who'll be involved in rescue missions how to think on the ground, what mistakes to avoid. And the myth of the rescue has grown over the years, passed down among airmen and others along with legends such as "Ripley at the Bridge" and the story of the downed Black Hawk in Mogadishu. Its component parts—the SAM's impact, the creation of the golf code, the journey to the river—each receives its moment, but it's Tommy Norris and Nguyen Van Kiet's crossing into enemy terrain that people tend to dwell on.

Over the years, the two men have been asked the same questions over and over, mostly by those who've never served: *Was the mission worth it, eleven lives to save one? What, after all, is the value of a single human life?* The two struggle to explain that, for them, the question is bewildering. It is as though one world were talking to another. "It's not the value of one life," Kiet finally exclaimed to one interviewer. "It's the principle that we as warriors, as comrades, will never leave our fellow soldiers behind enemy lines."

When the armored personnel carrier brought Hambleton to Dong Ha on the afternoon of April 13, 1972, journalists swarmed around the survivor, shouting out questions about the mission. After the airman was loaded aboard a chopper, one reporter turned and found Norris, dressed in his olive shirt and jeans, standing quietly off to one side. As it happened, this was the same overzealous dude who'd appeared at the bunker the day before, hoping to get an exclusive on the rescue, before Norris chased him off. Now the journalist brought his microphone up and said to the exhausted SEAL that he must be hoping never to go on such a mission again.

Norris had reverted to his shy-young-cleric manner by then, and he gave an almost embarrassed laugh at the question. ("I couldn't believe this guy," he admitted later.) But his response wasn't especially gentle. He looked at the reporter and replied that, if he thought he could get another American out, he would go back into the badlands that very night.

ACKNOWLEDGMENTS

My gratitude to all those touched by the Bat 21 mission who spoke with me or helped me in my research: Nguyen Van Kiet, José Astorga, Bill Henderson, Mary Lou Giannangeli, Robert Giannangeli, James Giannangeli. Brad Huffman, Hayden Chapman's sisters Beth, Carol, and Jean, Lee Kulland, Karen Wallgren, Leona Hauge, Ashley Kulland, Tim Alley, Buzz Busboom, Ty Crowe, Doug Brinson, Dennis Armstrong, Pam Forrest, Sharon Fitzpatrick. Martha Lorin Walker, Butch Hammond, Trent Wicks, Gus Evans, Rod Curry, Larry Potts, Joel Eisenstein, Paul Davis, Sandra Kolb of the United States Air Force, and Sharon Edgington at the Congressional Medal of Honor Society.

Thanks to Bruce Nichols and Ivy Givens at Houghton Mifflin Harcourt and Scott Waxman and Ashley Lopez at the Waxman Agency.

Special thanks to Jim Flessner, Donna Cutsinger and Mary Ann Anderson, sisters of Gwen Hambleton, who never failed to respond to my neverending questions with grace and humor.

Appendix A

CHRONOLOGY

SEPTEMBER 4, 1971: Lieutenant Colonel Gene Hambleton arrives at the Korat Royal Thai Air Force Base in northeast Thailand to begin his tour in Vietnam.

MARCH 30, 1972: The North Vietnamese launch the *mua he do lua* (red fiery summer), a significant mechanized attack on South Vietnamese and US forces. The Americans term the campaign the "Easter Offensive."

APRIL 2, 1972: Hambleton and five other crew members aboard an EB-66C aircraft are shot down over South Vietnam. The rescue operation commences minutes after Hambleton makes contact with a FAC orbiting over the crash site.

APRIL 2: First Lieutenant Byron Kulland and his crew aboard Army helicopter Blueghost 39 are shot down while trying to retrieve Hambleton. Three airmen are killed. José Astorga escapes the wreckage but is immediately captured by NVA soldiers.

APRIL 3: Captain Bill Henderson and First Lieutenant Mark Clark, aboard an OV-10, are shot down near Hambleton's location. Clark takes cover, while Henderson is quickly captured by NVA troops.

APRIL 4: A-1 and F-4 aircraft conduct airstrikes near Hambleton's position. Planners consider other options, including waiting for the NVA invasion force to move on past Hambleton. Several are seriously damaged.

APRIL 5: Bad weather continues. No rescue missions are launched.

APRIL 6: The Jolly Green 67 rescue crew attempts to pick up both Clark and Hambleton. The mission fails and the entire crew is killed when the craft is struck by enemy fire and crashes. General Creighton Abrams orders that no further rescue attempts be made by helicopter.

APRIL 7: No search and rescue forces launch. Planners meet to review the situation and to consider alternative methods of saving Hambleton and Clark.

APRIL 7: Air Force First Lieutenant Bruce Walker and USMC First Lieutenant Larry Potts, flying in an OV-10, are shot down over the DMZ area. Potts is not heard from again; Walker makes radio contact and begins escape and evasion maneuvers.

APRIL 7: USMC Lieutenant Colonel Andy Andersen calls Major General Winton Marshall and requests a meeting regarding the rescue situation.

APRIL 8: Marshall and Andersen meet in Saigon, and the general greenlights Andersen's overland rescue plan. Andersen makes contact with a Navy SEAL, Lieutenant Tommy Norris, and asks him to serve as tactical leader on the operation. Norris agrees.

APRIL 9: Andersen, Norris, and their team fly to Ai Tu Combat Base and brief General Vu Van Giai on the mission. They then move on to Dong Ha and are briefed by the commander of the First Armor Brigade before continuing on to their forward operating base on the banks of the Mieu Giang River.

APRIL 10: Mark Clark enters the river and begins swimming downstream toward the rescue team.

APRIL 10: Gene Hambleton begins his overland journey to the Mieu Giang. On the way, he's forced to kill a North Vietnamese man who confronts him with a knife.

APRIL 11: Norris, Petty Officer Nguyen Van Kiet, and other commandos locate Clark and bring him to the forward operating base. Hambleton reaches the Mieu Giang River. At dusk, he enters the water and begins swimming downstream.

APRIL 11: The team's forward operating base is struck by a North Vietnamese rocket and mortar attack. Andersen and many of the team members are wounded or killed. Andersen is retrieved by an armored personnel carrier and brought to a military hospital.

APRIL 11: Norris, Kiet, and two other commandos set out to locate Hambleton. They venture over a mile upriver but fail to find the airman and return to base.

APRIL 12: Two of the South Vietnamese commandos refuse to go after Hambleton that night. Norris and Kiet disguise themselves as Vietnamese fishermen and paddle upriver in a sampan. They find a dangerously malnourished and weak Hambleton and, after several encounters with enemy troops, bring him back to the forward bunker.

APRIL 12: Hambleton is taken by armored personnel carrier to a waiting helicopter and flown to an American base for treatment.

APRIL 18: Bruce Walker is killed by a Vietcong soldier after eleven days on the ground.

Appendix B

WALKER AND POTTS

The story of the pilot Bruce Walker and USMC First Lieutenant Larry Potts, who were shot down on April 7 while flying an artillery spotting mission just east of where the Bat 21 rescue was unfolding, quickly branched off from the rest of that operation. The full narrative is told here.

Larry Potts's road to the war was rougher than that of many of the airmen he would serve with in Vietnam. Born in Smyrna, Delaware, he was the product of a home broken by the early death of his mother. After her passing, Larry's truck driver father found it difficult to raise his children while earning a living on the road, and so the family split up. A few of the children ended up with relatives, others in foster care. "They were scattered all over," says Larry's nephew Trent.

Losing their parents and their home caused some of the Potts kids to go badly astray, at least in the eyes of the black middle-class families of Smyrna. A few of the kids got in trouble with the law or ended up dropping out of school. But Larry went to the home of his aunt Louise, who was known in her family as a "stern woman." Louise was a God-fearing, strict authoritarian with a college degree who brooked no mess whatsoever. "She put her all into him" is the how the family phrases it. And Larry came out right. More than right, in fact.

Track and field, church, choir, studies, dinner with Aunt Louise and her husband, Samuel — the young man didn't have a minute to spare for any kind of foolishness. Larry didn't drink or smoke or even cuss much. He didn't, as far as anyone could remember, even have a serious girlfriend until much later. No time! He was Aunt Louise's child, an honest-to-God choirboy, with his Buddy Holly glasses and his ramrod posture and serious nature. The whole family had their eyes on him. Some remarked that he seemed more like a young preacher than a warrior. "Very conservative, very intelligent, neat, clean, proper, well-groomed, well-mannered," said one Smyrna kid who took Larry as a role model. "He was one of the most well-respected young men ever in that town."

In fourth grade, Larry met Butch Hammond from the nearby town of Milford. They were both black, short, and tough. "He was like my twin," Hammond says. Years later, the two enrolled together at Delaware State University. Money was tight; sometimes Larry had to hitchhike the twelve miles from Smyrna to Dover, where the university was located. One day he and Butch decided to drive to Philadelphia and take the Marine Corps entrance exam, purely on a lark. They thought for sure they'd flunk it and it would be a story to tell their friends. After they finished, an officer came outside, gave the pair a look, and said, "Well, you two didn't set the world on fire. But you passed."

As they rolled back to Delaware State in Butch's maroon 1965 Chevy Impala with the 327-cubic-inch engine — Butch always managed to get his hands on the hottest cars — their laughter bounced off the white leather interior. The Marines thought they had the two boys from Delaware all wrapped up for delivery to Vietnam. Hell, they were college students now! But the more Butch and Larry talked about it, the less they laughed. Why *not* join the Marines? they thought. What exactly did middle-class life and the church and a job with GE or Palmolive or what have you offer to a pair of twenty-two-year-olds nearly bursting with testosterone?

They signed up. When Butch fell half an inch short of the five-foot-six height requirement, the slightly taller Larry took his friend's license (which, in the state of Delaware at that time, didn't include a picture) and walked onto the base's medical office to impersonate his pal. Butch got Larry infatuated with the Marines, but Larry got Butch into the Corps.

Some members of the Potts family were distraught. Why in God's name would Larry, who had before him a gleaming array of possible futures that many young black men in America could barely conceive of—lawyer, doctor, engineer, preacher—volunteer to join the Marines? And go to Vietnam? If the conflict was unpopular in white neighborhoods, it was downright scorned in some black ones. Muhammad Ali had gone to jail to avoid the draft, and here was Smyrna's own Larry Potts signing up to put his life on the line in a white man's war. Why?

The family never got a good answer. "I want to say that he really wanted to save his country," says his nephew Trent. Larry Potts believed in America despite its George Wallaces and its Strom Thurmonds, and he was going to fight for it no matter what anyone thought. Others met him and got the impression it was the Marine Corps that had him in its spell. "We had just a few encounters," says Gus Evans, a fellow Smyrna man who joined the Marines because of Larry's example, "and after I talked to him I knew that Larry was ready and willing to die for the Corps." Then again, just before his deployment Larry had split up with his most serious girlfriend yet, who he'd found out was his third cousin. "It broke his heart," Butch said. Maybe Larry wanted to forget all about it and Vietnam was a ready-made distraction. Maybe a lot of things went into it.

But there was something else. His best friend remembers Larry sidling up to him one day at the Marine base in Quantico, where they were the only black dudes in their respective platoons, and in that quiet way of his saying simply, "Butch, I want to be where the action is."

In 1972, to young Americans like Larry Potts, Vietnam was still a place to find out just what kind of man you were.

Bruce Walker's past could hardly have been more different from Potts's. His fate was seemingly set in place the moment he was born. He was the son of Colonel Charles Walker, a natural-born aviator, a man with "golden hands," as they said in the Air Force. Bruce would follow him into the service.

Bruce Walker didn't give off an air of entitlement or rock-jawed arrogance. He had friendly hazel eyes and a surprisingly high voice and came across as bitingly honest but open and friendly. "I couldn't imagine him having an enemy in the world," said a pilot who went through flight training with him. Walker's younger sister recalls him returning to Paris, where their father was stationed, after college and hauling a batch of 45s in his luggage so that she would have the latest American music and feel closer to events back home. She never forgot that gesture. What kind of older brother thought of such things?

While an undergraduate at Southern Colorado State College in Pueblo, Bruce met Martha Lorin, a self-described "weird bird," a fiery redheaded student who was at that moment having problems with a geology professor. When she'd tried to join his seminar, the man had told her, *Well, we're not really open to women in this field.* That was all Martha needed to hear. "I was impossible in that class," she remembers fondly. "I did everything to drive that guy nuts."

When she met Bruce—unwillingly at first, invited by a friend to go for pizza—she was intrigued by his friendly manner, his stories of growing up all across Europe, how *different* he seemed. Bruce was small, but he was strong and fit, a "rings" man for the SCSC gymnastics team and a ski coach up at Monarch Ski Area, where he could be seen cutting curves into the powder. He was bursting with vitality; "ruddy" is the word Martha used. And he had the most beautiful hands she'd ever seen.

The attraction was instantaneous, at least for her. When they first met, Martha was wearing cowboy boots and a Pendleton flannel shirt. Bruce thought she was "a dyke." But the next time he saw her she had changed her look completely and had on a nice dress and a long curly wig, all for his benefit. They were dying to make love. And they did.

Four months after they met, the two were married. And suddenly Martha Lorin Walker was an Air Force wife, something she was not particularly suited for. She hated "socializing with drunken women" while their husbands were trying to survive the instructors at Air Training Command, whose methods were neatly summarized by the guys as "Fear, Sarcasm, and Ridicule." The wives had afternoon parties where the gossip would begin as soon as you walked through the door and the liquor—gallons of it—arrived soon after. Martha was turned off. "I didn't give a damn if they drank. I just didn't want drinks pushed into my hand."

The two of them occasionally fought. Bruce resented the fact that she spent so much time with her mother, gambling at the dog track. One time Bruce dumped all her clothes on the front lawn and told her to get out. When he went to her mother's house to try to make up, Mrs. Lorin blocked her daughter's bedroom door. "It was like my presence was going to defile some holy temple," says the character based on Bruce in *Did I Say Goodbye*, a play Martha wrote later. "It was insane. *She* was insane." They broke up. Bruce drove back to his folks in Virginia, where his dad was now working at the Pentagon, until Martha called him to apologize and to beg him to come back.

But they were close, "almost psychic." When he was on a training mission one day, a feeling overcame her. "Lucy," she said to her friend, "I think Bruce just almost crashed." Her friend scoffed: How could she possibly know that? But later that night, she found out Bruce had been flying at that very moment when out of the corner of his eye he spotted a flock of turkey buzzards heading toward one of his intakes. He snapped the stick left and dove away, barely avoiding a crash.

Martha got pregnant. While they were on a weekend school break in Corpus Christi, she waded into the surf, happy and content despite Bruce's warnings that the waves could induce labor. At dinner that night, she felt the first contractions. They were 150 miles away from the base hospital. Bruce packed her into his Ford Falcon and sped across the wastes of south Texas, praying she wouldn't give birth in the desert among the rattlers and the mesquite. They just made it. Their baby daughter was named Lorin Marie.

As he came closer to getting his wings, Bruce had to decide what he would do. His instructors wanted him to stay and teach new recruits at Air Training Command. It was as safe as flying for Pan Am, a golden out. He could serve his country without ever hanging his ass over Vietnam. Martha told him she'd support him no matter what he decided.

But Bruce Walker was a born combat pilot, and the fate of his country was being decided in Southeast Asia. It was a matter of bloodline and duty. He was going to Vietnam. "Whatever you want," Martha said.

Martha was often a dissident from Air Force culture, but she knew its traditions. When she and Bruce drove to McClellan Air Force Base on the day of his shipping out for Vietnam, she walked with him toward the transport plane. At the appropriate spot, she stopped along with the other spouses and girlfriends, kissed her husband, then turned smartly and walked away. It's considered unlucky for Air Force wives to look back.

On April 7, Walker climbed into his OV-10 on the Da Nang flight line and flew to Hue to pick up Larry Potts, the artillery observer who would fill his backseat. Potts was celebrating his birthday. He was a bit edgy that morning; it was uncharacteristic — Potts was usually so positive. "It was a kind of a hot area," said his fellow Marine Gus Evans. "Larry wasn't nervous, but he was a bit apprehensive about it, a little shaky." Word had finally gotten out to the rank and file that the skies above Gene Hambleton were a veritable shooting gallery.

The Marine settled into his seat in the OV-10 behind Walker and the two set off, flying north. They were directed to an area around four miles north of the city of Dong Ha and ordered to inspect a firebase that had been abandoned during the North Vietnamese invasion.

As the two flew over the base, looking down at the green landscape, Potts was on the radio, talking to an artillery liaison officer on the ground. He was getting ready to start calling out artillery targets for one of the Navy ships offshore when, just after 11 a.m., the liaison officer heard Potts blurt out "Mayday! Mayday!" A SAM missile had hit the OV-10. The officer on the ground asked Potts to confirm the aircraft was in trouble. Potts said something — a string of rushed words — but he was speaking so fast that the officer couldn't make sense of them. The officer called again and again but Potts never came back on the radio.

A few seconds after the missile hit, Potts and Walker punched out of the burning plane and popped their chutes. Some of his fellow soldiers believe that Potts, who was terribly nearsighted, lost his glasses in the violent ejection. "I really worried about him being down there," said Lieutenant Colonel D'Wayne Gray. "Being in the badlands in immediate threat of capture and not being able to see would be a terrible thing to go through." Most likely, Potts's thick prescription glasses were lost and he hit the ground half-blind.

The efforts to move Walker to the river, where Tommy Norris might be able to reach him, soon failed. The Air Force determined that NVA units were too thick on the ground for him to get through. A fighter plane dropped a Madden pack to him, but it got lost in the elephant grass and he couldn't find it. It took four days for them to drop another. Famished, he ate the food and guzzled the water. But the supplies quickly ran out.

Martha had decided to pay a surprise visit to Bruce's parents in Clovis, New Mexico, in early April. It would give them a chance to see the baby. She was in the kitchen on April 8 when Bruce's father walked in.

"Do you want something to eat?" she asked him.

The older man shook his head. Then he said, "I've gotten a telex."

Martha turned to look at him. The expression on the older man's face ... she knew immediately. Every detail, every color in the room seemed to imprint themselves on her mind, from the shade of paint on the wall to the dress she was wearing to the "ugly yellow color" of the sunlight streaming in the window.

"Is he dead?" Martha said.

Bruce's father recited the details in the telex. Bruce was down, alive. and on the run in enemy territory. When he looked up, he could see the panic in Martha's eyes. "Oh, no," he said hurriedly, "they'll get him out of there." Bruce's father knew the code the airmen lived by. He believed the Air Force would stop at nothing to save his son.

But the Hambleton rescue had changed everything.

By April 16, the airman had been on the ground for nine days; he was undernourished and drinking muddy, contaminated water to survive. The weather had turned increasingly cold and wet. Sometimes at night, Walker would climb into the trees to hide from NVA patrols. The next day, rescue planners suggested moving Walker toward the east, traveling at night. Depending on Walker's location, Tommy Norris and his team would use the streams in that area or the shoreline itself to go up and snatch him.

Bruce's father talked to the base commander in Da Nang every day, getting updates. Martha stayed in her bedroom with the baby. She wasn't a "pokey" person, not someone who asked a million questions. "I separated myself from everything. Just closed down. Sucked it all in." She kept wondering if it was possible the Air Force would get him out. She felt numb.

The message from the Air Force was always the same: he's in good physical condition, we're talking to him daily, "we are continuing to try and effect his rescue."

But Bruce's father was becoming increasingly alarmed and embittered. Why hadn't the Air Force been able to save his son? Where were the rescue choppers? "He felt that Bruce was a pawn in order to get Hambleton back," said Martha. "They basically left Bruce with no protection. He was expendable." The conversations with the commander at Da Nang became so contentious that the man stopped answering Colonel Walker's calls.

The Air Force would have vehemently denied that they didn't do everything in their power to retrieve Walker. The skies around the pilot were still being raked with SAMS; one day, observers in the Navy ships offshore counted eighty-three launches in the area around the Mieu Giang. The Air Force did institute a small no-fire zone around Walker (whose exact position they didn't know, as he was constantly on the move), but the sector was declared unsafe for fighter planes or FACs, let alone the lumbering Jolly Greens.

The Hambleton mission had altered search and rescue policy in significant ways. The Air Force sent no helicopters in after Walker; there were no B-52 airstrikes to clear his way, though the big bombers were active in the area, hitting the NVA invasion forces. The commanders of the Seventh Air Force had learned a terrible lesson with Hambleton and were not eager to repeat it.

On the seventeenth, Walker agreed to the plan to move to the coast. He was going to rest that night and the following day, then strike out to the east. But when the FAC arrived back the next morning, Walker was gone. Something had happened during the intervening hours; perhaps the pilot had been spooked by enemy activity or he'd been discovered in the darkness. He'd set out through rice paddies and groves of trees and brush under cover of night.

After hours of slipping through the sleeping countryside, Walker stopped at a dike built by local farmers. As he rested there, he spotted an elderly Vietnamese peasant named Ta Van Can watching him. Walker approached the man and tried to communicate with him, but neither spoke the other's language. The pilot shook Can's hand and tried to ask for help, showing the farmer his Air Force ID card. Walker then reached into his pocket and pulled out some silver coins and tried to hand them to Can. The Vietnamese man refused but didn't run off.

Finally, after a few hours, and with morning breaking in the east, Walker began heading toward the coast with Can following behind him. The American soon outpaced the older man. Unbeknownst to the pair, Can's wife had spotted the two talking, and when they moved off, she ran back to the village, found the local Vietcong leader, and told him about the American pilot. The man gathered some fighters from the hamlet and set off in pursuit.

That morning, a young FAC, First Lieutenant Mickey Fain, drew the assignment of escorting Walker, who went by the code name Covey 282. Fain flew toward Walker's last known position in his O-2 just after daybreak and soon heard the American calling on the radio.

"Roger 282," Fain answered, "this is Bilk 35. How are you doing this morning?"

"I'm in a heap of trouble, Mickey."

Static fractured his words. "Say again. Over."

"I'm in much trouble," Walker came back. "I'm in deep shit." The pilot's voice was edged with panic. The fighters from the village had quickly tracked him to a rice field and were in pursuit.

"Push it all the way up!" Walker shouted. "Indigenous personnel coming . . . believed to be VC."

Fain radioed a FAC flying an OV-10, and the pilot dropped down from altitude and began firing his .30-caliber machine guns at the cluster of VC. Walker was watching the men advance. But the men didn't back away. "I am surrounded at this time," Walker radioed.

The FAC had few options left. He warned Walker that he was coming in with some white phosphorus rockets. "Hurry up," Walker said. "Just put it in right in close. They're coming at me. They keep coming at me."

Fain raced toward Walker's position. When he saw the American below him, he shoved his stick forward and descended to a dangerously low altitude, shooting phosphorus rockets at the VC soldiers. He felt the impact of bullets slamming into the O-2 as the enemy turned their guns on him. The phosphorus exploded in intense white flower bursts that left a cloud rising in their wake. But the soldiers emerged from the smoke and continued moving toward the American.

Walker keyed down the transmitter and Fain's ears filled with the sound of bullets. "They're shooting at me, babe," Walker cried. "They're shooting at me!"

Fain turned the O-2 and spotted Walker surrounded by VC. "Go ahead, Covey," he said.

Walker was holding down the radio transmit button. Fain could hear him screaming against a background of rifle fire.

"282, are you all right, babe?" Fain called.

There was no answer. Fain looked down and saw Walker sprawled in the grass hundreds of feet below. Out of Fain's sight, a VC fighter named Vo Van De was on his hands and knees, moving toward Walker with his AK-47 trained on the pilot. When he was twenty feet away, he fired six rounds with his AK-47 into Walker's body.

A flight of F-4s arrived over Fain, and he directed them to drop their bombs in the field around Walker. Pushed by the wind, the white phosphorus smoke from Fain's rockets drifted past the airman. When it moved away, Fain looked down and saw the pilot's body had disappeared. Low on fuel, Fain turned the O-2 toward Da Nang.

The final act of the Hambleton rescue mission was over.

Martha Walker was dazed by her husband's death. She wasn't a crier; she never shed tears for Bruce, except when she was alone. She later channeled her emotions into a play, *Did I Say Goodbye.* "It's just not very good anymore," she wrote in it, talking about the time after her husband's death. "Nothing seems to be." At a loss for what to do next, she agreed to move to Germany with Bruce's parents; his father had been appointed commander of the Hahn Air Base there.

While she was at Hahn, "terribly lost and crazed," she met Bruce's Vietnam hooch mate, who'd been close to the pilot in the months before he was shot down. The two talked about Bruce constantly. They began a relationship. "Sometimes we would make love and I didn't know whether it was you or him," she wrote in *Goodbye*. "It was like, I don't know, some kind of mystical thing, but in the middle it was like you were the same people . . . it sounds weird . . . I grew to hate him . . . I hated him because he wasn't you."

Eventually, Martha left the airman and returned to America. She took up jazz singing, an old love, and raised her and Bruce's daughter, who bore an uncanny resemblance to her father. Every time she moved, she would carry the boxes of Bruce's clothes with her; this went on for twenty years. And she continued to have dreams about him in which he appeared and stood stock-still in front of her. "Why did you go away from me?" she would ask. In these visions, Bruce never replied.

On April 8, a cluster of Air Force officers arrived in Smyrna, Delaware, and told the Potts family what had happened to Larry. Each member was affected by the disappearance in his or her own way. His aunt Louise, who'd taken Larry in as a young boy and raised him as her own, was admitted to a local hospital, suffering from shock. "She had a nervous breakdown," says Larry's nephew Trent Wicks. "She was never the same."

Many in the family dreamt about Larry for years afterward. Wicks, an Army infantry veteran, had one dream so vivid it seemed like a transmission from Larry himself. "I was in his place," he said. "I had got shot down, I was running through this tall grassy opening trying to get to a tree line. I couldn't see the enemy soldiers, but I could hear them. I was running and running and I felt my leg was on fire. I lay down, and I was thinking about my family. I'm all this way from home, thousands of miles away, and I'm going to die right here." Wicks woke up, breathing hard. "I was in his body. I could smell everything, I could feel everything."

Wicks compared losing his uncle to an abduction. "It's as if your kid or your wife goes missing, and they never find the body. It's a wide-open void."

NOTES

(ST) denotes an interview conducted by Stephan Talty. (DW) denotes an interview conducted by Darrel Whitcomb.

PROLOGUE: THE RIVER

page

xiii   *Gene Hambleton pushed himself away:* For Hambleton's stumbling onto the Mieu Giang, see Gene Hambleton with Marjorie Johnson, unpublished memoir manuscript, pp. 114–17 (hereafter unpublished Hambleton manuscript).

xiv   *"Thank you, sweet Jesus":* William Anderson, *BAT-21* (New York: Bantam, 1983), p. 168.

xv   *"What had looked like a godsend":* Unpublished Hambleton manuscript, p. 123.

xvi   *"You goddamn son of a bitch":* Interview with Major Donald Lunday, October 1994 (DW).

     "Damn, I didn't know they made 'em that small": Tom Norris and Mike Thornton with Dick Couch, *By Honor Bound: Two Navy SEALS, the Medal of Honor, and a Story of Extraordinary Courage* (New York: St. Martin's, 2016), p. 22.

     he'd managed to improve his vision: Interview with Tommy Norris and Mi-

chael Thornton, Academy of Achievement, http://www.achievement.org/
achiever/tommy-norris/#interview.

"He simply did not seem to notice": Norris and Thornton, *By Honor Bound*,
p. 5.

1. Midwestern

3   *Then a letter arrived instructing him:* Interview with Sharon Fitzpatrick,
July 2017 (ST).

4   *a company that bred and sold Percheron horses:* Ibid.

      "He was opinionated and bullheaded": Interview with Pam Forrest, June
2017 (ST).

      "soft and fuzzy": Interview with Sharon Fitzpatrick, July 2017 (ST).

5   *"a carbon copy of thousands of little communities":* Unpublished Hambleton manuscript, p. 38.

      "By a family's reputation from generations past": Ibid.

      "All my life I've been looking for the guy": Radio interview with Gene Ham-
bleton and Roy Leonard, undated, Hambleton family archive.

      "big boned and with perfect posture": For an account of the schoolroom and
the strap incident, see unpublished Hambleton manuscript, p. 37.

6   *He and his friends put a smoke bomb:* Ibid., p. 39.

      they occupied themselves by picking up: Ibid., p. 40.

      "In the most concentrated propaganda campaign": Transcript, March of
Time newsreel, January 21, 1938, quoted in "The March Toward War:
The March of Time as Documentary and Propaganda," http://xroads.
virginia.edu/~ma04/wood/mot/html/germany.htm.

      "'Hitler' was a name we were hearing": Unpublished Hambleton manu-
script, p. 23.

      "was no way for our country to stay out": Ibid.

      "'When the time comes, I'm going to get into the action'": Ibid.

7   *Gene Hambleton fully expected to be flying bombers:* Interview with Sharon
Fitzpatrick (ST).

      Chapman grew up in a plain farmhouse: The sketch of Chapman's child-
hood is drawn from interviews with Brad Huffman and the pilot's sisters
Beth, Carol, and Jean, August 2017 (ST).

8   *The military quickly sent him home:* Unpublished Hambleton manuscript, p. 23.

He found a job at the enormous Joliet Arsenal: Interview with Donna Cutsinger and Mary Ann Anderson, March 2017 (ST).

"She was the rock in that family": Interview with Joy Hukill (ST).

9   *When he was nine years old:* Interview with Donna Cutsinger and Mary Ann Anderson (ST).

"We always thought of her as a movie star": Interview with Sharon Fitzpatrick (ST).

10   *When he argued about his salary with his supervisor:* Interviews with Donna Cutsinger and Mary Ann Anderson (ST).

"We bet there are a lot of taxicab drivers": Quoted in Lieutenant Colonel Jay A. Stout, *The Men Who Killed the Luftwaffe: The U.S. Army Air Forces Against Germany in World War II* (Mechanicsburg, Pa.: Stackpole, 2010), p. 208.

Over the course of the war: Marilyn Pierce, "Earning Their Wings: Accidents and Fatalities in the United States Army Air Force During Flight Training, World War Two" (Ph.D. diss., Kansas State University, 2013).

"honest, truthful, reliable": Quoted in William Mitchell, *From the Pilot Factory, 1942* (College Station: Texas A&M University Press, 2005), p. 26.

11   *he flew thirty missions over Germany:* Interview with Sharon Fitzpatrick (ST).

"On top of his resentment over not becoming a pilot": Ibid.

"In 1945, I graduated": Unpublished Hambleton manuscript, p. 24.

2. ROCKET MAN

12   *"They would have been awesome parents":* Interview with Donna Cutsinger (ST).

"He was a delightful uncle": Interview with Pam Forrest (ST).

"I love you so damn much": Letters from Gene Hambleton to Gwen Hambleton, Hambleton family archives.

13   *"for five years or five stars":* Anderson, *BAT-21*, p. 49.

14 *"I'd been in targeting for most of my career":* Marv Wolf, "Bat 21: Down Near the DMZ," *Soldier of Fortune,* May 1991.

15 *Hambleton flew to Turkey:* Gene Hambleton service records, Hambleton family archive.

17 *"he'd even had a paper route":* Norris and Thornton, *By Honor Bound,* p. 20.
Tommy and his brothers heard on the radio: Ibid., p. 19.
"More than the other boys": Ibid., p. 21.

18 *he failed the crucial depth-perception test:* Interview with Norris and Thornton, Academy of Achievement.
"I rattled off": Ibid.
He washed out: Interview with Sharon Fitzpatrick (ST).
"It was devastating": Ibid.

19 *"too small, too thin and not strong enough":* Peter Collier, *Choosing Courage: Inspiring Stories of What It Means to Be a Hero* (New York: Artisan, 2006), p. 118.
Norris came down with a stomach virus: Norris and Thornton, *By Honor Bound,* p. 15.
"as tough as one man could be": Interview with Darrel Whitcomb, May 2017 (ST).
"Tommy's the nicest guy in the world": Ibid.

20 *He rarely drank:* Norris and Thornton, *By Honor Bound,* p. 4.
"A real gentleman, very engaging": Ibid.
"Probably more than any of the rest of us": Ibid., p. 15.

3. KORAT

21 *he might have spotted in the corner of his mirror:* For this and other details about life at Korat, see Colonel Dennis Ridenour, ed., *The Vietnam Air War: First Person* (self-published, 2016), especially the chapter "Early Days at Korat Flying the Thud" by John Schroeder. Also see Jay R. Jensen, *Six Years in Hell* (self-published, 1989), pp. 11–14.

22 *a visiting American nurse at another Thai base:* Dave Richardson, *Vietnam Air Rescues* (self-published, 2011), Kindle location 3338.

23   *One aspiring jock remembered the moment:* Lieutenant Colonel Jay Lack-
      len, *Flying the Line: An Air Force Pilot's Journey; Pilot Training, Vietnam,
      SAC, 1970–1979* (self-published, 2014), p. 20.

24   *And there was Roscoe:* Jensen, *Six Years in Hell,* p. 16.

25   *Sometimes you would see pilots and their navigators:* Ridenour, *The Viet-
      nam Air War,* Kindle location 1073.
      When he checked in, Hambleton learned: Interview with Hambleton, Febru-
      ary 1993 (DW).
      But the navigator scheduled to fly: Letter from Thomas McKinney to Gene
      Hambleton, undated, Hambleton family archive.

26   *"Our conversation usually runs to sharp banter":* Ed Cobleigh, *War for the
      Hell of It: A Fighter Pilot's View of Vietnam* (Paso Robles, Calif.: Check Six
      Books, 2016), Kindle location 439.

27   *"I'll tell you one thing":* Radio interview with Gene Hambleton and Roy
      Leonard, undated, Hambleton family archive.
      The CIA had secretly bought a Fan Song radar: Steven J. Zaloga, *Red Sam:
      The SA-2 Guideline Anti-Aircraft Missile* (Oxford: Osprey Publishing,
      2007), Kindle location 291.
      It was a simple, if terrifying, process: The description of jinking is drawn
      from Jensen, *Six Years in Hell,* p. 9; and Ridenour, *The Vietnam Air War,*
      Kindle location 1578.

28   *"Every day," said one airman, "was like going to the OK Corral":* Interview
      with Bill Henderson, March 2017 (ST).

4. The Boys in the Back

29   *"There is no way a SAM could hit my airplane":* "Air Force Veteran
      Recalls 12-Day Ordeal in Vietnam," *Arizona Daily Wildcat,* February 4,
      1982.

30   *passing them extra cash:* Remembrance of Levis posted by Lieutenant
      Colonel Hugh Miller on the Vietnam Veterans Memorial Fund site,
      http://www.vvmf.org/Wall-of-Faces/30499/CHARLES-A-LEVIS.

32   *"You crows in back wake up":* Anderson, *BAT-21,* p. 3.
      As they approached the DMZ: The account of the shootdown is drawn from

the unpublished Hambleton manuscript, various interviews with Hamble-ton, his after-action report, and Darrel Whitcomb, *The Rescue of Bat 21* (New York: Dell, 1999).

33 *Detachment 62:* This account is from a newspaper article, Xuan Viet and Dac Tu, "Vinh Linh Detachments Damage B52 Aircraft," *Nhan Dhan* (Hanoi), April 5, 1972.

"Avenge our murdered compatriots!": Ibid.

530 mph: Initial Evasion and Recovery Report on the Hambleton incident, p. 2. Hambleton reported that the EB-66C was traveling at 460 knots.

"Oh shit," shouted the pilot: Whitcomb, *Rescue of Bat 21,* p. 27.

34 *"SAM on scope!":* Unpublished Hambleton manuscript, p. 1.

"We were five seconds late": Ibid.

"Negative, negative, negative, move left, move left!": Buzz Busboom inter-view with Hambleton, November 1993.

5. THE TIME OF USEFUL CONSCIOUSNESS

36 *"tremendous noise":* "Training, Equipment Paid Off," *Las Vegas Sun,* April 26, 1972.

His windscreen melted away: Wolf, "Bat 21: Down Near the DMZ."

"the impatient jangle of a doorbell": Unpublished Hambleton manuscript, p. 3.

looking back and down at Bolte: Initial Evasion and Recovery Report on the Hambleton incident, p. 2.

37 *"It's gone," he thought to himself, "it's completely gone":* Buzz Busboom in-terview with Hambleton.

But the force of the blast had pushed him: Ibid.

38 *"Everything I did made me spin faster":* Ibid.

"I thought, I'm going to black out": Ibid.

"I'm going to hang here the rest of my life": Unpublished Hambleton manu-script, p. 22.

39 *Inside the plane sat First Lieutenant Bill Jankowski:* Interview with Bill Jankowski, August 1990 (DW).

"'Bat 21 Alpha'": Ibid. Jankowski was the only service member who re-ported hearing Bolte's call on the radio that day.

40   *"Look up," Hambleton said:* Hambleton repeated this response in several interviews and, in a slightly altered form, in the unpublished Hambleton manuscript, p. 5.

   "It about blew my mind": Interview with Jankowski (DW).

   "The great opportunity to end the U. S. war of aggression": "Appeal to All VC Cadre, Soldiers and People," Hambleton family archive.

41   *"I could see troops all around me":* Interview with Hambleton (DW).

   "I said to myself, 'Don't breathe'": Undated newspaper clipping, Hambleton family archive.

6. Ernie Banks

43   *Hambleton knew he couldn't stay:* Hambleton's moves immediately after the shootdown are drawn from the unpublished Hambleton manuscript, pp. 6–13.

   he estimated there were 150 to 200 enemy soldiers: Ibid., p. 26.

   "I'm sitting in an airplane six and a half miles up": Hambleton radio interview with Roy Leonard, Hambleton family archive.

   The Air Force would drop over twice as much ordnance on Vietnam: Stuart Auerbach, "Wide Devastation by Big Bomb Told," *Washington Post,* December 28, 1971.

44   *"I had information that they must know":* Jensen, *Six Years in Hell,* p. 41.

45   *Moscow also sent a team of specially trained operatives:* Ilya Gaiduk, *The Soviet Union and the Vietnam War* (Chicago: Ivan R. Dee, 1996), p. 64.

   At one point they even located and recovered the intact cockpit: Merle L. Pribbenow, "The Soviet-Vietnamese Intelligence Relationship During the Vietnam War: Cooperation and Conflict," working paper, Wilson International Center for Scholars, December 2014.

46   *"How could we find and attack their SAM sites?":* Merle L. Pribbenow, "Who Interrogated American Electronic Warfare Specialists in North Vietnam During the War: The Riddle of the *Task Force Russia 294 Report,*" December 11, 2014, http://www.washingtondecoded.com/site/2014/12/tfr294.html.

   "six or seven": Buzz Busboom interview with Hambleton.

47 *"What is your dog's name?"*: Anderson, *BAT-21*, p. 11.

"It started to look like the Fourth of July": Interview with Jankowski (DW).

7. BLUEGHOST 39

48 *Born in Tijuana, Mexico, Astorga had immigrated:* Astorga's story is drawn from several interviews with him, March–August 2017 (ST).

49 *"What's-his-name's sick"*: Ibid.

He'd grown up in rural northwestern North Dakota: The account of Kulland's boyhood and service is drawn from interviews with his brother Lee Kulland, his sister Karen Wallgren, and his wife, Leona Hauge (ST).

"We would walk down the street in New Town": Interview with Karen Wallgren, July 2017 (ST).

"We used to wrestle": http://arlingtoncemetery.net/bkkulland.htm.

"It was like it was out there somewhere": Interview with Karen Wallgren (ST).

50 *"One day we had gone someplace after dark"*: Interview with Leona Hauge, August 2017 (ST).

51 *"Rescue choppers are airborne"*: Anderson, *BAT-21*, p. 32.

52 *"was being rapidly converted"*: Whitcomb, *Rescue of Bat 21*, p. 35.

"Sir, there's a lot of smoke coming out of the engine": This and all subsequent quotations from Astorga are from interviews with him (ST).

56 *"It was almost like the time for the shift change"*: Unpublished Hambleton manuscript, p. 14.

"They were looking and looking hard": Ibid., p. 11.

"It was dark as pitch": Ibid., p. 12.

57 *"My crew and I ran out to the airplane"*: Interview with Dennis Constant (DW).

"I was thinking this guy sounds cool as a cucumber": Ibid. The quotations that follow are also from the Constant interview.

58 *"I'd never seen so much ground fire in my whole life"*: Interview with Don Morse, May 1993 (DW).

"Every hill looked like a Christmas tree": Robert E. Stoffey, *Fighting to Leave: The Final Years of America's War in Vietnam, 1972–1973* (Minneapolis: Zenith Press, 2008), p. 32.

59 *"I'd gotten five and couldn't see number six":* Interview with Gary Ferentchak, April 1993 (DW).

"I was like, 'Holy shit, man'": Interview with Constant (DW).

In the early evening of April 2: The account of the downing of Blueghost 39 is drawn from interviews with José Astorga (ST); and Whitcomb, *Rescue of Bat 21,* pp. 32–38.

60 *"Can you dig in for the night?":* Anderson, *BAT-21,* p. 34.

61 *"It was the worst night of my life":* Interview with Morse (DW).

8. Tucson

62 *Gwen Hambleton was cleaning up:* The account of Gwen Hambleton is drawn from Anderson, *BAT-21,* pp. 23–24.

64 *One time near Hanoi:* This anecdote is from Jensen, *Six Years in Hell,* p. 14.

"99 percent of the family": http://arlingtoncemetery.net/bkkulland.htm.

In the small Minnesota town of Wadena: This account is drawn from an interview with Karen Wallgren (ST).

65 *In Colorado Springs, the younger Giannangeli children:* This account is drawn from interviews with Dennis and Robert Giannangeli and Mary Lou Giannangeli, March–September 2017 (ST).

9. Blowtorch Jockeys

68 *"It was dark dark":* Interview with Hambleton (DW).

He woke and raised his head: Unless otherwise noted, the details in this chapter are drawn from the unpublished Hambleton manuscript, pp. 12–35.

72 *"Blowtorch jockeys," he called them:* Anderson, *BAT-21,* p. 29.

73 *"almost been a computer game":* Ibid., p. 31.

"Dropping a bomb from a plane": Hambleton obituary, *Los Angeles Times,* September 27, 2004.

"Turning healthy human beings": Ibid.

10. JOKER

77 *"I had clear instructions"*: Interview with Major General John Carley (DW).

79 *"were the sole combat element"*: Neil Sheehan, *A Bright Shining Lie* (New York: Vintage, 1988), p. 762.

"At my side, I had an Army liaison": Interview with Daryl Tincher, June 1993 (DW).

80 *"This has been part of American society"*: Colin Daileda, "The Military History of 'Leave No Man Behind,'" Mashable, June 14, 2014, https://mashable.com/2014/06/14/bowe-bergdahl-are-american-military-soldiers-ever-left-behind/#QYhi2v9VwGq3.

"We knew who he was": Interview with Tincher (DW).

Hambleton could have been some pogue lieutenant: This sentiment is repeated in interviews with Bill Henderson (ST) and with Tommy Norris (DW), among others.

81 *"the Very Nice Air Force"*: The term was in common usage among USAF personnel and is mentioned in Cobleigh, *War for the Hell of It,* Kindle location 831.

"There is nothing *over here worth an American life"*: Interview with Whitcomb (ST).

"I would have ripped": Interview with Ferentchak (DW).

"The feeling when you get": Interview with Lieutenant Colonel Lachlan Macleay, February 1993 (DW).

82 *One crew flying a nighttime mission:* Stoffey, *Fighting to Leave,* p. 43.

"We were in full-scale war": Interview with David Brookbank, August 1990 (DW).

"He read the message carefully": Whitcomb, *Rescue of Bat 21,* p. 43.

83 *"You've got to shut it down"*: Interview with Jerry Turley, June 1993 (DW).

"We were deeply involved in a war": Ibid.

"My god, my god": Ibid.

"Where are the American planes?": Whitcomb, *Rescue of Bat 21,* p. 118.

"People were just begging for artillery": Interview with Brookbank (DW).

"Mass hysteria": Turley in "Just One Man," *Battlefield Diaries*, episode 7, Military Channel, 2008.

84   *"One?" he said. "Just one man?":* Interview with Turley (DW).

"*I said, Screw you, I'm not going to do it*": Ibid.

"*This was the attitude*": Interview with Brookbank (DW).

"*They would have killed you*": Ibid.

85   "*I was absolutely up the wall*": Interview with D'Wayne Gray (DW).

"*I would rather lose two ARVN divisions*": Ibid.

11. YESTERDAY'S FRAT BOY

86   "*yesterday's college frat boy*": Bernard Fipp, *Triple Sticks: Tales of a Few Young Men in the 1960s* (self-published, 2014), p. 2.

The son of a World War II flight engineer: The details of Henderson's boyhood and war service are drawn from an interview with the pilot (ST).

90   "*Break it off, break it off!*": Interview with Bill Harris, February 1993 (DW).

Crowe experimented with the speed: The details of Jay Crowe's mission are drawn from an interview with the pilot, April 1993 (DW).

91   "*Extreme, intense fire*": Ibid.

"*Where in God's name had those guns come from?*": Anderson, *BAT-21*, p. 33.

"*Like a busy anthill that had its top kicked off*": Ibid., p. 34.

92   "*like some melancholy emblem*": Ibid., p. 35.

12. "THEIR GLOWING TRAJECTORIES"

93   "*Fliers used every trick to confuse ground detection*": Whitcomb, *Rescue of Bat 21*, p. 69.

94   "*triumphant*": *Newsweek,* April 17, 1972, p. 20.

"*The loss of the EB-66C*": Ibid.

"*The EB-66C contains highly secret electronic equipment*": *Times* (London), April 22, 1972.

95   *Bill Henderson continued orbiting above the clouds:* Unless otherwise noted, the account of Henderson's shootdown and capture are drawn from an interview with the pilot (ST).

At that moment the missile appeared: Letter from Captain Fred Boli to Darrel Whitcomb, May 28, 1990. Boli was the pilot who watched the SAM pass over his aircraft.

96 *"There were a lot of people":* Evasion and Recovery Report, Mark Clark, Part III: Ejection/Bailout.

97 *"SAM, SAM, vicinity of Khe Sanh!":* Whitcomb, *Rescue of Bat 21,* p. 61.
"something really big": Interview with Warrant Officer Ben Nielsen, May 1994 (DW).

98 *"The shit lit up":* Interview with Henderson (DW).
"The 'war is over' syndrome was rapidly evaporating": Lieutenant Commander Jay Crowe, after-tour report submitted to Rear Admiral J. W. Moreau, United States Navy, April 27, 1973.
"big into researching things": Interview with Ty Crowe, September 2017 (ST).
The pilot grabbed a ride aboard the Jolly Green: Interview with Jay Crowe (DW).

99 *"There aren't any SA-7s in-country":* Ibid.

13. TINY TIM

100 *On the ground, Hambleton heard the FAC:* Unless otherwise noted, the details and quotations in this chapter are drawn from the unpublished Hambleton manuscript, pp. 29–54.

103 *While this was going on, Bill Henderson:* Interview with Henderson (ST).

14. FUTILITY

106 *"In my opinion, this gave the enemy":* Quoted in Whitcomb, *Rescue of Bat 21,* p. 112.

107 *"In early 1972," Nixon wrote:* Richard Nixon, *No More Vietnams* (New York: Arbor House, 1987), p. 140.
"That's one determination I've made": Douglas Brinkley and Luke Nichter, *The Nixon Tapes* (New York: Houghton Mifflin Harcourt, 2014), p. 383.

108 *"It looks as if they are attacking in Vietnam":* Ibid., p. 429.
"only barely able to control his temper": Ibid., p. 436.

"What is his job out there?": Ibid., pp. 436–37.

109 *"Haig says, correctly," Kissinger told Nixon:* Ibid., p. 451.

"We want to see more B-52s": Ibid., p. 382.

"a rapid global mobility response": Matthew Brand, "Airpower and the 1972 Easter Offensive" (thesis, U.S. Army Command and General Staff College, Fort Leavenworth, 2007), p. 15.

110 *"reckless and wrong":* Nixon, *No More Vietnams*, p. 147.

"has thrown down the gauntlet of nuclear war": Ibid.

up to ninety sorties a day: Southeast Asia SEA (CHECO) Office, *Project Checo Southeast Asia Report: Search and Rescue Operations in SE Asia, 1 April 1972–30 June 1973*, p. 38.

"I want Abrams braced hard": Brinkley and Nichter, *The Nixon Tapes*, p. 441.

"If this isn't fought more aggressively": Ibid., p. 457.

"It was my understanding": Interview with Cecil Muirhead (DW).

15. "I Know We're Going to Die"

112 *"Fear is nibbling at your gut":* Fred Boli in "Just One Man."

Alley was from Plantation, Florida: Details of James Alley's boyhood are drawn from an interview with Tim Alley, June 2017 (ST).

"On any given night": Author interview, July 2017 (ST).

"He was drafted in the Army": Letter from Alley's mother to Hambleton, Hambleton family archives.

113 *"I think he thought they would be lonely":* Interview with Tim Alley, June 2017 (ST).

"I know we're going to die": Alley's words in this section are from an interview with Doug Brinson, September 2017 (ST).

114 *"When conditions are right":* Whitcomb, *Rescue of Bat 21*, p. 59.

115 *"I was like, 'Oh, really?'":* Interview with Brinson (ST).

What Alley said was: "I'm not going": Ibid.

116 *"You're either going to get on the chopper":* Ibid.

"Today," he believed, "was the day of his deliverance": Anderson, *BAT-21*, p. 76.

16. Low Bird

117   *"It was my turn"*: Bill Harris in "Just One Man."

    Not long before, Chapman had been the low chopper: Interview with Harris (DW).

118   *His tour was up and he'd received orders:* Interview with Brad Huffman (ST).

    "I briefed the crew that they should not make an attempt": Interview with Crowe (DW).

119   *Brinson spotted a sixth figure waiting to board:* Interview with Brinson (ST).

    The aircraft headed to a point southeast of Quang Tri: The details of the Jolly Green 67 mission are from Whitcomb, *Rescue of Bat 21*, pp. 70–76.

    "The good Lord was showing His favor": Unpublished Hambleton manuscript, p. 72.

120   *"I was just stunned":* Interview with Crowe (DW).

121   *"I'm hit! They got a fuel line":* Whitcomb, *Rescue of Bat 21*, p. 73.

    "We're taking hits, we're taking hits!": Interview with Brinson (ST).

    "I knew right then we were in deep trouble": Unpublished Hambleton manuscript, p. 73.

    "Turn south, Jolly, turn right": Whitcomb, *Rescue of Bat 21*, p. 74.

122   *"Jolly's down, Jolly's down!":* Interview with Captain Mark Schibler, November 1992 (DW).

    "Anyone getting out would be the result of a miracle": Unpublished Hambleton manuscript, p. 74.

    "I hate to see a grown man cry": Buzz Busboom interview with Hambleton.

    "I felt it necessary to talk it over": Unpublished Hambleton manuscript, p. 70.

    "You are by yourself": Ibid., p. 71.

123   *"I really cocked this up":* Whitcomb, *Rescue of Bat 21*, p. 75.

17. The Division

124   *"It's been a bad two days":* Harold Icke cassette tape courtesy of Darrel Whitcomb.

    "We now had two survivors": Interview with Crowe (DW).

    "not move out of Cam Lo": Whitcomb, *Rescue of Bat 21*, p. 63.

125   *"[We] found this impossible to accept after so much sacrifice"*: Crowe, after-
tour report.

"the Recovery Studies Division": The Division's unclassified name was the
Joint Personnel Recovery Center.

"short, stocky, fiery": George J. Veith, *Code Name Bright Light: The Untold
Story of U.S. POW Rescue Efforts During the Vietnam War* (New York:
Dell, 1999), p. 321.

126   *"He burned to rescue a fellow American"*: Ibid.

18. The Real John Wayne

129   *April 7 brought no relief to Hambleton:* This account of Hambleton's
actions is drawn from the unpublished Hambleton manuscript,
pp. 82–92.

131   *"had a fire burning"*: Interview with Captain Bob Covalucci, January 1995
(DW).

"bold and perhaps dangerous decision": Whitcomb, *Rescue of Bat 21*, p. 85.

One major who planned to go with Lieutenant Colonel Andersen: Interview
with Lunday (DW).

132   *"It couldn't have been better"*: Crowe, after-tour report.

"do it black": Interview with Paul Broshar, June 1993 (DW).

133   *"It was, 'we're going to do something* special'": For the remaining quotations in this chapter, see ibid.

19. The Hurricane Lover

135   *"Well, it just so happens, he's sitting right here"*: Norris and Thornton,
By Honor Bound, p. 14.

136   *"Tom," Dorman recalled, "was chomping at the bit"*: Ibid.

20. When the Moon Goes over the Mountain

140   *"I felt like a corporate exec"*: Ibid., p. 15.

"This guy knows something that they want back": Interview with Norris
(DW).

140 a "superb, hard-charging" officer: Whitcomb, *Rescue of Bat 21*,
p. 89.

141 "E & E"—escape and evade: Interview with Muirhead (DW).
"My concern was, well, suppose we don't get him": Interview with Norris
(DW).
"I would have liked to have him say": Ibid.

142 "We function much different than they [the Navy] do": Ibid.
"What Andersen said didn't affect me": Ibid.
"I don't mind saying": Norris and Thornton, *By Honor Bound*, p. 18.
"Nothing else really mattered": Ibid., p. 30.

143 "He . . . told us, directly in his broken English": Ibid., p. 26.
"They didn't know what was happening": Interview with Major Gerald
Bauknight, October 1994 (DW).

144 "We are going to have to do something different": Unpublished Hambleton
manuscript, p. 85.
"What have you been smoking?": Interview with Hambleton (DW).
"the damnedest thing I had ever heard": Ibid.

145 Not once during the long and complex journey: Unpublished Hambleton
manuscript, p. 92.
"This is a decision that is going to be entirely up to you": Ibid., p. 86.
"If this succeeds," Kissinger told the president: Brinkley and Nichter, *The
Nixon Tapes*, p. 458.

146 "Every great power must follow the principle": Ibid.
In Moscow, Dobrynin's superiors were equally disturbed: The account of
the Soviet reaction to the Easter Offensive is drawn from Gaiduk, *The
Soviet Union and the Vietnam War*, pp. 218–38.

147 "If the mission had failed": Interview with Major Donald Lunday,
December 1994 (DW).
"I want to know some success": Veith, *Code Name Bright Light*,
p. 321.

148 "In the early years, I felt free": Interview with Nguyen Van Kiet, November
2017 (DW).
he announced he would shoot anyone: Whitcomb, *Rescue of Bat 21*,
p. 93.

149 "It was understood amongst them": Interview with Norris (DW).

"I thought of the . . . men who had been lost": Unpublished Hambleton manuscript, p. 86.

"I'll go with the plan": Ibid.

"tremendous numbers" of people: Evasion and Recovery Report, Mark Clark, Part III: Ejection/Bailout. Clark's words in this section are from the same report.

21. THE FIRST AT TUCSON NATIONAL

152 *Hambleton could just make out the moon:* The details in this section are drawn from the unpublished Hambleton manuscript, pp. 93–95.

153 *"It scared the living hell out of me":* Evasion and Recovery Report, Mark Clark, Part III: Ejection/Bailout.

154 *Hambleton looked around his hiding place:* The details in this section are drawn from the unpublished Hambleton manuscript, pp. 95–103; and Anderson, *BAT-21,* pp. 127–47.

22. DARK ENCOUNTER

159 *"I'm still on my way down":* Evasion and Recovery Report, Mark Clark. Part III: Ejection/Bailout. Unless otherwise noted, the quotations in this section are from the same document.

"I just about drowned myself": Interview with Mark Clark, January 1993 (DW).

160 *Hambleton stood stunned:* The material in this section is drawn from Anderson, *BAT-21,* pp. 147–48.

161 *"Actually killing a man face to face":* Ibid., p. 154.

"galloped off like a wild fool": Ibid.

162 *Tommy Norris and his team:* The material in this section is drawn from Norris and Thornton, *By Honor Bound;* an interview with Norris (DW); and Norris and Thornton interview, Academy of Achievement.

"I said, 'Uh-oh, I'm not going to put my guys in that'": Interview with Norris (DW).

163 *"We'd burned up so much time":* Ibid.

164 *"Oh, Jesus, why me?":* Ibid.

23. The Grove

165 *"He was a fifty-three-year-old man running around up there":* Interview with Tincher (DW).

166 *"was the most intense we had ever seen":* Letter from an airman named Batte, Hambleton family archives.

"I had five sets of controllers on that mission": Interview with Tincher (DW).

167 *"like the crazy-looking Road Runner bird":* The material in this section is drawn from the unpublished Hambleton manuscript, pp. 108–9 and 112–18.

170 *"I was so damn excited":* Buzz Busboom interview with Hambleton.

24. Clark

173 *"a-huffing and a-puffing":* Norris and Thornton, *By Honor Bound,* p. 39.

"All I could see were blackened faces and wide eyes": Ibid.

174 *"I've really done it now":* Interview with Norris (DW).

"He got past me," he told Andersen: Ibid.

175 *"I'm sitting out there in the middle of no-man's-land:* Interview with Tommy Norris, Pritzker Military Museum and Library, Chicago, November 9, 2006.

176 *"For a second," Kiet said:* Interview with Kiet (DW).

"Mark, I'm an American": Norris and Thornton, *By Honor Bound,* p. 42.

"Oh good Lord": Evasion and Recovery Report, Mark Clark, Part IV: Initial Actions on the Ground.

"I'm here to take you home": Norris and Thornton, *By Honor Bound,* p. 42.

177 *"No, no, no, he's with me":* Ibid., p. 43.

"If I drop, you drop; if I turn, you turn": Ibid.

178 *"I wouldn't have gone in there after me":* Interview with Clark (DW).

25. Places Like the Moon

179 *Bill Henderson was marching toward Hanoi:* The details in this section are drawn from an interview with Henderson (ST).

"I gave him that": *Stars and Stripes* did publish the name and rank of captured soldiers, but not serial numbers.

180 *"There were lots of bombs":* Interview with Nguyen Quy Hai by Khuyen
   Tuong, Hanoi, June 2017.

   "After the bombs fell, some soldiers died": Interview with Doan Cong Tinh
   by Khuyen Tuong, Hanoi, June 2017.

   "Go South," it went, "and die": Michael Lee Lanning and Dan Cragg,
   *Inside the VC and the NVA: The Real Story of North Vietnam's Armed
   Forces* (College Station: Texas A&M University Press, 2008),
   p. 31.

   "There were many bombs": Interview with Nguyen Thi Uong by Khuyen
   Tuong, Hanoi, June 2017.

182 *"They took me to a village and decided to execute me":* This material is
   drawn from an interview with Astorga (ST).

26. ZEROED IN

183 *Hambleton spent the morning of April 11:* Details in this section are drawn
   from the unpublished Hambleton manuscript, pp. 118–22.

184 *"We've got big trouble":* Interview with Norris (DW).

185 *"A big piece of shrapnel went through his right arm":* Ibid.

   "Lieutenant Colonel Andersen has been hit": Ibid.

27. ESTHER WILLIAMS

188 *As nightfall approached, Hambleton heard a surge:* Details in this
   section are drawn from the unpublished Hambleton manuscript,
   pp. 122–28.

192 *"They wanted to go back":* Details in this section are drawn from Norris and
   Thornton, *By Honor Bound,* p. 54.

   "It seemed all the muscles in my body": Details in this section are drawn
   from the unpublished Hambleton manuscript, pp. 128–33.

195 *Finally, Norris signaled Kiet that they would head back:* Interview with
   Norris (DW).

   Hambleton's progress was pitiful: The details in this section are drawn
   from the unpublished Hambleton manuscript, pp. 133–38.

28. "Some Kind of Rescue"

201 *"You want what?":* Norris and Thornton, *By Honor Bound,* p. 52.

"You goddamn dummy": Interview with Hambleton (DW).

202 *"This guy is losing it":* Ibid.

Norris spent the afternoon getting ready: The incident with the reporters is told in Norris and Thornton, *By Honor Bound,* beginning on p. 52.

203 *"They said it was too dangerous":* Ibid., p. 53.

204 *"They had lost their fighting spirit":* Interview with Kiet (DW).

"No, Dai Uy, *I'm going with you":* Interview with Norris (DW).

Hambleton had been asleep for hours: The details in this section are drawn from the unpublished Hambleton manuscript, pp. 139–42.

His weight was down to 125 pounds: "Training, Equipment Paid Off," *Las Vegas Sun,* April 26, 1972.

29. The Sampan

207 *After a few hours of agonizingly slow progress:* Unpublished Hambleton manuscript, pp. 143–45.

209 *"It was like pulling into a bus station":* Norris and Thornton, *By Honor Bound,* p. 60.

210 *"There can't be a hill there":* This account is from the unpublished Hambleton manuscript, pp. 145–50.

212 *"the most beautiful thing he had ever seen":* Dwight Jon Zimmerman and John D. Gresham, *Beyond Hell and Back: How America's Special Operations Forces Became the World's Greatest Fighting Unit* (New York: St. Martin's, 2007), Kindle location 1711.

30. Journey's End

214 *"It was like diving to the bottom of the sea":* Interview with Kiet (DW).

215 *"I also told them that we were going to need some air cover":* Norris and Thornton, *By Honor Bound,* p. 62.

216 *a hoarse shout from the riverbank:* Interview with Kiet (DW).

Three armed North Vietnamese soldiers: Interview with Kiet, Operation Report, Camp Pendleton, July 13, 1975.

"It sent chills up my spine": Nguyen Van Kiet in "Just One Man."

217   *"the greatest pair of eyes of anyone I know"*: Unpublished Hambleton manuscript, p. 153.

"starting to moan and babble": Norris and Thornton, *By Honor Bound*, p. 64.

218   *"We really need some air support"*: Ibid., p. 65.

219   *"Where are we?"*: Interview with Hambleton (DW).

"They felt like two chunks of ice": Unpublished Hambleton manuscript, p. 158.

220   *"What the hell have you gotten me into?"*: Interview with Hambleton (DW).

"I was overcome with a flood of emotions": Undated clipping, Hambleton family archives.

"Kindness needs no words in a time like that": Unpublished Hambleton manuscript, p. 158.

31. "Lay That Man Down"

222   *"It was a hell of a price to pay for one life"*: "Hell of a Price to Pay," *New York Times,* April 22, 1972.

"Fifteen or 20 in all swarmed over me": Unpublished Hambleton manuscript, p. 162.

223   *"I was again given the royal treatment"*: The account in this section is drawn from ibid., p. 163.

224   *"Well, I'm going over"*: This and subsequent quotations in this section are drawn from an interview with Major Gerald Bauknight, October 1994 (DW).

225   *"Hang in there, Gene"*: Unpublished Hambleton manuscript, p. 173.

"Gwen Hambleton speaking": Anderson, *BAT-21,* p. 209.

"We've just received a message": Ibid.

226   *"I've had some pretty sensitive jobs"*: Undated newspaper clipping, Hambleton family archives.

"We're the O-2s and the FAC boys": Unpublished Hambleton manuscript, p. 167.

227   *"I had always bragged I wasn't the emotional type"*: Ibid.

228   *"But for joy"*: Ibid., p. 173.

"*I'm no believer in ESP*": Ibid.

"*This episode absolutely stunned the rescue community*": Interview with Whitcomb (ST).

"*I am an Air Force man*": Unpublished Hambleton manuscript, p. 174. The remaining quotations in this section are from the same source, pp. 174–77.

230 *A photographer for the local paper:* The photos are in the Hambleton family archives.

231 "*She suffered worse than I did*": Interview with Hambleton (DW).

32. Beyond a Normal Call of Duty

232 "*RESCUED U.S. NAVIGATOR BARELY ESCAPED N. VIETS*": *Arizona Daily Star*, April 21, 1972.

"*11 DAYS BEHIND ENEMY LINES*": Undated clipping, Hambleton family archives.

"*brought jubilation to headquarters officers*": Undated clipping from the *Los Angeles Times* news service, Hambleton family archives.

"*It's kind of embarrassing, actually*": *Sawadee Flyer* (Korat Royal Thai Air Force Base), May 13, 1972.

233 "*how great it was*": "Rossville Native Survives War Ordeal," *Champaign Urbana News Gazette,* April 21, 1972.

"*He thought enough of this country to fight for it*": Undated clipping, Hambleton family archives.

"*For some reason,*" *wrote one columnist:* Undated clipping, Hambleton family archives.

"*fantastic . . . miraculous*": Undated clipping, Hambleton family archives.

"*He wasn't a bragger*": Interview with Dennis Armstrong (ST).

"*I was really shocked*": Letter to Hambleton from Captain James Vornberg, Hambleton family archives.

"*SOME PEOPLE WILL DO ANYTHING*": The telegram is in the Hambleton family archives.

"*You never know how strong you are*": Wolf, "Bat 21: Down Near the DMZ."

234 *"I always thought it was Gene's way":* Interview with Sharon Fitzpatrick (ST).

"I certainly admire the man": Interview with Hambleton (DW).

The first 25,000 copies sold out: William Anderson, "Selling a Military Picture to Hollywood," *Retired Officer Magazine,* August 1988.

235 *"The world is hungry for heroes":* Undated clipping marked "Calif. Paper," Hambleton family archive.

"He wouldn't have gotten out of there": Interview with Norris (DW).

"Well, I'm a son of a . . . you're black!": Anderson, *BAT-21,* p. 216.

"Charlton Heston, Dean Martin, and The Rockford Files' *James Garner":* Unidentified clipping dated February 18, 1981, Hambleton family archive.

236 *"Gene would have no part of that":* Interview with Mary Ann Anderson (ST).

"He was a better me than me": Hambleton radio interview with Roy Leonard, undated, Hambleton family archive.

"Are you still in touch with Captain Bartholomew?": Ibid.

237 *"I think I'm pretty much the person":* Ibid.

Four years after he returned: Interview with Mary Ann Anderson (ST).

he would hear a little plink *sound:* Buzz Busboom interview with Hambleton.

238 *"This was our only son":* Letter to Hambleton from Syble Alley, Hambleton family archive.

Hayden Chapman's sister Beth was returning home: This account is drawn from interviews with Chapman's sisters Beth, Carol, and Jean and his nephew Brad Huffman (ST).

239 *"Please keep in touch if there is ever anything":* Letter from Hambleton to Barbara Serex, September 21, 1986, Hambleton family archive.

"I have been all over the country": Undated newspaper clipping, Hambleton family archive.

240 *"We cannot accept the fact that our son is dead":* Letter from Mrs. Alley to Hambleton, Hambleton family archive.

241 *"He was always very much embarrassed":* Interview with Dennis Armstrong (ST).

33. The Returns

242 *"You are murderers!"*: Gaiduk, *The Soviet Union and the Vietnam War*, p. 239.

243 *"For all the bombast and rudeness"*: Ibid.

"A FIRST STEP, BUT A MAJOR STRIDE": *New York Times*, May 27, 1972.

245 *"I was depressed, I was hallucinating"*: Interview with Astorga (ST).

"People didn't understand": Ibid.

"It was worth it": Ibid.

After marching for days: The details in this section are drawn from an interview with Henderson (ST).

34. "As Comrades"

247 *"She fought for every day"*: Interview with Mary Ann Anderson (ST).

"He told me he had a spot on his lung": Interview with Pam Forrest (ST).

"Honey, I do love you and always have": The card is in the Hambleton family archive.

248 *"I knew when she died, he wouldn't make it a year"*: Interview with Dennis Armstrong (ST).

"BAT 21 HAS BEEN RESCUED": Photo, Hambleton family archive.

"My dad had the perfect family": Interview with Tim Alley (ST).

"He was this hero I could never live up to": These quotations — and the account of Alley's trip to Hawaii and the wake — are from an interview with Tim Alley (ST).

251 *"The whole side of his head was completely gone"*: Interview with Norris and Thornton, Academy of Achievement.

"Mike, there's no way he's gonna make it": Ibid.

"We didn't think we were gonna save you": Ibid.

252 *"My injury"*: Ibid.

"conspicuous gallantry": Medal of Honor citation.

"I don't feel that I was anybody special": Interview with Norris and Thornton, Academy of Achievement.

254 *"I did not want anyone to know"*: This account is from an interview with Kiet (DW).

255 *"Due to Petty Officer Kiet's coolness":* Navy Cross citation.

257 *"It's not the value of one life":* Nguyen Van Kiet in "Just One Man."

   "I couldn't believe this guy": Norris and Thornton, *By Honor Bound*, p. 70.

Appendix B. Walker and Potts

262 *Larry Potts's road to the war was rougher:* Potts's story is drawn from interviews with Butch Hammond, Trent Wicks, Gus Evans, Rod Curry, and a nephew of the Marine officer also named Larry Potts (ST).

263 *"He was one of the most well-respected young men":* Interview with Gus Evans, June 2017 (ST).

264 *Bruce Walker's past could hardly have been more different:* Walker's story is drawn from an interview with Martha Lorin Walker (ST) and from her play *Did I Say Goodbye.*

267 *Some of his fellow soldiers believe that Potts:* Interview with Gray (DW).

INDEX

Abilene golf course, 157

Abraham Lincoln National Cemetery, Illinois, 248

Abrams, Creighton
  downed airmen and, 77, 110
  Marshall/Andersen rescue attempt and, 132
  Nixon and, 108–9, 110
  stopping air rescues of Hambleton/ Clark, xvi, 123, 140, 149
  Vietnam War and, 77, 108–9

Ai Tu Combat Base, 82, 84, 142

Alley, Jim
  background/cars and, 112, 113, 248, 249–50
  cameraman/Vietnam, 112–14
  death premonition/talking about and, 113–14
  father after Jim's death, 237–38, 248
  flight to Da Nang and, 111–12
  Hambleton mission/death and, 119, 122
  Hambleton's talks and, 239
  mother correspondence/Hambleton, 240–41
  mother/Jim's remains, 250

mother's illness and, 248
  parents, 112, 113, 237–38, 248
  parents adopting child and, 113, 248
  parents after son's disappearance, 240–41
  parents receiving death notification, 237–38
  refusing of Hambleton mission and, 115–16
  remains returned/funeral, 248–50
  schedule for returning to States, 115, 116, 118
  See also Hambleton, Gene rescue Jolly Green 67

Alley, Tim
  brother's remains/funeral and, 248, 249–50
  childhood/adult career, 248–49
  parents' promise to Jim and, 248, 249

Andersen, Andy
  description/traits, 125, 131
  Hambleton rescue possibilities and, 126, 130–31
  issues with MACV/rescue and, 143

Recovery Studies Division and, 125
success and, 125, 137, 147
Andersen, Andy and Clark/Hambleton
    rescue missions
after rescue, 224–25
air strikes and, 184
escape from hospital, 186
Marshall and, 131–32, 186
Norris meeting, 140–42
Norris progress report and, 163
NVA hitting bunker area/injury and,
    185–86, 224
ordered out of the Hambleton mis-
    sion, 186
questioning Norris (Clark mission),
    175, 177–78
tactical leader/characteristics needed,
    133–34
threat to shoot anyone abandoning
    post, 148–49, 185
traveling to position, 147
Zerbe and, 143, 224
See also Clark, Mark rescue/"ground"
    mission; Hambleton, Gene
    rescue/"ground" mission
Anderson, Mary Ann, 9–10, 247
Anderson, William, 234–35
Andrews Air Force Base, 18, 118
Ap Bia Mountain, 78
Apollo program/crews, 8, 14
Arizona Daily Star, 233
Armstrong, Dennis, 233, 241, 248
Arnold, Hap, 10
Astorga, José
background/helicopter roles, 48
description/traits, 48
Hambleton rescue and, 48–49, 51,
    52–54
Huey shootdown/injury and, 52–54
Astorga, José post-shootdown
crewmates/families and, 245
on Hambleton rescue, 245

Henderson and, 182
life in United States, 244–45
physical/mental condition and, 182,
    245
as POW, 54–60, 106, 182, 244
PTSD and, 245
atomic bomb, 11
Avery, Allen, 122

Bartholomew, Captain (fictional charac-
    ter), 235, 236
BAT-21 (book/Anderson), 234–35
Bat-21 (movie), 235–37
Battle of Hamburger Hill, 78
Bauknight, Gerald
after Hambleton's rescue, 224,
    225
Andersen's rescue mission and,
    143
Zerbe and, 143, 224
Bloomington Pantagraph, 232
"blowtorch jockeys," 72
Boli, Fred
after failed rescue attempt, 132
as on-scene commander (Hambleton
    mission), 119, 120, 121, 122
supplies for Hambleton and, 119
See also Hambleton, Gene rescue
    Jolly Green 67
Bolte, Wayne
death, 37–38
description/traits, 29
SAM mission and, 29, 32, 34, 35,
    36, 37–38
"Bravo" meaning, 39
Brezhnev, Leonid
meeting with Nixon/Kissinger,
    242–43
other leaders and, 146–47
US relations, 45, 107, 146,
    242–43
Vietnam War, 45, 107

bridge at Dong Ha/Ripley, 83, 166
Brinson, Doug
    Alley/death talk and, 113–14
    background, 113
    Hambleton rescue and, 113, 115,
        119
    See also Hambleton, Gene rescue
        Jolly Green 67
Brookbank, David
    Easter Offensive vs. no-fire zone,
        82–85, 106
    position, 82

Call, John Henry, 122
Can, Ta Van/wife, 270
Carley, John, 77–78
Carson, Johnny, 101
CBS Evening News, 31
Chapman, Carol, 7, 238–39
Chapman, Peter ("Hayden"), II
    aborted infantrymen rescue and,
        117–18
    Beth, Brad, Julie, Carol and, 238–39
    family/sisters learning of death,
        238–39
    Hambleton mission/death and, 117,
        118, 121, 122
    Hambleton on, 239
    Hambleton's talks and, 239
    Harris and, 117, 188
    pilot training/becoming military
        pilot, 8
    schedule for returning to States,
        118
    "Special Air Mission" and, 118
    See also Hambleton, Gene rescue
        Jolly Green 67
Chapman, Peter ("Hayden"), II, child-
    hood
    flying/planes and, 7, 117
    location, 7
    sisters and, 7
Cherry, Don, 156

China and Vietnam War
    communications/information and,
        146
    Easter Offensive and, 146
    Soviet Union and, 45
    United States relations and, 107, 146
    violating peace accords, 244
Cigli Air Base, Turkey, 14–15
Clark Air Base, Philippines, 227
Clark, Mark
    Abrams ending rescue missions, 123
    calling in strikes and, 150
    ejecting/landing, 96
    health and, 149, 150
    Jolly Green 67 mission and, 120, 123
    post-shootdown, 106, 149–50
    SAM hitting aircraft, 95–96
Clark, Mark rescue
    ARVN and, 124
    "impossible" chances and, 124–25
    Nielsen plan and, 97–98
    See also Henderson, Bill/Hambleton
        rescue mission
Clark, Mark rescue "ground" mission
    after rescue, 177, 178
    Andersen and, 163, 175, 177–78
    bunker return and, 177
    code/geography and, 150–51
    "Esther Williams" and, 150
    FACs and, 150, 159, 174, 175
    leaving hiding spot, 151
    life preserver inflating and, 153–54
    making noise in river and, 173–74
    Mieu Giang River and, 151, 153,
        159, 162, 163–64, 173–77
    NVA and, 162–63, 164, 173–74, 177,
        178
    problems with river, 159, 162, 163
    See also Norris, Tommy ("Flipper")
        and Clark rescue
Cobeil, Glenn, 44
Cobra helicopter description, 97
Cold War, xiv, 26, 46, 146

Combat Achievement Medal, First
    Class (North Vietnamese), 44
Constant, Dennis
    calling in help and, 56–58
    Hambleton rescue and, 56–58, 59–60
    SAMs/jinking and, 59–60
Crowe, Jay
    Andersen/Marshall meeting and, 132
    background, 98
    briefing Jolly Green 67 crew, 118,
        120–21
    on Clark/Hambleton rescues, 124,
        125
    description/traits, 98
    Hambleton rescue mission and, 89,
        90–91, 98
    knowledge of invasion force and,
        98–99
    landing helicopter and, 90–91
    See also Henderson, Bill/Hambleton
        rescue mission
"crows" defined, 26
Cuban Missile Crisis, 15, 26

Da Nang Air Base
    uses, 51, 60, 81, 88, 95, 98, 111, 114,
        115, 124, 133, 140, 165, 186,
        201, 202, 215, 218, 219
    Walker/Potts and, 267, 268, 269, 271
Da Nang hospital, 223, 225
"dark knights" term (US aviators), 79
Davis-Monthan golf course, 154–55
De, Vo Van, 271
Dobrynin, Anatoly, 146
Dorman, Craig
    as new to Vietnam, 135
    Norris and, 135–36
Dragnet (television), 235

"E & E" (escape and evade) rescue, 141
Easter Offensive (North Vietnamese)
    aerial view description, 82
    China and, 146

descriptions, 40, 78, 79, 82, 98–99,
    180
Hambleton location/rescue and, 40,
    43, 55–56, 57–60, 68, 69–73,
    89, 90–92, 95–96, 97–99, 132,
    136, 141, 142
hospitals description, 180
no-fire zone around Hambleton and,
    79, 81–85, 106
rescuers not told about, 89, 98–99
South Vietnam and, 243
Soviet Union and, 146, 185
villagers (south of DMZ) and, 83
Eighty-ninth Military Wing ("Special
    Air Mission"), Andrews Air
    Force Base, 118
Enola Gay, 11

FACs (forward air controllers) de-
    scribed, 39
Fain, Mickey, 270–71
farming in United States
    farm boom and, 4
    Great Depression and, 4
    See also specific individuals
Ferentchak, Gary
    Hambleton rescue and, 59
    SAMs/jinking and, 59
Flessner, Gwendolyn Mae
    description/traits, 8–9
    Donna (sister), 12
    Kenneth (brother), 9
    Mary Ann (sister), 9–10, 247
    parents and, 9
    See also Hambleton, Gwen
Flessner, Kenneth
    accident/death, 9
    death effects on family, 9
Fonda, Jane, 93
Ford, Gerald, 252
Foster, Stephen, 144–45
French and Indian War (1750s-1760s),
    80

French Indochina, 77
Frink, John
  Astorga and, 245
  death, 53
  Hambleton rescue and, 48, 49, 53

Gagliano, James, 253
Gandhi, Rajiv, 253, 254
Gatwood, Robin F.
  background, 30
  death, 37–38, 106
  description/traits, 30
  SAM mission, 30, 37–38
Gemini program, 14
Giai, Vu Van, 142–43
Giannangeli, Anthony
  background/fishing with sons, 30
  death, 37–38, 106
  description/traits, 30, 31
  SAM mission, 30, 31–32, 37–38
Giannangeli, Dennis
  anger at Hambleton, 67
  father "missing" notification and,
    66–67
  school announcement/father missing,
    66
  sports and, 66–67
Giannangeli family
  Colorado Springs and, 30–31
  "missing" notification and, 65–67
  mother/wife and, 65–66
Giannangeli, Robert
  father's knife and, 31, 65
  fishing/relationship with father,
    30–31
  friend's death/funeral and, 65
  "missing" notification of father and,
    65–66
  as Vietnam War opponent, 30–31
Glenn, John, 8
Goebbels, 6
Grant, Cary, 8

gravel mines description/consequences,
    68–69
Gray, D'Wayne
  no-fire zone vs. Easter Offensive, 85
  on Potts, 267
  Vietnam War views, 85
Great Depression, 4

Hackman, Gene, 235–36
Hai, Nguyen Quy, 180
Haig, Alexander, 109
Hambleton, Frances, 3
Hambleton, Gene
  basic training/physical and, 8
  buying Tucson home, 16
  children and, 12, 241
  description/traits, 9, 10, 16, 62
  elopement, 10
  flight school/Air Corps and, 10–11
  golf and, 16, 122, 137–39, 152–53,
    154–55, 156, 157, 161,
    247
  Gwen relationship, xiv, 8–10, 12–13,
    16, 22, 122, 160–61, 171, 205,
    220, 224, 225–26, 228, 230–31,
    247–48
  jungle survival school, Philippines,
    31
  Korat Royal Thai Air Force Base/
    daily routine, 16–17, 21–22,
    24–27
  Korean War, 12–13
  meeting Gwen/relationship begin-
    nings, 8, 9–10
  munitions factory work and, 8, 10
  navigation school/skills and, 11
  Pam (niece), 4, 9, 12, 247
  Peoria life, 12
  position, 16
  role/activities summary, 43
  SAC/rockets and, 13–16
  Sharon (niece), 9, 11

sibling rivalry/father and, 11, 232–33, 234

teeth problems and, 8, 10–11

top-secret background and, xiv, 13–16, 80, 140, 226

Vietnam/Southeast Asia arrival/situation, 16–17

World War II ending and, 11–12

Hambleton, Gene after rescue

arrival in Arizona/Gwen and photos, 230–31

BAT-21 (book) and, 234–35

change in, 247

correspondence with families of dead rescuers, 239, 240–41

debriefing, 226

earthquake and, 227

father and, 232–33

food/drinks, 223–24, 226

Gil and, 234

Gwen communication and, 227–28

healing, 227–28

health/anniversaries and, 237

as hero/response, 228–31, 232–37

hospital visitors, 224–25, 226–27

hospitals, 223–25

illness/death, 247, 248

Kiet and, 256

Korat/rescue techniques and, 228–30

medals, 232

medevac helicopter, 222

movie and, 235–37

newspapers and, 232–33

Norris on, 234

NVA rockets hitting hospital, 117

reporters/questions and, 222

rescuers/deaths and, 222, 239–41

rescuers funerals and, 240

rescuers remains returning and, 239–41

retirement, 234

routine, 247

Sharon (Gil's daughter), 234

story/as hero, 165–66, 202, 224, 228–29, 232

survivor's guilt, 241

talks/vanity license plate and, 233–34, 239–40, 241

Hambleton, Gene (Iceal) childhood

changing name, 5

description/traits, 4–6

father and, 4, 111

flying/planes and, 3, 6–7

locations, 3, 5

pranks and, 5–6

school/schoolhouse and, 5–6

Hambleton, Gene post-shootdown

B-52s bombing area/effects, 130

bridge at Dong Ha/Cam Lo and, 83

calling in strikes/seeing dead, 71–73

capture/torture and, xiv, 44, 46, 111

combat experience and, 43

depression and, 129, 130

Easter Offensive/enemy activities and, 40, 43, 56–57, 58–60, 68, 69–73, 89, 90–92, 95–96, 97–99, 132, 136, 141, 142

emotional effects/seeing dead NVA, 73

enemy "reviving" and, 91–92

flares (enemy) and, 69–70

gravel mines and, 68–69, 101

hiding spot, 47, 54–56, 100, 102–3

Huey shootdown and, 60–61

hunger/food and, 100, 101–3

injuries, 46

landing/area, 40, 41–42

moving, 43, 54–55

NVA soldiers around, 43, 56–57, 68

parachute on ground and, 46, 47

peasants searching for, 68, 69

physical condition and, 129–30

Hambleton, Gene post-shootdown (*cont.*)

radio communications, 40, 47, 51, 60, 68, 71, 72, 100–101

sleep and, 68

supplies and, 46, 55

surroundings, 101–3

See also SAM mission/Bat 21 (April 2, 1972)

Hambleton, Gene rescue

Abrams ending air rescue missions and, xvi, 123, 140, 149

B-52s use, 130

Constant communicating with, 57

Easter Offensive/enemy activities and, 40, 43, 56–57, 58–60, 68, 69–73, 89, 90–92, 95–96, 97–99, 132, 136, 141, 142

enemy activity in area and, 51–54, 57–61

fog and, 47

"impossible" chances and, 124–25

intelligence on activities in area and, 57

Korat alert and, 56–57

need to rescue three men and, 97, 100

no-fire zone and, 79, 81–85, 106

operation as highly classified, 106

Potts/Walker attempt and, 129

size/costs summary, 106

story/as hero, 165–66, 202, 224, 228–29, 232

top-secret background and, xiv, 13–16, 80, 140, 226

views on rescue missions, xv–xvi, 123, 124–25, 131

See also Jankowski, Bill/Hambleton rescue; Joint Rescue Coordination Center/Hambleton; SAM mission/Bat 21 (April 2, 1972); *specific individuals*

Hambleton, Gene rescue Blueghost

Cobra attack helicopter and, 50, 51–52, 60–61

crew of Huey, 48–50

flight to Hambleton location/precautions, 50–51

shootdown/deaths and POW, 51–54, 60–61

Hambleton, Gene rescue "ground" mission

activities before leaving hiding spot, 149, 151

Andersen monitoring, 172

Andersen/Norris meeting with Giai, 142–43

attacker and, 158, 160, 161, 183, 204

banana grove/water and, 169

boots and, 189–91

at bunker following rescue/APC taking, 219–21

chicken/rooster and, 158, 160

"Esther Williams"/"Charlie the Tuna" and, 144, 186, 188, 191

FAC vs. Hambleton versions, 198–99

FACs and, 133, 144–45, 149, 152, 154, 155, 156, 161, 168, 171–72, 188, 191, 192, 195, 198, 201, 204, 205, 206, 208, 210, 211

fear of creatures/disease from river, 188–89

fear of going in wrong direction, 167–68

finding the river/FAC finding position, xiii–xiv, 170–72

golf as code, 137–39, 152–53, 154–56, 157–58, 161

Hambleton's decision on rescue, 145, 149

hiding spots and, 195–96

hunger/thirst and, xiii, 149, 158, 167, 169, 183, 195, 196, 197, 198

injuries and, 160, 161, 214

invasion force/enemy activities and, 132, 136, 141, 142

irritable stupor, 193

leech and, 197

lessons learned from, 228, 256, 268, 269

maps problem, 141

Mieu Giang River and, 132, 133, 136, 137, 138, 143, 147, 183

military phone calls to Hambleton's friends/family and, 136, 137, 138

moving through village, 156–58

myth of, 256

need for code, 136–39

NVA and, 193–94

out in daylight/danger and, 201–2

physical/psychological problems, xiii, xv, 149, 154, 155, 156, 157, 160–61, 167, 168–72, 186–87, 188, 190, 192–93, 194, 195, 196–97, 198–99, 200, 201–2, 204–6, 207, 208, 210, 211–12, 214, 217, 218, 219–20

pop-culture code and, 144–45

positions and, 133

religion/Jesus and, 183–84

river crossing/problems and, 188–91

river travel/problems and, 192–95, 204–6, 207–8

secrecy and, 132–33, 165

sleep and, 157, 192, 193, 204, 205, 206, 208

snakes and, 189, 207

success possibilities and, 142, 143

supplies and, 151, 189

survival package and, 196, 197–98

"Swanee" and, 144–45, 188, 198

talk of his situation/rescue and, 165–66

turtle and, 194

vision problems, 154, 155, 161, 170

wood piece, 194–95, 205, 211

See also Norris, Tommy ("Flipper") and Hambleton rescue; *specific individuals*

Hambleton, Gene rescue Jolly Green 67

Alley's refusal and, 115–16

briefing/trap possibility and, 114–15

calling in resources for, 111–12, 113–14

crew boarding, 119

enemy activity and, 119–20

Hambleton and, 116, 120, 121, 122–23

Hambleton's expectations, 116

helicopter shootdown/deaths, 121–22

reactions to shootdown/deaths, 122–25

resupply purpose/Crowe briefing, 118, 120–21

switch to rescue mission, 120–21

weather and, 114, 115, 116, 119

Hambleton, Gil

after Gene's rescue, 234

birth, 3

as father, 12

flight school/World War II and, 11, 12, 234

Hambleton, Gwen

after Gene's rescue, 233, 247–48

children and, 12, 241

description/traits, 62

elopement, 10

Gene relationship, xiv, 8–10, 12–13, 16, 22, 122, 160–61, 171, 205, 220, 224, 225–26, 228, 230–31, 247–48

Hambleton, Gwen (*cont.*)
  Gene's Arizona arrival/photos,
    230–31
  golf and, 153
  ground rescue and, 136
  illness/death, 247–48
  Mary Ann (sister), 9–10, 247
  meeting Gene/relationship begin-
    nings, 8, 9–10
  notification of Gene's rescue,
    225–26
  notification of husband's shootdown,
    62–63
  Peoria and, 12
  preparation for Thailand trip, 62
  Vicky (niece) and husband, 237
  visiting Gil/family, 234
  See also Flessner, Gwendolyn Mae
Hambleton, Iceal, Sr.
  childhood/college and, 3
  description/traits, 3, 4
  as father, 4, 111
  on Gene/rescue, 232–33
  Great Depression and, 4
  marriage/children, 3
  Midwest farm and, 3
  Pam (granddaughter), 4
  Percheron horses and, 4
Hambleton, Stella
  children, 3
  description/traits, 4
  See also Wilbur, Stella
Hammond, Butch, 263
Hanoi Hannah (Trinh Thi Ngo), 93
Hanoi Hilton, 44
Harris, Bill
  aborting mission, 91
  Chapman and, 117, 118
  Hambleton rescue mission, 89–90,
    91
  Jolly Green 67/Hambleton rescue
    mission and, 117, 118

  See also Henderson, Bill/Hambleton
    rescue mission
Henderson, Bill
  childhood/swimming, 86–87
  college, 87, 181
  description/traits, 86, 87–88, 95, 96,
    103, 105, 181
  father, 86–87
  flying and, 87–88
  marriage/child, 87
Henderson, Bill/Hambleton rescue
    mission
  ejecting/landing, 96–97
  enemy activity/invasion force and,
    89, 90
  flying and, 88–89
  knowledge on invasion force and, 89
  at location, 89
  mission plan, 88, 89–90
  refueling/second attempt, 95
  SAM hitting aircraft/injuries, 95–96,
    100
  timing, 86
  See also specific individuals
Henderson, Bill post-shootdown
  Astorga and, 182
  back in United States, 246
  captors/interrogation and, 179,
    181–82
  change in, 246
  Cobra attempt to rescue, 97, 98
  ejecting/landing, 96–97
  escape plan, 104–5
  on Hambleton rescue, 246
  health problems and, 245, 246
  hiding places, 96, 97, 103, 104, 105
  injuries and, 95, 103, 179
  marches/transport to Hanoi, 106,
    179, 180, 181, 245
  NVA finding, 105
  NVA/machine gun plan, 104–5
  parachute and, 96–97

as POW/conditions, 179–82,
245–46
"why are you here?" question,
181–82
Heston, Charlton, 235
Heyser, Richard, 15
Hiroshima, 11
Hitler, 6
Hogan, Ben, 156

Icke, Harold, 124, 256
irritable stupor, 193
It's a Wonderful Life (movie), 9

Jankowski, Bill/Hambleton rescue
Broadcasting call for help, 48
during parachuting and, 41
help call and, 48, 56–57
Huey shootdown and, 60–61
identification/questions, 47
parachuting and, 38–41
pinpointing position, 47
radio communication and, 40, 47,
51, 60
Jensen, Jay
shootdown, 44
torture/interrogation, 44–45, 46
tricking interrogator, 46
"jinking" described, 27–28
Joint Rescue Coordination Center
Easter Offensive knowledge and, 78,
84
location, 77
mission/power, 77, 79
See also specific individuals
Joint Rescue Coordination Center/
Hambleton
no-fire zone vs. Easter Offensive, 79,
81–85, 106
top-secret background and, 80
Joker. *See* Joint Rescue Coordination
Center

Jones, Miss (teacher), 5–6
jungle survival school, Philippines,
31
Jupiter rockets, 14, 15

Kennedy, John F., 15, 26
Kennedy, Robert, 15
Khrushchev, Nikita, 15
Kiet, Nguyen Van
after Americans left Vietnam, 254
Clark rescue and, 148, 174, 175–76
description/traits, 148
family and, 254, 255–56
Hambleton rescue and, 148, 186,
191, 192, 195, 204
on leaving no one behind, 257
myth of rescue and, 256, 257
Navy Cross award, 255
Norris and, 255, 256
as refugee, 254–55
in United States, 255–56
See also Norris, Tommy ("Flipper")
and Hambleton rescue with
Kiet
Kissinger, Henry
China relations and, 146
meeting with Soviets, 242–43
NVA invasion/Hambleton rescue
and, 107–8, 109, 110, 145
peace negotiations/North Vietnam,
78
Soviet relations and, 107, 242–43
Knives (21st Special Operations Squadron), 88
Korat Royal Thai Air Force Base,
Thailand
clothing/fabric and, 22
danger and, 23–24, 26–28
fighter pilots and, 22–24
food/drink, 21–22
identification method, 23
maps of target areas, 24–25

Korat Royal Thai Air Force Base, Thailand (*cont.*)
nurse incident, 22–23
officer daily routine, 21–22
Roscoe (dog), 24
snakes and, 21
See also specific individuals
Korean War, 12–13, 80
Kulland, Byron
Astorga and, 245
background, 49–50
death, 53
description/traits, 49–50, 65
Hambleton rescue and, 48, 49, 50–51, 53
Hambleton's talks and, 239
Harlan (brother), 49
Leona (girlfriend/wife), 49, 50
"missing" notification to family, 65
Silver Daggers and, 49
Vietnamese aviators/Hai and, 50
Kulland, Karen
background, 64
on brother, 49–50
father and, 65
notification of brother missing and, 65
Kulland, Leona, 49–50

Le Duan, 146–47
"leave no man behind" idea
history, 79–80
Kiet on, 256–57
Norris on, 257
Vietnam/motivation for, 80–81
Levis, Charles
background, 29–30
death, 37–38, 106
description/traits, 30
SAM mission, 29–30, 37–38
Literary Guild American, 234–35

Lorin, Martha
description, 265
See also Walker, Martha Lorin

McKinney, Thomas, 25
MACVSOG (Military Assistance Command, Vietnam—Studies and Observation Group), 125
Manhattan Project, 12
Mao, 146–47
March of Time newsreels, 6
Markle, Peter, 235
Marshall, Winton W., 131–32
Martin, Dean, 235
Martin, Graham, 244
Masters golf course, 156
Military Assistance Command, Vietnam-Studies and Observation Group (MACVSOG), 125
Moorer, Thomas, 108
Morse, Don
enemy activities in area and, 58–59, 60–61
Hambleton rescue and, 58–59, 60–61
Muirhead, Cecil, 78

Nakhon Phanom Air Base, Thailand, 86, 111
Napoleon, 141
New York Daily News, 10
New York Times, 243
Newport News (cruiser), 251
Newsweek, 93, 94
Ngo, Trinh Thi (Hanoi Hannah), 93
Nielsen, Ben
enemy attacks/mission abortion, 97–98
rescue attempt, 97
Nixon, Richard
election (1972), 243–44
nuclear arms race and, 146, 243

Nixon, Richard/Vietnam War
China relations and, 107, 146
diplomatic gathering (April 10, 1972), 146
escalation/views, 109–10
getting out of Vietnam and, 87
intoxication/Moscow dinner, 243
meeting with Soviets, 242–43
NVA invasion/Hambleton rescue and, 107–8, 110, 145
other leaders and, 146–47
Soviet relations and, 107, 145, 146, 242–43
Vietnamization, 16, 40
Norris, Tommy ("Flipper")
after Hambleton rescue, 250–54
description/traits, xvi, 19–20, 140, 251, 252–53, 254
FBI and, 252–54
fear and, xvi, 19–20
Kiet (after rescue mission), 255, 256
as legend, 252, 253, 254, 256
Medal of Honor, 251, 252, 254
SEALs decision and, 18–20
Sikh terrorists and, 253–54
Vietnam injury/recovery, 250–52
Walker rescue possibility, 135, 267
Norris, Tommy ("Flipper") and Clark rescue
Anderson progress report and, 163
Anderson questioning, 175, 177–78
missing Clark on river and, 173–75
rescuing, 175–77, 252
team travels to river, 162–64
traveling to position with Anderson, 147
See also Clark, Mark rescue "ground" mission
Norris, Tommy ("Flipper") and Hambleton rescue
Andersen meeting, 140–42
commandos mutiny and, xvi, 192, 203–4

commitment to, 135–36, 142
concerns about South Vietnamese commandos, 148–49, 184–85, 192, 195, 200
concerns about weapons, 147–48
FACs and, 200, 201, 209
on Hambleton/rescue, 234, 235, 257
Hambleton's talks and, 239
military commitment and, 140
NVA hitting bunker area/casualties and, xvi, 184–86
preparation for second night, 202
realization of difficulties/risk, 142
reporter after rescue, 257
reporters and, 202–3, 257
restriction area and, 141–42, 163
selection as team leader, 135–36
team turning back first night, 195
travel to position, 147
travels to river, 191–92, 208
See also Hambleton, Gene rescue "ground" mission
Norris, Tommy ("Flipper") and Hambleton rescue with Kiet
air support and, 215, 218–19
decision to go together, 204
disguise, 208, 209
FACs and, 215, 218, 219
finding sampan, 208
gun fire and, 217–19
NVA soldiers spotting/actions, 216
NVA soldiers/tanks near river and, 209, 210
relationship, 200, 203–4
return trip with Hambleton, 214–19
river channels and, 209
sampan idea, 200–201
sampan travel to Hambleton, 209–10, 212–13
strike call, 219–21
travel to position, 147

Norris, Tommy ("Flipper") childhood
  description/traits, 17, 18
  hurricane and, 17
  locations, 17
  vision and, xvi, 18
  wrestling, 17–18

"Old Folks at Home," 144–45
Only Angels Have Wings (movie), 8
Operation Paperclip, 14

parachuting
  hypoxia and, 38
  spinning/stabilizing and, 38
Paris Peace Accords, 243
Paschall, Mark, 64
Paschall, Ronald
  Astorga and, 245
  background, 48
  death, 53
  Hambleton rescue and, 48–49, 53
  "missing" notification to family, 63,
    64
Paschall, Ruth
  background, 64
  notification of son missing, 64
Pearson, William Roy, 122
Percheron horses, 4
Phantom, F-4, 71–72
Pierre (dog), 47, 137, 225, 226
Podgorny, Nikolai, 242–43
Potts, Larry
  Aunt Louise/description/traits, 262
  Aunt Louise/Uncle Samuel and,
    262–63
  childhood/family break up, 262–64
  Delaware State University, 263
  description/traits, 262, 263, 264
  family notification of death/reactions,
    272
  signing up with Marines/reasons,
    264–65

Potts, Larry/Hambleton rescue attempt
  assumed dead, 129, 135
  shootdown, 129, 135
Powers, Francis Gary, 26
Prater, Roy, 122
Presley, Elvis, 93

Quang Tri, 58, 82, 105, 145, 168

Radio Hanoi
  description of broadcasts, 93–94
  report on downing of Hambleton's
    EB-66C and, 93–94
Reader's Digest, 18, 235
Recovery Studies Division
  Hambleton/Clark information/rescue
    and, 126
  record, 125–26
  rescue role, 125
  See also Andersen, Andy
Redstone Arsenal
  during/after World War II, 14
  Hambleton and, 13–15
  weapons/rockets and, 14–15
Reed, Donna, 9
Reed, Jerry, 235
rescue missions
  changes/lessons learned, 228, 256,
    268, 269
  photographers and, 115
  See also specific rescue missions
rescuers/Hambleton
  remains and, 239–40
  See also specific individuals
Ripley, John, 83, 166
Rockford Files, The (television), 235
Rogers' Rangers, 80
Roosevelt, Franklin D., 10
Roscoe (dog), 24

SAC/rockets and Hambleton, 13–16
SALT 1 treaty, 243

SAM missiles
  aircraft to protect from, 25, 26
  CIA/Fan Song radar investigation
    and, 27
  Cuban Missile Crisis and, 26
  danger/fear and, 26–28
  "jinking" described, 27–28
  Russia and, 26
  sites/NVA and, 25, 27
  target aircraft signal/warning lights
    and, 26
SAM mission/Bat 21 (April 2, 1972)
  enemy optical-only launch and, 34
  enemy SAMs/aircraft and, 32–35
  jamming/monitors and, 32, 34
  jinking and, 32–35
  men/crows with Hambleton, 29–30
  plan/purpose, 25, 26
  plane (Hambleton's) on fire/crashing,
    36–38
  planes involved, 25, 32
  Radio Hanoi and, 93–94
  significance of downing EB-66C/
    Hambleton, 94
  See also specific individuals
SAM mission/Bat 21 (April 2, 1972)
    and Hambleton
  "Bravo" meaning, 39
  enemy missiles/aircraft, 33, 34,
    35
  enemy shooting at, 41
  landing/landing area problems, 40,
    41–42
  parachuting/conditions, 36–37,
    38–41
  plane fire/crashing and, 36–38
  preparation/flight, 25–26, 29, 32
  significance of downing EB-66C/
    Hambleton, 94
  See also Hambleton, Gene post-
    shootdown
Saturn V, 14

SEALs
  description/traits, 141–42
  US military methods vs., 141–42
  See also specific individuals
Serex, Barbara, 239
Serex, Henry M. ("Mike")
  background, 30
  death, 37–38
  description/traits, 30
  SAM mission, 30, 37–38, 239
Shaw Air Force Base golf course,
  155
"She Got the Goldmine (I Got the
  Shaft)" (Reed), 235
Sheehan, Neil, 79
shock waves effects, 71
Sikh terrorists/plan, 253–54
Smokey and the Bandit (movie),
  235
Soviet Union
  nuclear arms deal and, 243
  nuclear arms race and, 146
Soviet Union and Vietnam War
  China and, 45
  communication/information and,
    145, 146
  Easter Offensive and, 146, 185
  SA-7 missiles, 99
  supplies, 45, 99, 184
  timing, 45
  torture/interrogation and, 45, 46
  United States relations, 107, 145,
    146, 242–43
  violating peace accords, 244
  war booty and, 45–46
"Special Air Mission" (Eighty-ninth
  Military Wing), Andrews Air
  Force Base, 118
Special Operations Squadron, 21st
  (Knives), 88
Springer, Paul, 80
Sprouse, Tim, 97

Stalin, Joseph, 13

Stars and Stripes, 93, 179

Strategic Air Command (SAC) role/
   components, 13

Tan Son Nhut Air Base
   location/history, 77
   people at, 131, 135

Tet Offensive (1968), 78

Thieu, Nguyen Van, 40, 243–44,
   254

Tho, Le Duc, 78

Tho, Lieutenant
   description/traits, 140
   Hambleton/Clark rescues and,
      140–41, 162, 175
   NVA hitting bunker area and, 184,
      186
   See also Hambleton, Gene
      rescue/"ground" mission

Thornton, Michael, 250, 251

Time magazine, 93

Time of Useful Consciousness, 38

Times, The (of London), 94

Tincher, Daryl
   Hambleton rescue and, 79, 80
   Joker/position, 78
   no-fire zone establishment and, 79
   talk of Hambleton/rescue and, 165,
      166

Tinh, Doan Cong, 180

Tiny Tim, 101

Tonight Show, The (television), 101

torture/interrogation by North Viet-
      namese
   description, 44–45
   guard selection and, 44
   Jensen tricking interrogator, 46
   Soviet Union and, 45, 46
   wizard's war men and, 44
   See also specific individuals

Tucson National golf course, 152

Turley, Jerry
   background/description, 83
   disobeying no-fire zone, 84
   Easter Offensive vs. no-fire zone,
      82–84

Uong, Nguyen Thi, 180

US military
   downed Americans/airman and,
      77–78, 80–81
   "missing" vs. "presumed dead" noti-
      fications/reasons, 63–64
   views of South Vietnamese/army, 81
   *See also specific events; specific indi-
      viduals*

USS *Constellation,* 109

USS *Hancock,* 165, 218

USS *Kitty Hawk,* 109

Valdez, Juan, 244

Vietnam
   French and, 77
   *See also specific individuals; specific
      locations;* Vietnam War

Vietnam War
   air vs. ground fight, 78–79
   American POWs and, 244
   Americans leaving and, 243–44
   conflict in United States over, 30–31,
      80–81, 87, 93, 166, 250, 264
   embassy scene/Americans leaving,
      244
   heroes/talk and, 165–67
   history (summary), 78–79
   North Vietnamese people on, 180
   Paris Peace Accords, 243
   red fiery summer casualties, 242
   reporters and, 166–67
   situation (1972), 78
   soldiers situation, 78–79
   training Vietnamese aviators/vomit-
      ing incident, 50

US Air Force ordnance, 43–44
"war winding down" view, 87, 98, 109
"why are you here?" question and, 181–82
See also specific events; specific individuals/countries; specific locations
Vietnamization
    "Easter Offensive" and, 40
    Nixon and, 16, 40
    US Air Force and, 16
Vogel, Mike
    Alley/death talk and, 113–14
    description/traits, 113
    Hambleton rescue and, 113
    See also Hambleton, Gene rescue Jolly Green 67
von Braun, Wernher, 14

Walker, Bruce
    childhood, 264–65
    description/traits, 264–65
    military before Vietnam, 266
    sister and, 265
Walker, Bruce/Hambleton rescue attempt
    death, 271
    FACs and, 269, 270–71
    possible rescue of, 135, 267
    post-shootdown, 129, 135, 267–68, 269–71
    shootdown, 129, 267
    Vietnamese peasants and, 270
    white phosphorus rockets and, 270–71
Walker, Bruce/Martha
    Bruce shipping out for Vietnam, 266–67
    Lorin Marie (daughter), 266, 268
    relationship, 265–66, 272
Walker, Charles, 264, 268, 269

Walker, Martha Lorin
    as Air Force wife, 265
    Bruce's death and, 271–72
    description/traits, 265, 266, 268
    Did I Say Goodbye (play of), 266, 271
    visiting Bruce's parents/learning of Bruce's shootdown, 268–69
Washington Post, 17
Wayne, John, 8, 17
Webb, Jack, 235
Webster, William, 252
Whitcomb, Darrel
    Arlington ceremony/Hambleton and, 240
    documentary/Hambleton rescue, 256
    on Norris, 19
    rescue mission changes and, 228
Wicks, Trent
    on Potts family, 262, 272
    on uncle, 272
Wilbur, Stella, 3
    See also Hambleton, Stella
Williams, Hank, 9
"wizards' war"/men, 16, 44
World War I, 4
World War II
    Air Force ordnance, 43
    atomic bomb/*Enola Gay,* 11
    Battle of the Bulge, 109
    Douglas A-1 dive-bombers, 69
    Easter Offensive comparison, 70
    end, 11
    Gene Hambleton and, 6, 11–12
    Gil Hambleton, 11, 12, 234
    men left behind, 80
    newsreels, 6
    Operation Paperclip and, 14
    Redstone and, 14

Yeager, Chuck, 27

Zerbe, Frank, 143, 224